THE MILLIONAIRE MENTOR SERIES

Frank and Andrea Cooke

Real

Wealth

An investment
story describing
the road to
wealth through
rental real estate

PUBLISHER'S NOTE

This publication is designed to provide accurate and authoritative information in regard to the subject matter covered. It is sold with the understanding that the publisher is not engaged in rendering legal, accounting or other professional service. If legal advice or other expert assistance is required, the service of a competent professional person should be sought.

Cypress Publishing Group, Inc.
11835 Roe #187
Leawood, KS 66211
www.cypresspublishing.com

Library of Congress Cataloging-in-Publication Data

Cooke, Frank and Cooke, Andrea
Real Wealth / by Frank and Andrea Cooke
p. cm.
ISBN: 0-89447-339-5

   1. Real estate investment 2. Rental housing I. Title.
II. Title: Real Wealth: An investment story describing the
road to wealth through rental real estate
332.6324   2002

Printed in the United States of America

November 2002
10 9 8 7 6 5 4 3 2 1

Dedicated to Frank's brother Walter
and to all who strive to achieve
through learning, working and
applying common sense.

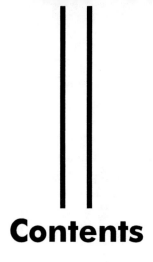

Contents

score. Update and compare to track progress as you accumulate wealth.

PART 2. NECESSARY KNOWLEDGE

evaluation and exploration of financing possibilities and closing costs. Determining cash-on-cash return using various prices and financing plans. At least three trials should be performed. Maximum price to be paid to get an adequate return is determined.

PART 3. ACTUAL ACQUISITIONS

Introduction

Want to be a millionaire? Want enough money to do almost anything you desire? Buy anything you need? Want to retire in a comfortable manner with no financial worries?

This book, based on facts but written as a fictionalized account to keep your interest, will tell how, as an ordinary Joe or Jane, you can achieve financial independence. You can become Joe or Jane Millionaire. You can have piles of money. Putting into practice the uncomplicated techniques contained on the following pages enabled the authors to acquire 115 residential rental units and to become multi-millionaires. All of the techniques described as part of the wealth-building process are true to life. Each acquisition story is based on a buy actually made by one or both of the authors or by a client under the guidance of Frank Cooke as a Realtor. No material facts have been changed in the fictionalization, only names, locations and some numbers.

The authors accumulated their residential rental properties one building at a time. Frank, while working full time at a salaried job, started with a duplex, then another duplex and so forth. Andrea, who prefers the nickname "Andy," started with a quadraplex. Andy, before marrying Frank, was also working full time in a salaried job when she acquired her first rental.

Wrapped up in full-time jobs. Sound familiar? Moving on up to become multi-millionaires before age 60? Not so common. But read on and learn. You can do it, too.

In his mid-forties Frank became a licensed Realtor. He still is, although retired. Andy never was a Realtor. Both authors have fielded hundreds of questions concerning rentals and how this or that could be done. We have helped many people get their start in the residential rental business. We told them what to do and what not to do. We encouraged them to act and to keep moving forward when they had successes. We consoled them and gave advice when troubles arose. We became mentors in practice.

It's our feeling that anyone with reasonable intelligence, common sense and a willingness to make diligent efforts should be able to master the techniques described. The practical knowledge you need is woven into the book's storyline. Understand the story and you absorb the lessons. Both ordinary men and women can and do become wealthy, as singles and as couples.

Becoming wealthy through rental real estate is not an overnight process. This book doesn't describe any "get rich" schemes. However, adherence to the easy lessons you'll learn from the story which follows can enable you, with no real estate experience, to become Joe or Jane Millionaire within 10 to 25 years of today. You can start putting the book's lessons into practice at any age: 25, 35, 45, 55, or whenever you decide to get started. Think about it. How old are you now? How old will you be when your net worth has at least six zeros following a one? Author Frank started his real estate wealth-building program as a side venture when he was 35.

Perhaps you've already gotten started. Perhaps you've accumulated 3, 4 or 12 rental homes or a building housing 10 or 16 apartments. If so, this book will suggest what you ought to do next.

As an average American, you probably have completed high school but may not have completed four years of college. Whether you have or not, your academic record will show middle-of-the-road achievement with maybe an occasional A but mostly Bs and Cs.

The ordinary interested investor is a wage earner employed by someone else but may be self-employed. In either case his or her income is "average" (that is, before absorbing the lessons of this book).

What if your personal or family income is currently lower than normal? Don't despair! You can still make it! In fact, you'll have greater motivation than others. Keep reading.

Enjoying higher than average income? Good for you. You should be able to get off to a quicker start, but keep reading.

Typically you will be between 27 and 60 years of age when you start thinking seriously about how to make it big to achieve financial independence. You may be very money-oriented before 27 but primarily in the sense of earning all you can and spending even more. Don't travel down an impossible road to wealth; you can't become wealthy just by spending as if you already are. Even if you have what seems like a zillion obligations you can and must put a wealth-building plan into effect to have any real hope of becoming a millionaire.

You may have taken a stab at making it big already, but failed. Possibly you were missing some aspect of the wealth-building process and will find the lacking ingredient in this book. While it is true that, because of inflation, a million dollars "just ain't what it used to be," it still is a sizeable amount. Becoming a millionaire is still a worthy objective and a formidable one. Between four and seven percent of American households are in the millionaire category. This book will guide you towards becoming a "sustainable" millionaire, meaning being able to remain in that status indefinitely once it is achieved. To stay there requires significant sustainable income for personal living expenses. In this book a sustainable millionaire is considered as one with a constant, personal-use annual income of not less than $100,000.

Due to inflation, in ten years or so you may need two million and an annual income of $200,000 to be in the same condition as today's millionaire with $100,000 income. In a sense, it doesn't matter. The wealth-building process put forth in this book and the underlying investment recommended— direct ownership of residential rental real estate—is essentially inflation-proof. Yes, property and all expenses will cost more over time but rents will be higher as well. It is the revenue, or the cost and profit relationships, which are most important and the relationships will remain intact regardless of inflation. The essential process will endure despite changing conditions. It is timeless.

Depending upon where you live in the United States, property values and rents may be much higher or lower than in this book, but specific dollar amounts given as prices, costs, and rents don't matter to the wealth-building process advocated. In this book it is the approach, the financial plan and percentages which are the keys. They apply equally . . . anywhere in the country.

To make this how-to book more readable and to avoid a tiresome textbook flavor, fictional characters were created named Joe and Jane Anderson. Readers get to follow their steady progress toward becoming millionaires. It's not necessary to have a spouse to become a millionaire, but a spouse can help. A spouse can help a lot.

Joe attended a two-year community college. He was a B-student but dropped out before earning his two-year degree. Jane has about the same amount of formal education from a different college.

You meet Joe when he is age 30 and working for a security firm earning a salary of $25,000 a year. Jane is 28 and earns $21,000 at a meeting planning company. Their total income equals the average U.S. household income for the year this is being written. If they lived in the northeast U.S. or California, they would earn more for the same jobs but Mr. and Mrs. Anderson live in a southern city with about 200,000 other people.

This book shows step by step how Joe and Jane Anderson become permanently wealthy. How much wealth is enough? Most people want to become at least "go to hell wealthy," which is when a person has enough money to not have to endure aggravations from others. It's the point at which you can afford to say "no, and don't bother me anymore." The point at which you can cease being nice solely because you're fearful of financial damage if you're not. Most people are satisfied with life and themselves when they become permanently financially independent through their own efforts.

Two other fictional characters you'll meet are Fred and Wendy Madison who are the alter egos of the authors, Frank and Andy. The Madisons are in their mid-fifties and have "made it" financially through residential rentals. Recently they retired...earlier than most.

Joe and Jane met the Madisons at a church dinner. Fred saw something of himself in young Joe. In fact, Fred was a little excited when he heard Jane saying to Wendy that Joe was reading a how-to book on rental real estate. Joe apparently wanted to get somewhere faster and farther than his primary job was likely to take him.

Fred has a hankering to tell someone how he would do things if he had a chance to start over. Fred has done well. Nevertheless, Fred feels if he knew then what he knows now he would have done much better much sooner. Now he yearns to convey to others the benefits of his experience.

It is presumed that the typical reader of this book knows little or nothing about residential real estate, so it explains the necessity of having dreams and setting goals, devising a wealth-building plan and keeping score as wealth increases. Of course, it explains why real estate is a super investment for industrious people with little start-up money. Advice is given as to what type of properties to buy, how to analyze them and most importantly, how to determine the maximum price to pay for them.

Fred and Wendy Madison then mentor Joe and Jane Anderson through their purchase of their first rental, a duplex. Next the Andersons buy a quadraplex and reside in one of its four apartments. From there they use a novel approach to buy and improve a single-family detached house as their primary residence. Next comes a financial stretch as they boldly buy two quadraplexes. A three-way trade, or tax-deferred exchange, is used to acquire yet another quadraplex. Then Fred guides his protégés through a no money down purchase of a tired 24-unit apartment. A five-way trade to acquire a 47-unit building and improve its profitability follows. Finally, just before they become millionaires, Fred mentors them through discounted early payoff of a loan.

The book is divided into three sections:

> Part 1. Getting Yourself Together
> Part 2. Necessary Knowledge
> Part 3. Actual Acquisitions

Ideally the book will be read and absorbed from start to finish and this is what the authors recommend. However, some readers may already feel competent in all or some part 2 knowledge areas and, to avoid boredom, jump ahead to the more exciting acquisitions section. Do so if you wish. Just remember, it's okay to refer back to part 2 if you get confused.

PART 1:

GETTING YOURSELF TOGETHER

1

You've Got to Have Goals and a Plan

Fifteen years before they would become millionaires, Joe and Jane Anderson, just past the stage of calling themselves newlyweds, were an absolutely ordinary couple. They were typical—basically happy but with few possessions and no specific goals. They were somewhat confused about what they should be doing for the long run and given to squabbling in a minor way. It was a Thursday. After they watched an evening news item concerning the high amount of debt carried by the typical household, Joe turned to his wife and said, "You know, Jane, for people our age without college degrees, we're doing okay."

"Guess you're talking financially again. I swear, Joe, you're obsessed with money."

Joe had always been interested in money, although he had never had much. He had always been somewhat of an entrepreneur starting with a lemonade stand at age eight, selling kites in middle school and T-shirts in high school. Once into his junior year he had a part-time job some days after school and on weekends as well. Jane's exasperated tone annoyed him.

"No, I'm not. But finances are something everybody ought to take an interest in, including you. It's just that . . . if you put us both together . . . we're making something like $46,000 a year. To me that's a lot. Oh, I know the papers talk about new graduates getting jobs starting at 50 or 60 thousand, but that isn't us, Jane. At 28 and 30 we've already got a start. Of the couples we know, we're doing as well as any. We're struggling, but we're doing okay."

"Okay, so we're doing all right by your standards but I sure don't think we're raking in the big bucks. What are you really getting at?"

There was a longish pause as Joe evaluated his wife's slightly irritated attitude. He knew that he had been talking a lot about money lately, but it wasn't the only thing he thought about. He thought about having kids, too, just like Jane. It ruffled Joe when Jane seemed to dismiss talk about finances. It was also strange, considering she did such a good job handling their household budget. In fact, Jane was the one who got them to actually use a budget—something none of their friends did, so far as he knew.

Thanks to Jane they had a good idea of what their money was going out for as well as what was coming in. The out matched and occasionally exceeded the in, but they agreed that using the budget made it seem like having 10 to 20% more money. He thought of their in-laws the Archers and friends the Repaskys. Both couples bragged about making a lot more than the Andersons but they never seemed to have any money available. He and Jane took in a movie and had dinner out once a week, but half the time the Archers and Repaskys said they couldn't afford to go with them. On the other hand, the Repaskys were always having pizzas delivered and sometimes the "takeout taxi" brought entire meals to their house.

It had only been in the last six or eight months that Joe had begun thinking seriously about money. Before that he and Jane were preoccupied with furnishing their apartment with the basics. Now they had enough to get by on; the place no longer looked totally empty. Compared to the homes of their parents their apartment was still pretty sparse. Everyone said not to worry about it; the finer things would eventually come. After all, it was only about a year and a half ago that they finally landed steady, full-time jobs that seemed likely to last.

It had been much worse just after they married. For almost eight months it was first Joe and then Jane who was out of a job. Not their faults for the most part. A little company would hire one of them then fold. Or, the particular job they were hired for was dissolved. Or, once they started a job, it would be clear it had been totally misrepresented and they would feel compelled to quit.

They realized that their lack of educational credentials barred them from even applying for most good sounding jobs. That was simply the way it was, but being content with recent progress, they weren't complaining. However, Joe had started to think that there must be a way to get going faster... and farther. He was halfway through reading his second real estate how-to book. The concepts seemed to make sense, but Joe still didn't entirely grasp how to implement them. How could they ever get started? Was it really feasible?

Discussions with Jane had so far been, well, unsatisfactory. For some reason there was conflict. It wasn't as if she were against the hope of somehow making it big, she just didn't seem to let herself go and dream as he did. He could visualize himself driving a big car or traveling to Singapore or Egypt. Jane kept nodding agreement but didn't get swept up with his imagination. A couple of weeks ago they had even had an argument about their differences in dreaming. Finally Jane had concluded the discussion with the declaration that if he were so wrapped up in making it big he ought do something about it or stop talking about it.

"Joe," she had said. "I'm not against your hopes. Why would I be? It's just that I keep hearing you dreaming out loud, but I'm not seeing any action. Are you only going to talk about how great it's going to be and never actually do anything? I'm getting a little tired of hearing you go on and on when you don't have anything specific in mind. Am I married to a dreamer or a man of action?"

Her question had certainly ended their discussion and his hopes for other activities that night. Since being put down, Joe hadn't been able to stop thinking that Jane might be right. Her question might be the basis of the conflict between them, but he didn't want to admit it. What could he do to prove her wrong? What should he do?

Jane had the habit of saying: "You've gotta have goals and you've gotta have a plan. You've gotta have goals and a plan." Joe found her mantra annoying but conceded she was probably right. Jane had picked up the goal-and-plan thing from her father who apparently told her, probably repeatedly, to never start any big project without identifying what she wanted to accomplish, thinking it through and writing down a plan.

Joe's habit had always been to decide to do something then just start doing it, working toward some favorable outcome. Of course, he often hit snags but generally worked things out as he proceeded. Now that he thought about it, he really was a man of action. Why didn't Jane see it! Then, doubts rolled in again. Yes, he admitted, he was a man of action on small projects but he was stymied as to how to go about making the Anderson family the well-off Anderson family. If only he had someone to talk to about it!

Time for fate to intervene. On a Wednesday evening, the Andersons attended one of the pot-luck dinners held once a month in the social hall of their church. Joe liked to go to them sometimes so he could gorge on some of the finest dishes the parishioners could prepare. Jane always took a batch of her famous bread-pudding dessert as the Andersons' contribution to the feast. Besides the compliments her dessert always received, Jane loved the friendly sociability of the events.

After shuffling through the food line, Joe and Jane took the two remaining seats at one of the large round tables spaced throughout the hall. They knew one of the couples already seated. As was customary, they introduced themselves to the two other seated couples whom they had seen at church but didn't know. One of the couples was Fred and Wendy Madison. Jane sat next to Fred.

As they prepared to leave about 40 minutes later, the Andersons began bantering with the Madisons, who had turned out to be unusually friendly.

"Joe," Fred called out. "Jane tells me you're on the verge of doing something big but you're not sure what it's going to be. You know, if you don't know where you're going, any path will take you there!"

Joe reddened slightly because Fred had caught him mulling over his dilemma, but Joe was generally pretty quick on his feet. "It's not that," he shot back as they walked toward the parking lot. "I'm just trying to identify the path of least resistance."

Fred and Wendy chuckled. Jane tilted her head and eyes heavenward. Then Joe added in a serious tone, "Actually, Jane's basically right. I feel there's a way we can make it big financially but frankly, I'm not sure how. Real estate sort of appeals to me but it also confuses me."

Fred caught Joe's serious edge under the quips. "You know, Joe," he stated. "You've gotta set some goals and develop a plan."

Joe stopped in his tracks, his mouth half opened. That's exactly what Jane always says! This was getting scary! Uncanny! He quickly recovered. "That's just what I was debating in my head, Fred. You got any ideas?"

Fred, ever ready to spout off advice when asked, threw out an off-hand "course I do."

By the time they reached the Madisons' Cadillac, parked three spots closer than the Andersons' Honda, it had been arranged for Fred and Joe to meet Sunday afternoon to toss around a few ideas.

Fred lived in a house that would be called nice but not extravagant or even large. It was well located, in a sense. It was in an older, pleasant neighborhood within a mile or so of the city's center. It was convenient for the Madisons, considering what they liked to do and where they needed to go. On the other hand, it was not in one of the wealthy neighborhoods where Joe thought people with money always wanted to be. The wealthy areas were miles from the city center and featured large lots with prestigious looking houses. Right away, Joe started to wonder about Fred. Was he really as well off as the crowd said?

As if reading Joe's mind, Fred offered a quick, partial tour of his house since it was Joe's first visit. The Madisons' home was well furnished but the items weren't fancy let alone opulent. They had every modern convenience and most entertainment devices but not state of the art stuff. The Archers had a much larger TV and the Repaskys had elaborate setups for playing video games. The Madison rooms were a bit messy; there were piles of books in many places and lots of family photos in standup frames on almost every horizontal surface. The walls had lots of watercolors, some oils and some prints. Overall, the impression was of a comfortable house, well-lived in and in slight disarray.

While they toured, Fred explained that he and Wendy had lived in the 70-year-old house for about 15 years. It was plenty big for the two of them and they liked it and their neighborhood as well as anything they had seen elsewhere. So, why move? His attitude was typical of true millionaires—most are firmly planted and have lived in the same house for years.

In answer to Joe's questions Fred revealed he was retired . . . for the second time! He had done well enough to retire by age 40. Then, after two years of almost no productive activity, he felt the need to plunge back in and get busy. He had started a second career in a field entirely different from his first. Now, at age 56, he had retired again! But Fred was quick to point out that this time he had no intention of sitting on his duff being unproductive. Fred described his new approach as "redirecting himself."

"I didn't make up redirecting as a new buzzword," said Fred. "I think I picked it up in the book *Real Age*. But it fits my situation to a tee. Wendy and I hope to do lots of things we enjoy. Maybe I'll make a little money as we go along, but fortunately money-making doesn't have to be our focus."

Fred clearly liked to talk and his stories were interesting, but Joe wanted to get to his own situation. "Okay, Fred," he said. "It's plain to see you've done well and I'm impressed. Now how do Jane and I get started?"

Fred asked what Joe had in mind when he said he wanted to make it big financially. Joe's responses were vague, partly because Joe didn't want to appear greedy or money-hungry.

Fred finally waved him off. "Look, Joe," he commenced. "You're talking in generalities. You need to have specifics in mind as well as an overall intention. It is quite all right to dream. In fact, motivational experts galore will tell you straight out that to achieve you must have a specific goal, one you can visualize. I agree with 'em. Just think, you're being encouraged to dream! But dream specifically about tangible items. Oh, it goes without saying you want a happy, healthy, rewarding life for you and your family. And, oh yes, you want to earn respect and establish a reputation as a good, charitable, tolerant, responsible man. I take those as givens. Every clear thinking person wants those things. Let's go beyond givens."

For the next hour, Fred and Joe discussed and defined some specific goals for Joe beyond the givens. Joe thought he was in a cafeteria being encouraged to select whatever desserts he wanted with everything being free. Joe thought his oh-so-practical Jane would have been amazed at Fred's encouragement to more or less "blue sky" his desires. They made a list:

- House with a two-car garage, fully equipped
- Swimming pool
- New cars of their choice at least every five years
- Travel out of the country every second year
- Memorable in-country vacation other years
- Fund college educations for eventual two-three kids
- Good quality wardrobes, kept up to date
- Freedom from constant money worries
- Being well set up for retirement
- Becoming my own boss
- Retire early—maybe at 55
- Eat out whenever and wherever
- Do what I want when I want

The list wasn't nearly as long as it could have been. Fred wouldn't let Joe write down all the small stuff he mentioned. Fred told him the small luxuries would take care of themselves once the big things were achieved. Joe told Fred the goals made him feel guilty since they so obviously required a lot of money. Was he supposed to be crass? Wasn't it a sin or something? What about charity? Aren't you supposed to give excess money to the poor and just keep enough to satisfy basic needs?

"I'm not against charity," explained Fred, who went on to state that he and Wendy gave a considerable amount to quite a few charities each year.

"Joe, I don't like to talk about our giving, but I will do so only to make a point. What we give now is far, far more than we could have given in our early days. If we had given away all excess beyond our basic needs from the start, we could never have built any wealth. The charities we help support now get a lot more help from us in one year than we could have afforded in ten of our early years.

"You've got to use whatever talents you're blessed with. If you have entrepreneurial talent that enables you to start a business and employ others, you sure as heck ought to do it.

Why? Because most people can't start a business and keep it running. So, you perform a worthwhile service to mankind just by running a legitimate business profitably. Even if you don't have any employees of your own, buying goods and services from others employs people.

"Similarly, making money through direct real estate investment is a talent which ought to be utilized once it's recognized. You can't make money in real estate without spending money. If you buy a new appliance, get a survey, hire someone to cut the lawn or have a new roof installed you're helping the economy. Spending helps others as well as yourself.

"It would be wrong if you make money and then bury it. Burying money helps no one and glorifying money itself rather than what can be accomplished with it is wrong also. It would only mean you're satisfying a selfish, greedy tendency. You must put money to use. What you use it for is up to you if you earned it, won it or it was given to you. Course, you do have a few tax laws to contend with but then it's up to you. If you choose to give a lot to charity so be it. But remember, if you grow wealth properly you'll be able to give a lot more in the future if you re-invest as many funds as possible during your growth period."

Joe liked what he was hearing. It seemed he wasn't morally wrong just for wanting things or even buying them for that matter. He would think about it more later. In the meantime, doubts and uncertainties about his hopes were fading.

Then, Fred jolted him back to reality. "Now that you've made your goals list, Joe, forget about getting any of the things on it for a while. We didn't do this to help you decide which goodie to buy first. Of course, that's exactly what many people do. They decide what's most important to them right now and then put all their resources and energy into getting it. For example, the large-enough house with a swimming pool is to remain your dream goal for the time being. If you put your mind to it, plus all of the resources you can muster, I'll bet you can purchase a house right now fulfilling all your home desires. Much more house than you two need at the moment.

Once you have the house, you'll spend any remaining resources you have and others you'll borrow in order to furnish each and every room.

"If you do, you'll be following the course taken by thousands of other young couples. But also, you'll be making it much, much harder to ever achieve financial independence. Yes, if you buy a house now you'll get out of paying rent to some landlord. Nevertheless, I suggest staying in your apartment and trying first to buy a property to use as a rental. If you simply must buy something to live in yourself, make it a very modest starter house at this time. Or, buy a duplex and live in one half and rent the other."

"But Jane and I want a *nice* house of our own!" protested Joe.

"I fully understand, and you shall have your house. Enough house to satisfy any realistic desires you conjure up. It's just that you shouldn't get what I'll call your dream house now. You have to get started with a plan to travel the road to wealth."

"Well then, why did we bother with the list of goals now?"

"The likelihood of achieving your goals will be much higher if you have specific items in mind. The list allows you to visualize things. Visualize yourself cruising around in whatever kind of car you want. Look at cars in the showroom if you want. Take a test drive now and then. After all, you are a buyer, just not an immediate buyer. Get a magazine that shows all the new car models including the one you're dying to own. But don't buy the car...yet. Visualize until you can just about taste it. But wait until you can afford it—or anything else you want—comfortably, without derailing your train to wealth."

Joe was almost stunned. Here was Fred, apparently a successful guy, telling him to blue sky it! Telling him to dream about what he wanted! It was so unlike what Jane said to him. Jane seemed to stifle his dreams. And the funny thing was, Fred hadn't said anything about Joe needing to be a man of action. Unbelievable!

But then Fred started up again.

"You know, Joe, I want you to dream about the things you want real bad as a means of keeping you going. You know, motivated. The goodies you want are the carrots needed to keep the donkey moving forward. Guess what? Joe, you're the donkey!" Fred laughed mightily at his own humor while Joe turned pink.

"Aw, don't take things so seriously, Joe, just having a bit of fun . . . at your expense!" Fred chuckled softly again but stopped abruptly when he noticed Joe's tight lips.

"Now, Joe, don't get bent out of shape on account of my failed attempts at humor. I'm trying to make some points here that I think are important."

Fred continued: "Point number one is that you'll keep on track better if you have specific, tangible goals in mind. They'll keep you striving. If you think of letting up once you're headed towards wealth, you'll immediately remember that by giving up you're giving up your hopes of a fancy car or an exotic vacation. You won't give up your dreams easily once they're visualized and firmly implanted by thinking about them week after week.

"Point number two is that once you've got your goals set, you've got to have a plan. How are you going to reach your goals? What things can you do to help you attain them? What things should you not do because they're things which may prevent or delay you achieving your goals? It will become obvious the more you think about it. Everything brought to your attention, if it involves finances or time you could spend on your goals, will have to be evaluated. Think about everything in terms of whether it will or won't help you get where you want to be. Don't become obsessed, but evaluate everything you're asked to do and every cent you're asked to spend. Question whether it will help toward reaching your goal or work against you."

"Keep in mind what I said about not becoming obsessed. You and Jane won't have much fun in life if you go overboard trying to make it big. You've gotta have balance. For example, don't give up on annual vacations just because you're dreaming about having a spectacular cruise to Tahiti some time in the foggy future. Keep the dream, but your family needs a vacation every year. Heck, Joe, you need a vacation every year! But let's say you should be taking only economy vacations year by year until you make it big.

"A successful life must be a balance between demands and desires that are often at odds with each other. You must balance the yin and yang of things, as the Buddhists say. Don't become obsessed with making it big financially. You can't deprive yourself, your wife and your kids of all present enjoyments just so you can devote all your resources to the future. Some people say the future never comes; only the present is reality. We're only living in the present so we must live in an enjoyable, satisfying way even as we dream about and save or build for the future. Don't become an obsessed maniac.

"By the way, Joe, how old are your kids?"

"Don't have any."

"Really?"

"Yeah. It's not as if we don't want any. At least one day. Jane's more anxious than I am to have a couple. But I don't know how they would fit in with the big plans we've been discussing. What do you think?"

"Well," began Fred, stretching it out. "Kids have got good points and, uh, kids certainly can have bad points." He hesitated, thoughtfully. "Kids aren't for everyone," he declared as he looked penetratingly at Joe, "but most couples have them. My opinion is that kids are part of the great scheme of things and that if a couple has a hankering for them, they ought to have them.

"Now, you've suggested, Joe, that Jane is getting a little antsy about having children. Biological clock thing I suppose. But you can't ignore it, Joe; something like that is immensely important to a woman. And anything which is immensely important to either one of you has to be immensely important to you both as a couple. You must be together on the big things if you're going to be a successful couple. That's certainly true as far as getting wealthy together through real estate. No, wait a minute, I'll take that back to make a little change. You must be together on the big things if you are going to be a *happy*, successful couple. Notice I put in the word happy? Very important!

"An old friend of mine wanted to get into buying rental properties but his wife wanted no part of it. Well, he started buying anyway, but it just didn't work out the way he had planned. His rentals were successful enough, but all the joy was gone because his wife didn't even want to hear about them. Anyone with rentals ends up with a million stories. Some funny, some tragic. Lots of setbacks but lots of victories, too. But what if you didn't have anyone to share your experiences with?

"Now it would be one thing if my friend had been single. He wouldn't expect to be going home at the end of the day to tell someone all about his rental trials and tribulations. He would wait until he got together with other landlords for a beer or lunch or a meeting or whatever. Then they would all bemoan their fates or brag about how well things were going. But my friend was married! So the damned thing was he had someone to go home to talk to about the day's events, but his wife didn't want to hear anything about rentals! It was maddening to him. Took all the joy out of something very important to him. It was a big thing that they weren't together on as a couple."

"So what happened?" ventured Joe.

"Well, they eventually got divorced, that's what. Oh, it wasn't strictly on account of not seeing eye to eye on rentals but that was definitely a factor. I know it was, because one time while the divorce proceedings were underway my friend rambled through all his complaints against his wife. Item number four was she never had any interest in his real estate ventures. It really hurt him. Of course, looking at it from her perspective—and I liked them both—her item number four might have been how he dumped all their extra money into real estate gambles even after she had told him she didn't want to invest in rentals. My point, young man, is a couple needs to be in accord on big issues. One can lead and one can follow but they sure need to be in agreement as to the direction they're going."

"Yeah, well, I guess I agree with you, Fred. Jane wants me to go for something and will support me if I act instead of just talking about it. Oh, wait a minute. Probably I should say she'll support me if I define some goals and make a plan first."

"Actually, Joe, I don't think you should assume she'll support you just because you come up with goals and a plan. Jane strikes me as pretty level-headed and sensible. I think you'll have to come up with mutual goals and a darned good plan to convince her and get her full support."

"Yeah, you're probably right."

"Think about everything we've talked about today, Joe and feel Jane out about her general mood toward investing in rental real estate. But get serious with her about the children issue, too. Seems to me you probably should try to do both. That is, if both issues are important to both of you. You don't want to end up wealthy but not happy. Could happen if you both want kids but don't have them because you think they'll interfere too much with your plans. Remember balance, Joe.

"Let's get together again in a week or two or whenever you and Jane have reached agreement on some of these big issues. Okay?"

"Yeah, sure, Fred," Joe mumbled with uncertainty. "You've given me a whole lot to think about. But it sounds right." Joe had gotten up and was slowly making his way to the door with Fred behind him. He opened the front door and stepped out, then stopped.

"Yeah, Fred, I think you're absolutely right. Jane and I have got to put our heads together about a lot of things . . . including kids and rental real estate. We'll get into it, and once we've decided in a general sense what we want to do, I'll give you a call."

"Sounds good, Joe. Whenever you're ready, call me."

Joe and Jane had many discussions over the next few weeks about investment goals, major hopes for their lives, and, to a lesser extent, strategies for making it big financially. They didn't talk much about strategies because they agreed early on to be guided by Fred if, in fact, they decided to invest in real estate. First, however, they had to decide more specifically than simply health and happiness on what they wanted to achieve together.

Achieving goals *together* took on a prominent role in their discussions. Joe had taken to heart Fred's admonishments that to be happy as a couple they had to be in close harmony about all big issues.

Together they decided to try to get their first child under way. Having a child was to be considered a priority and all other matters would have to fit around it. However, they also decided together, that making it big financially was even more important if they were going to have a growing family. They vowed to provide a good life for their entire family even if they ended up with several children. What constituted a good life remained undefined. In general, besides good moral values and help thy neighbor type of satisfactions, Joe and Jane wanted to have the items on the wish list developed by Joe with Fred's guidance.

Joe and Jane, after considerable give and take as to what was most important to them, agreed to make a multi-year try at making it big. They would sacrifice and work as hard as necessary and adhere to whatever self-disciplines were necessary for several years. If, at the end of three years they hadn't made noticeable progress toward accumulating wealth, they would relax their efforts. If progress over three years looked good, they would stay the course.

The gradual formulation of a plan drew Joe and Jane closer together. More than ever before they discussed with each other their hopes and dreams. And they seemed to appreciate and respect each other more. They both wanted to make it big financially and were willing to make a strong joint effort. They knew it would not always be easy and they would undoubtedly make mistakes and false starts. The fact that they would support each other in the quest toward a common set of specific goals made all the difference. Both were eager to get going on their plans: to have a child and to make it big financially.

About four weeks after Fred and Joe had their first meeting, Joe called Fred and said: "We're ready. Can we get together about a rental real estate investment plan?" Fred proposed the two couples get together at the Madisons' house the coming Sunday afternoon, April 20th.

To this point, Joe and Jane Anderson, who were filled with conflict and doubt, and wondering if they would ever make it big financially, learned they should first make a "blue sky" list of desires. As motivation, they were encouraged to visualize specific tangible goals. They learned they must reconcile their wish list with their hopes of having children since this is a typical source of conflict between couples. The need for family agreement on goals and balance between wealth-building and other activities was stressed.

2

Why Real Estate Is Best

Joe and Jane Anderson were excited as they arrived at the Madisons' home Sunday afternoon, April 20th, of what would turn out to be their wealth-building year number one. As they took their places around a patio table, both Fred and Wendy could almost touch the enthusiasm which virtually bubbled out of their younger friends.

"My, oh my," said a bemused Fred. "Looks like we've got a couple of live ones here! Wendy, get me one of my blank contracts. Looks like time to sell some property! Yes, indeed, lambs to the slaughter. Yes, indeed!" He wrung his hands in a greedy manner, as if anticipating a big killing. The Andersons recoiled, mouths agape.

"Wa . . . wa . . . wait!" stammered Joe. "We . . . we . . . we're not ready to buy anything yet! Not today at least. We just. . . ."

Fred cut him off. "Just kidding!" He exploded in laughter at their reactions. "No, no, no, I'm just kidding and have no intention of selling any real estate to you two."

Wendy saw the problem. "Oh, don't mind Fred," she explained, as she looked at him disapprovingly but fondly. "Sometimes he gets carried away with what he thinks is funny. He's harmless . . . really." She turned back to the Andersons. "We're certainly glad to see you though. Fred tells me you may try to make it big financially through real estate. I don't know how big 'big' is in your minds, but we've done all right in real estate ourselves. Fred loves to talk about it. He told me he was looking forward to helping if you really want help. He said he would tell you everything he wished someone had been willing to tell him when he was your age."

The Andersons looked relieved.

"That's right," Fred offered. "Sorry if I came on too strong. Sort of like a used car salesman, wasn't I?" This time they all laughed easily. Fred continued.

"Let me clear things up before you start getting suspicious of me again. First, I do have an active state real estate license in good standing. Second, I'm retired from brokering except maybe for my own account. Third, I *am* willing to act as your mentor, to tell you what I know. But, I'm not your broker and I'm not trying to be. I'm not trying to sell you anything. And, as I said, I don't have anything to sell anyway—nothing of mine and no listings either.

"Real estate investing is my favorite subject. If I can help you get into it successfully that would be great. Wendy and I have done well at it and it would give me great pleasure to help someone else do well too."

"Sounds great, Fred," said Jane. "We'd like a mentor if that means you'll tell us what to do and give us all the money!" This time she and Joe laughed while Fred was taken aback. "Just kidding!" she added, and they all laughed. They had sized each other up. From now on they could talk easily.

"Okay," Fred began. "Let me tell you a bit about rental real estate and point out some advantages as I go along. Now, I'm assuming you know little or nothing about real estate. Also, I assume you're typical young Americans with little or no money. Am I right?" He looked at Joe and Jane for their reactions.

"Right on both counts," said Joe. Both he and Jane nodded.

"Fine. Okay on both counts. You know, I'm really enthusiastic about residential rentals for young, ambitious people. I mean those who have some dreams, are industrious and willing to do some work. For quite a long time it's work you can do in your spare time, on weekends or at night. From what little I know of you, you appear to be the type who could do well at it. You both seem energetic, level-headed and practical. Also, ambitious and goal oriented.

"Jane, Joe and I had quite a talk when he came over some weeks ago. We made a list of all the things he felt you both wanted. It was quite a list. It'll cost you a lot of money to get everything on it. Did you discuss it? Most important, are you both in agreement? Do you want to go for it?" He eyed Jane.

"Well, Fred, for the most part we are," said Jane. "We have some disagreements with details such as the items on the wish list you guys came up with and on priorities. We *do* want to make it, well, 'big,' as you say, but we weren't kidding about not having much money."

Wendy consoled her. "It would be great if you had a big bag of money to work with, Jane, but most young people don't have those resources. We didn't when we were your age. But where there's a will there's a way. And you two look as if you've got the will."

Fred began to talk about the advantages of residential real estate as a means of getting wealthy from a no-money, standing start. You just had to have a little to start, he said, plus a regular program of putting money aside. He outlined a road to financial independence. Joe and Jane listened silently, totally absorbed. Occasionally they asked a clarifying question, but for the most part they just let Fred speak. He obviously liked his subject and talking about it.

Fred explained: "Historically, real estate ownership has been the sustaining basis of most of the great family fortunes in the United States. Regardless of how a wealthy family made its original money—steel, chemicals, cosmetics, manufacturing, or whatever—a major part of the family's funds was eventually transferred into real estate. Real estate, in its many forms—office buildings, warehouses, apartments, stores, raw land or houses—possesses a stability other investments lack. In addition, the long-term price trend of well-located real estate is always up.

"In recent years, fortunes made quickly though high tech ventures and stocks have grabbed the limelight, but real estate is still a place for good investments. Why, even the new high tech millionaires are grabbing up fabulous properties. Bill Gates himself sank forty-two million dollars into a place to lay his head at night!

"Real estate is tangible. The owner can touch it, stand on it and control it to a large extent, although not completely. Control, in my opinion, is the number one reason why real estate is better than other investments. The owner can change its use, within restrictions, to make it more valuable. Or, the owner can make it less valuable through negligence. Real estate can be a super investment for young people who don't have a lot of money.

"For instance, if you invest in a duplex, you have considerable control over its value which is totally different from the stock market where the little guy has absolutely zero control over his stock holdings except to sell them. After you've bought the duplex you can stand on its front lawn if you want. You can embrace its mailboxes if you want. You can kick the building in the side. It'll feel solid.

"More importantly, you can evaluate your duplex as bought and decide how to improve its value. Does it need landscaping? New paint? New tenants? Should the rents be raised? Should you change lawn services? Perhaps discontinue lawn service and do it yourself? Induce a tenant to do the lawns?

"The point is, *you yourselves* call the shots. There are many things you can do—or have done—which will affect the profitability of your duplex. It's profitability that determines the rental's value to you and others. Which investment do you have most control over, stocks or rental property? It's a no-brainer. It's no contest. Rental property is the winner.

"Another critical difference between buying stocks and rental real estate is that with rentals you can determine the intrinsic value of the property. Most people can't determine the value of the business behind stock they wish to buy and don't even try. They end up buying price to chase a hoped for higher price. For rental real estate, I'll show you how to determine value fairly accurately before you buy. Value in rentals is related to the generation of profits. That's key to investment success. Determining the value of rental property allows you to determine an appropriate price to pay for it. That's the way stock purchases should work but don't. With stocks, for most people, the price is the price; there's not necessarily any rational relationship between price and stock value.

"Using a little money to control a lot of value is using what is called leverage. The possibility of using high leverage in financing the purchase of residential real estate is the second major reason why it is a superior investment. Let me explain leverage.

"Joe, suppose Jane asked you to lift the front of your refrigerator so she could get an earring that dropped and rolled underneath. You know you couldn't easily do the job with your bare hands. What you'd probably do is slip a strong, thin piece of wood under the leading edge of the fridge like a pry bar. You'd then put a small block of wood, say a piece of two by four, under your pry bar close to the fridge. Then you'd press down on the far end of your pry bar with just one hand and easily raise the front of the refrigerator. With your other hand you would retrieve Jane's earring and become a hero.

"To raise the refrigerator you would have been using leverage. With a lever placed over a pivot point called a fulcrum, you can lift a heavy object with little physical effort. The longer the lever from fulcrum to free end, the easier it is to lift or control the heavy load on the other end. If you make the comparison to financing, the load is the value of what you're trying to purchase and a loan is the lever used to help make the purchase. The higher the percentage of loan to value, the longer the lifting lever. The easy effort enabled by the long lever, or high percentage of loan to value, is analogous to the relatively small amount of cash you have to come up with to make the purchase.

"Let's assume for the moment that you two, as beginning investors, had somehow saved $10,000 and decided to put it into a rental duplex. Forget for the moment the acquisition or closing costs connected with the duplex purchase.

"You should fairly readily be able to buy a $100,000 property using your $10,000 as a 10% down payment. Upon closing, you'll own and control the $100,000 duplex. As mentioned before, you can, if you wish, stand on its front lawn and embrace its mailboxes. You can stand there chanting a mantra: 'It's mine, all mine. It's mine, all mine . . . .'"

The others all laughed at Fred's chant and he smiled with pleasure at the success of his humor. He continued: "Oh sure, a financial institution holds your promissory note for $90,000 with a mortgage on your duplex as its collateral, which is the backing for your loan. Nevertheless, the official public records in the county courthouse show you two—and you two alone— as owners. What a feeling! And guess what? The financial institution doesn't want to take it away from you! They want you to own it! That is, they do providing you don't do something stupid to materially decrease the value of their collateral or, even dumber, neglect to make loan payments.

"The tremendous importance of being able to own $100,000 in property for a mere $10,000 down is worth emphasizing. Not only do you own the real estate, but you can *control* it, to a large extent! Think about the total lack of control you would have over an investment of the same size in stocks, gold, silver, coins or commodities. As I've said, with such investments you have zero control other than to sell.

"So what, you say. How do you benefit from the use of high leverage in a real estate purchase? First answer is the obvious one—without leverage you wouldn't be able to buy the duplex, period. Second answer is that leverage magnifies the power of your own money, meaning your $10,000 down payment. Here lies the real power of real estate leverage and it truly is awesome.

"Consider your duplex going up 10% in value over a period of time. Its appreciated value is now $110,000. But you owe $90,000 to your lender and, in fact, a little less due to mortgage payments you made. Wow! Subtracting your $90,000 loan from the property's new value of $110,000 gives a difference of $20,000! The $20,000 difference between actual value and what you owe is known as your equity, meaning the portion you own."

Fred went on: "While the property increased just 10% in total value, due to leverage, your $10,000 original equity *doubled!* Doubling your equity from ten to twenty thousand dollars means you enjoyed a 100% gain!"

Jane interjected, "Sounds good, Fred, but how long would it take to double our equity?"

"With real estate it can take virtually no time at all. Perhaps the duplex, when you bought it, looked shabby. Maybe that's partly why you had to pay only $100,000 for it. Paint was peeling, grass was as high as an elephant's eye and bushes around it had gone haywire. You get the picture—an eyesore. Using not much money, maybe only about $150 for paint, plus effort and sweat, you could improve the property's appearance mightily. You make the buildings and its surroundings look so much better that other real estate buyers would easily pay $110,000 for the freshly-painted, sharp looking duplex.

"A main reason why Wendy and I got into and stuck with residential rental real estate is that it can become your own cash cow. A rental can sort of be like your own goose that keeps laying golden eggs. Stocks, if they pay a dividend at all, might give you a yield of between 2 and 7% a year. Providing you buy and operate your rentals correctly, you should receive anywhere from 15 to 40% cash-on-cash return, or more, on your investment per year. I'll prove it to you once we get into the specifics of a particular rental property purchase.

"The spendable money you get from a rental property is the rent money you take in less all the money you pay out to operate and maintain the property and to service your debt. It's what's left in your pocket. Buy and operate correctly and there should be a good percentage of money left in your pocket or purse at the end of the year.

"You want cash flow out of your rentals so you can buy other rentals and for living expenses as well. And, oh yes, also to buy all the luxuries you want. Once you're into retirement, you'll need a steady flow of cash to live the way you were accustomed to before retirement. In fact, you may wish to live even better after retirement as you travel to faraway places. That kind of travel can get really expensive."

"Questions!" exclaimed Joe.

"Me too," added Jane a second later.

"Well, okay," said Fred. "Guess you're not sleepin' after all! Fire away."

Joe began: "Why did you say cash-on-cash? Why didn't you just say return? And, our friend Marty Repasky told us one problem with investing directly in real estate is that it goes up in value slowly. Is that so?"

Fred responded: "Joe, whoever told you real estate appreciated slowly was correct for the most part. Oh, some properties zoom in value spectacularly. Different growth cities and certain areas get hot from time to time. You hear about frantic bidding by buyers and sellers getting offers for more than they were asking for their houses. Those cities are the exception, and those hot times may be short lived, like maybe two to four years, until supply and demand come back into balance. On the other hand, real estate markets can certainly become depressed and values stagnaie for years.

"There is no doubt, however, about the value of well-located property going constantly upward, long term. Of course, when I say well-located I'm excluding those cities, usually northern, which have lost their industrial base and gone into major decline. The city of Cleveland is, or at least was, an example. Cleveland went into a terrible decline that sent real estate values into a tailspin. But guess what? Cleveland is coming back! It's being revitalized and real estate values are rising again.

"In an overall sense, well-maintained residential rental property in normal growth areas is typically increasing in value at the rate of between 2½ to 10% a year. Think of maybe 6% overall compared to the 11% long-term growth rate for stocks. So it would seem to be slower growth all right but overall value increase doesn't tell the whole story. You see, it doesn't take into consideration the tremendous value of leverage as applied to real estate financing. Leverage in rental real estate is better than for any other type of investment. Let me give you an example.

"Let's go back to your hypothetical $10,000 and the alternatives of investing in stocks or a duplex. Using the maximum margin in purchasing stocks—which I strongly recommend *against* for beginning investors like you—you could buy twice as much stock as your own money would buy. In essence, you can borrow up to half of the total value of the buy. So, if you have $10,000 of your own, using maximum margin you can buy up to $20,000 worth of stock. Suppose in a year the price goes up 11% so the value is now $22,200. Your equity, after paying back the broker's $10,000 loan, is now $12,200. Your $2,200 gain represents a 22% increase.

"Alternatively, you buy a $100,000 duplex with $10,000 down and have a mortgage of $90,000. This kind of leverage is definitely recommended for the beginning real estate investor. At the end of the year the duplex goes up 6% so it is now worth $106,000. What's your equity now? Well, if you had to pay back the $90,000 mortgage you would have a remaining equity of $16,000. That's a $6,000 or 60% increase on your original $10,000!

"Real estate is the obvious, hands-down winner for the beginning investor, even if you buy the stocks on maximum margin. And remember, the beginner with no holding power shouldn't be buying stocks on margin, as any ethical stockbroker will tell you. I'm sure you know people can and do lose a lot of money in the stock market even though in the long term, good quality stocks appreciate. Stock prices are relatively volatile and can go down at any time. Real estate values, on the other hand, are pretty stable. In a declining stock market, use of margin causes you to lose money very rapidly. If our example stocks hadn't been bought on margin, the results contrast would be even more dramatic: an 11% equity increase from stocks versus 60% from the duplex.

"So you see, even though the rate of total value increase is lower for real estate than it is for stocks, it doesn't mean stocks are better for the beginning investor. If leverage is properly used, the equity increase through stocks is not even close to what is possible from real estate."

Joe and Jane looked at each other and at Wendy. Wendy nodded her agreement.

"My question is," Jane said, "How can there be such a range of returns from the rental property? You said returns could be from 15 to 40%. That's an incredible range. Do we have a choice? If so, we'll go for the 40%!" They all laughed.

"Plus, tell us how to get those high returns. Also, do the returns you're talking about from rentals correspond with the interest or yields from other investments? Are we talking apples and apples here or do the profit measures differ depending upon which type of investment?"

"Good questions, Jane. Yes, absolutely we are talking about the same kind of returns because obviously it's very important only to be comparing apples with other apples. That's also why I use the term cash-on-cash. I want to emphasize the *total* cost of an investment, and I want to reduce the acquisition cost to the common denominator that allows alternative investments to be properly evaluated. The common denominator is cash invested. Once you know that, you need to know how much cash you get from your investment in a year."

Wendy elaborated: "In other words, given the total cash cost of acquiring an investment—whatever it is—how much cash does it earn for you over the course of one year?"

Fred took over where Wendy had left off. "Now, notice at this time we're not talking about the total cost of the investment, only the cash needed to acquire it. Think back to the duplex we discussed. The duplex cost $100,000, but we only want to consider—at this time—the $10,000 cash we must put down to own it. You see, we'll automatically be taking into consideration whatever degree of leverage we chose to use or, rather, can use.

"So, let's suppose you get $1,950 in cash flow in a year's time from your duplex. I'll show you later how cash flow is actually calculated. But for the moment, accept that you get $1,950 cash from your $10,000 invested cash, or 19.5%. This cash flow return, and remember we're talking about annual return at this time not growth or appreciation, is directly comparable to returns from alternative investments. For example, you might get 2.5% interest if you kept your $10,000 in a savings account. That would be $250 cash on your $10,000 cash. From a one-year certificate of deposit, or CD, you might be paid $500 cash interest on your $10,000 cash. That's 5% cash-on-cash. From dividend-paying stocks you might get a 5.5% yield or $550 cash on your $10,000 cash. Invest in gold bars or coins and you won't get any cash-on-cash annual return. Cash-on-cash is an important concept and should definitely be used in comparing alternative placements for your hard-earned money.

"Now I'll get to Jane's original question and then throw a fly into the ointment. First, you may wonder why I just used 19.5% as the cash flow from the duplex in my comparison of yields from other investments—I wouldn't want you to invest in direct ownership of any rental real estate unless you calculate a cash-on-cash return of not less than three times the then current one-year CD rate. Got that?"

Joe and Jane looked quizzically at each other, then at Wendy, then at Fred. Fred went on. "Suppose you calculate the cash-on-cash you're likely to get from a rental property you're considering buying. What I'm telling you is that you shouldn't buy it unless you clearly can see a return coming out of it of at least three times the rate that one-year CDs are pay-ing. If a CD will pay you 5%, you shouldn't buy rental prop-erty unless it will pay you at least 15%."

"Wow!" interrupted Joe, "we'll never be able to find any-thing like that! How about two times the CD rate?"

"No, Joe. It has to be at least three times the annual CD rate for the twelve months immediately following the closing. You can do it. I'm going to explain why and how, but just bear with me for now. Here comes the ointment fly I promised you."

Joe and Jane sat back in their chairs looking worried.

"In the real world you can't get away with paying $10,000 cash for a transaction, even if the deal is supposed to be 10% down on a $100,000 duplex. There are essential front-end expenses called closing costs to contend with. Closing costs could very well add 2.5 to 5% of the total property cost on top of your down payment. To keep it simple, let's say the various closing costs required to acquire the $100,000 duplex amount to 3%. It means you will need $3,000 plus $10,000, or $13,000, to acquire the duplex.

"The total cash required must be used in the cash-on-cash calculation for any investment. In this case, the duplex still generates $1,950 cash flow a year but on your $13,000 cash, not just $10,000. The true return is therefore 15%, not 19.5%. And yes, in my opinion the true cash-on-cash return, based on total cash required, must exceed three times the an-nual CD rate to make it an acceptable deal. And, mind you, three times the CD rate is needed just to make it an *acceptable deal*; it doesn't mean it's a *good deal!*

"So why do I say three times the one-year CD rate is the minimum acceptable return from residential rental property? Well, to begin with, if you just left your money in a one-year CD you'd get 5%. Right?"

Joe and Jane nodded. They remembered that 5% had been used earlier as an example yield from a one-year certificate of deposit.

"Well, then," continued Fred. "You wouldn't cash in the no-effort, virtually risk-free CD to buy residential rental prop-erty unless it would pay you more than 5%, would you?"

"Course not!" declared Jane.

"No, of course not!" echoed Joe a moment later.

Fred continued: "Figure that the work to operate your rental property yourself is worth 5% on its own. After all, holding the CD required no effort whatsoever. On the other hand, the rental property will require lots of attention: Fix and clean apartments, show them, rent them, collect rents, bookkeeping, etcetera, etcetera. Surely all that is worth something! I'd say it's worth 5% at least."

The Andersons nodded.

"Let's go further," Fred said. "Holding a CD is pretty well risk-free. Owning your rental property won't be. Oh, there may not be any appreciable risk of losing it, providing you buy right and in a decent location, but there is still the risk of turnover and vacancies. Plus, you might have apartments occupied, but the occupants might decide not to pay you. All of these things are risks to your profits. You can minimize the risks to a low, quite acceptable level by managing properly, but the risks remain.

"In addition, there's an aggravation factor associated with owning residential rentals. Despite good screening of prospective tenants, some loony is bound to get in sometime or you rent to what seems to be a stable married couple and they split up. The husband or wife moves out and the other whines to you that they can't handle the apartment on their own. All manageable aggravations and all solvable but aggravations nevertheless. To me, the risk factor and aggravation factor together are worth at least another 5%.

"Basically, I'm saying that to make it worthwhile to endure the work, risk and aggravation of being an owner, it's got to provide a return at least three times greater than you could enjoy with no risk, no effort and no aggravation. But hold on a minute. I suppose I better put in a qualification. Here it is: the three times rule only applies when you're going to manage the property yourself. And I know that's what you two plan to do.

"However, at some point, when you have enough property to be burdensome, you may want to pay someone else to manage it for you. If so, a professional manager's fee—say 5 to 12% of rents collected—has to be factored in as an operating expense for any property you're considering. When this is done, reduce your minimum expectations of profit from the new property. Reduce it from three times the annual CD rate to two times to allow for at least some of the amount you'll pay the manager. It's reasonable to accept only two times the CD rate as profit because you'll have less stress, aggravation and work with a professional manager.

"Actually, I'm not the only one who thinks the return from rentals you're considering buying and managing yourself should be at least three times the current annual CD rate. During my years as a real estate broker I worked with scores and scores of serious rental property buyers. As I worked with them and analyzed prospective properties with and for them, I got to know their expectations. Now, no one outlined their rationales in the fashion I just did for you. You know—effort, risk, aggravation and so forth. But they did have an intuitive feel for what return would convert them from lookers to buyers.

"In any big-ticket selling situation, the salesperson has got to be looking for the price at which the prospective buyer will act. Buying a rental property should be based on analysis and determination of annual rate of return on the total cash required to acquire the property. Many factors go into a proper analysis and all have some effect on return. Whatever cash-on-cash return a prospect seemed to perceive as adequate steered me to the all-important price that I, as broker, had to find in order to get the buyer to act. The price asked for the property is merely one ingredient. Terms and money down are at least as important. Someone once said they would pay any price asked for anything as long as they could set the terms of purchase!

"In any event, gradually I came to understand that even buyers who couldn't or wouldn't say what return they wanted would act if they saw a calculated return acceptable to them. I noticed the acceptable return price-point varied somewhat in tune with what interest rates prevailed at the time. It's natural enough. If rates for bank borrowing are running high, interest rates to bank depositors are also high, although much lower and lagging behind borrower rates. Gradually I began to notice a correlation between interest paid on one-year CDs and the cash-on-cash return which would cause buyers to act. My conclusion, even though buyers wouldn't state it as such, was that buyers will start to buy when the return shows as at least three times the annual CD rate.

"My conclusion was not scientifically determined. It's what is known as an empirical conclusion, meaning based upon practical observation. I certainly had good, practical data. At one return point a buyer wouldn't budge, but at another—at least three times the one-year CD rate—I could start to smell commission. Nothing more practical than that!"

"Are you saying no one bought unless you could show them a three times CD rate of return?" asked Joe.

"No, no exactly. What I mean to say is that many times my hesitant prospects became active buyers once they saw a level of return which ignited their interest. My repeated observation was that the ignition level was a return equaling three times the annual CD rate. I reached my three times conclusion a number of years ago, but before that I couldn't say for sure at what return point buyers would buy.

"Also, while I've always been big on analysis, the same is not true of all other brokers and salespeople. Good heavens, a good many salespeople don't seem to have a clue as to how to even make a thorough analysis! Yet, they sell properties. On what basis it's hard to say. Be assured I'll make sure you two will know how to do an analysis.

"Firsthand and secondhand I've heard from and about buyers who bought stupidly, in my opinion. Owners have told me they bought on a break-even basis or even at a monthly loss. I can't imagine myself doing either. Never have, never will. I advocate buying only on the basis of a decent profit—or return—starting with the day of closing."

"But, Fred," said Jane. "How well did it sit with those sellers you were representing if you insisted on buyers getting such a high rate of return?"

"Not really at odds, Jane. A basic real estate fact is that, barring forced or distressed sales, the only sales/purchase price that works is the fair one. It's the proper price for the property at that particular time. My experience is that sellers won't accept a price they're not really happy with. Of course, they would all like to get more, but they know no one is forcing a buyer to buy. Likewise, a buyer will only pay a price he or she is comfortable with. Now remember, we're talking about investment purchases here, not homes for the buyer's family to live in. In the case of homes, emotion and status enter into the decision.

"Purchases of rental properties are, or should be, non-emotional. The knowledgeable investor goes by the numbers. They'll only pay the price the numbers tell them will result in an acceptable deal. Acceptable means lots of different things to different buyers. I already told you no buyers ever told me precisely what return they would accept and what they wouldn't. I say this knowing the buyers themselves knew definitely what they wouldn't accept. Understandably, they wanted the exact opposite of sellers. Buyers want the lowest price and highest return possible. But reasonable buyers know that if they want the property, it's unlikely they'll be able to steal it. They know they'll have to pay a fair price.

"The broker is in the middle. The honest broker does what he can to affect a sale/purchase, but neither the buyer nor the seller has to accept any deal they don't want to accept. The seller is properly served when the broker puts together a sale that satisfies the seller. Similarly, a buyer is properly served when the broker puts together a purchase that satisfies the buyer.

"But I remember, Jane, you still want to know about getting 40% returns. Jane, let's suppose at a time when one-year CDs are paying 5% interest you purchase a duplex which will give you 15% cash-on-total-cash return over the first twelve months you own the duplex. Now, let's suppose you also do a cosmetic fix up of the duplex and put in some sweat. The minor cost of the fix up is treated as normal maintenance and doesn't diminish your expected cash flow. Why? Because you had budgeted money for maintenance when you did your calculation of expected return. The cash flow you projected was *after* paying for maintenance. Please accept that you can greatly improve the appearance, and therefore the value, of your duplex with a little money and a lot of sweat. More relevant to my point is the fact that your improvements may enable you to easily raise rents $25 per month for each side of the duplex. Your cash flow thus goes up by $50 per month or $600 a year on your original investment.

"Say you had originally projected $1,950 cash flow from a $13,000 total cash investment to give you a 15% return. Now your cash flow is up to $2,550 but since your cash investment remained at $13,000, your annual return rate is now 19.6%! But don't forget the growth component of your investment. If your improvements added 6% to the overall value of the duplex, it's now worth $106,000. Since you still owe $90,000 or thereabouts, your equity is now $16,000. A $3,000 increase in equity represents more than 23% growth of your original $13,000 cash investment.

"Just think, my friends," Fred said, happily. "Within the first twelve months of owning your duplex you're enjoying almost 20% annual rate of return plus a growth in equity of 23% or so!"

"Bravo, Fred!" exclaimed Joe. "Let's buy it! Where do I sign up for this duplex? We've got to get started. We can't afford to be sitting around drinking coffee!" They all laughed at Joe's exuberance.

"Joe! Joe! Joe!" cried Fred with a downward motion of his half-outstretched arms. "Get control! I'm just talking about a hypothetical situation here. Besides, you don't have $13,000!" Again, they all laughed.

"But don't lose your enthusiasm either," Wendy added. "Fred was painting a hypothetical scenario but it was an entirely realistic one. We've done what he described and even better. You can, too. Not only that, your annual return rate will get better and better as the years pass. Just think, rents will continue to go up, but your investment remains essentially the same. Yes, your costs will go up, so you won't get to keep every penny of your rent increases, but you'll keep a reasonable percentage. If your investment remains the same your rate of return has got to get higher and higher. Given enough time, your annual return can become 40% and even higher.

"Also, as Fred said, the growth component of your investment should be fantastic as well. Is there any doubt a well-located $100,000 duplex, if properly maintained, will eventually be worth $125,000? None whatsoever, given enough time. No more than maybe seven years at the most and maybe just three. Plus, since you're paying down loan principal as you make monthly mortgage payments, by the time the property is worth $125,000 you may only owe $87,000. Your equity in the duplex would then be $38,000. Seems to me that would mean your original $13,000 cash investment would have almost tripled—a 300% increase! Not too shabby, I'm sure you'll agree! Three hundred percent in seven years is almost 43% per year."

The Andersons were stunned. Both of them could see how it could happen. They could suddenly see themselves climbing up the ladder toward financial independence. The Madisons hadn't said anything the Andersons didn't think they could handle. The Andersons had faith in the Madisons. They trusted them to be telling them the plain truth.

As if reading their minds, Fred declared. "You're probably having a hard time believing all this is true, but Wendy and I can attest it is absolutely so. We didn't overstate our case. I can guide you into making such real estate investments a reality for you. Not only that, I haven't even described all of the advantages real estate has over alternative investments. There's depreciation and there are other great tax aspects. There's pride of ownership and there's satisfaction in supplying shelter—one of the basic human needs. Plus, to us, rental property ownership seems to be the ideal, inflation-proof retirement plan. You can't beat it.

"But hold on now. Let me remind you there are also some negatives to direct investment in real estate. We won't deny it. For one thing, it's an investment you have to work at. How well you do will depend a great deal upon how much you put into it, and that includes some actual sweat. At least until you're doing well enough to hire other people to do anything physical. You don't have to do anything to be invested in CDs or stocks.

"You also have to put up with tenants—your customers—and some of their shenanigans will curl your hair. Don't get me started! You don't have to deal with tenants if you deal in gold coins. It's largely a matter of your temperament and attitude. Some people just aren't cut out to be landlords. Others, like Wendy and me, enjoy it. Of course, every type of business has its share of aggravations and the residential rental business is no exception. But when I talk to my buddies in other businesses, they have some awful things to contend with also. In business you kind of pick the poison that most agrees with you. Wendy and I prefer rental property poisons. In fact, for the most part we enjoy the rental business very much.

"One big thing to consider with direct ownership of real estate of any kind is the lack of liquidity. What do I mean? Well, cash in your pocket is very liquid. It can, and probably will, flow out of your pocket like water drains through a hole. On the other hand, if you have money tied up in a property, you can't easily or quickly get it out if an urgent need arises. Your funds are not 'liquid.' Sure, you can sell the property, but unless you go for fire-sale prices to get an instant sale, it's going to take two to three months minimum to get your money out. With publicly traded stocks you've got a huge ready market and you can have your funds in hand within days of deciding to sell. Liquidity is definitely an advantage of the stock market. The stock market certainly has problems but liquidity ain't one of them.

"There are some answers to the real estate liquidity problem but they're not perfect. The very fact you have equity in an income producing property will probably get you a small, short-term, unsecured loan from your bank. If you need a sizeable amount, there are second mortgage loans and refinancing, but both of these alternatives take time to arrange. You won't have to sell your property but it's still not instant cash. Keeping in mind the lack of liquidity with any real estate—including your own house if you have one—means you should keep a larger amount as cash reserves to handle the unexpected. Naturally, as your holdings grow—providing you don't get greedy and grow too fast—your liquidity problems should fade away. In fact, I can envision the day when you'll have so much cash coming in it will be a problem. Kind of a nice problem, but a problem nevertheless."

Joe and Jane started to smile.

"No joke, I'm serious!" Fred quickly added. "There are more real estate pros and cons we'll discuss as we think of them. But I guess that'll have to wait until we have another session," he said, glancing at his watch in an obvious manner.

Wendy chimed in. "We haven't exaggerated any of the advantages of real estate. In fact, it can get much, much better. Just think if you had a bunch of different properties. What if you had not just a duplex with two rental units but 20 rental units or 50 or 80 or 110! If Fred and I can do it, you can, too."

Fred beamed. He was happy to help someone. He would be delighted to help the Andersons—and anyone else—get started on the road to financial independence. Besides, he chuckled to himself, they would have to do all the hard work; all he had to do was to give advice!

The two couples chatted amicably for ten more minutes then agreed to get together again in a week. As they were driving home, Joe and Jane agreed they could hardly wait for their next investment session. It was getting exciting! Why, the way Fred and Wendy put it, the Andersons' wealth train seemed ready to pull out of the station! Were they ready to go?

Joe and Jane Anderson had been very excited when they met with multi-millionaires Fred and Wendy Madison. As their new mentor, Fred had explained that residential rental real estate is tangible, can be accurately evaluated and can be controlled by the owner in marked contrast to stocks. Through judicious use of leverage they could obtain a far greater cash-on-cash return than from stocks they bought on risky margin. In addition, they learned that operating cash flow from rentals far surpasses yields from stocks, CDs, money market accounts, etc. Fred also had explained why the maximum price to be paid for rental property is the one that results in a cash-on-total-cash return equaling at least three times that produced by one-year CDs. Fred outlined some negative aspects of rental properties as well.

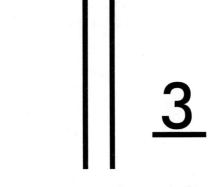

3

Getting Ready

The first Saturday in May, after pleasantries, the Madisons and Andersons sat down around the Madisons' patio table. Sipping coffee, they quickly got to the business of how the Andersons should go about becoming wealthy.

Pragmatic Fred started in a solemn tone. "Before we come up with a specific real estate buying plan, we need to go over a few basics. Things that will get you ready to work on becoming wealthy. Establish your foundation, so to speak. Becoming wealthy will depend upon having a good foundation, goals and a plan to follow. It will depend on how well you carry out your plan once devised. It'll depend upon how diligent you are, how disciplined you are, how bad you want to achieve your goals. Whether or not you're willing to get your hands dirty, literally as well as figuratively. You've got to be alert and aware of possibilities. You've got to have stick-to-itiveness and not be an easy quitter. You've got to be energetic." He eyed them both to gauge reactions.

Jane responded: "Fred, I can't thank you enough for all you said to Joe about goals back in March and for your explanation about real estate advantages a couple of weeks ago. I can say we're determined to give the getting wealthy business a damn good try. We're ready—both of us—to follow your recommendations. And, I think we've got all the qualities you say are essential. So . . . lay it on us!"

Wendy jumped in. "Good for you two! Fred and I haven't really regretted anything big we've done together. Oh, we've made mistakes, but since we got into things together we've never wasted much time blaming each other for messes. We just figured out what we did wrong, then straightened things out. Luckily, Fred and I are pretty optimistic. I hope you are, too. If you're optimistic, then a setback doesn't throw you too bad. You just revise plans and move on."

"Glad you said that!" Joe exclaimed. "Sometimes I've a tendency to be very cautious for fear of making a mistake. Are you giving us the green light to screw up every once in a while?"

"Honey," Wendy said, "you just check with Fred on any of the big things you're unsure of. At least until you get confidence in yourself. Fred's pretty confident—sometimes I think he's overconfident—but he wasn't always so. We've had lots of practice so we feel okay about any real estate decisions we make now. Once upon a time we were where you are now."

Fred cut in. "Okay, everyone, let's get down to business. Joe, how much money do you have?"

Joe shot a glance at Jane. He hesitated then started. "Ah, I . . . that is . . . we . . ."

Jane cut him off. "Other than what's in our checking account, we've got about $3,000 in a savings account, and we're trying to add to that each month."

"Good enough. Now we've got a starting point. $3,000 and growing. Terrific. How fast is it growing, Jane?"

"Depends on the month. Sometimes we've got a good surplus and we put up to $500 into our nest egg. Sometimes we can't put anything in it. And to tell you the truth, sometimes we draw money back out."

"Uh, oh," said Fred. "Bad answer. But typical. It's part of why most people don't get anywhere." Fred held up his hand to stop the defensive protests he saw Jane about to unleash. "Jane, don't take offense. What you two do concerning your nest egg is just typical, that's all. Heck, I give you real high marks for creating a budget. Joe told me you have one and live by it. Most families don't have a formalized budget, but they should have."

"Well at least we try to live by it," explained Jane. "It's hard sometimes."

"Oh, we know all about tight budgets, don't we, sweetie?" Wendy asked, looking at Fred and giving him a calming pat on the forearm. "There were plenty of times when it was a real struggle and pain in the rear to stick to our budget. To be perfectly honest, Jane, sometimes we didn't stick to it despite what Fred would have you believe." She said this with a smile and another calming pat to Fred's forearm. Fred's eyebrows bunched and he looked wryly back at Wendy.

"Yeah," conceded Fred, "Wendy's right . . . again. We had fits and starts getting out of the gate. But that was way back when. We've had smooth financial sailing for years and years ever since." Fred raised his head slightly and gazed into the distance. After a few moments he added wistfully, "Maybe that's why I'm keen on helping you guys. And, of course, if you want the help. Wendy's always telling me not to give advice unless it's asked for. But I think you kinda were asking. Weren't you?"

"Oh yes! Definitely!" chimed the Andersons. "We're so confused as to what we should do and how to get started. We want advice. You're the expert as far as we're concerned"

"Hold on a minute!" cried Fred with a shake of his head. "I'm not used to anyone calling me an expert!"

"Except yourself," jabbed Wendy, and they all laughed. Wendy went on: "But in defense of my loquacious hubby . . . dear, you are an expert . . . compared to Jane and Joe!" They all laughed again. "Seriously though, Fred is an expert. I mean, he's not the world's foremost expert but he knows what he's doing in the field of rental properties and he'll keep you from going very far wrong. How many real estate deals have you done, Fred? I mean not just concerning our stuff but altogether?"

Fred had worked first as a general commercial realtor and then, for his last ten years as a broker, had specialized in small residential rental properties. "Small" to Fred had meant properties having no more than 70 apartments.

"Well, since you're asking," began Fred in his aw shucks tone, "I've probably been involved in around 150 real estate deals that successfully closed. And at least that many that didn't. The no-goes include deals that really didn't get off the ground to ones that almost made it all the way. Damned if I haven't had a deal or two blow up at closing! Now, that kind of thing gets to you. A very successful broker once told me that mistakes in real estate can really cost you. She was absolutely right. Her point was that they cost so much, and it hurts so much, that you learn harsh lessons very, very well. You sure as hell avoid making the same mistake, or anything like it, twice.

"Gradually, you get better at what you're doing; gradually, you make fewer mistakes. You get to know the signs of trouble and can see early on what's not going to work. You learn when to extract yourself or pull the plug on an unsalvageable, losing proposition. Sort of like knowing when to fold in a poker game. It gives you plain old experience—which is what you need in any field to become good at it. Course, I mean successful experience is what makes you good at something, not just doing the same dumb thing over and over. Someone said experience is what you get when you don't get what you're trying to get. It's sort of a consolation prize. Jane, I'll try to give you the benefit of my successful experiences."

"Great and thanks," said Jane.

"Can we get on with it?" prompted Wendy.

Fred started talking. "I'm glad you've got $3,000 to spend, but I hope you've also got a rainy day fund. I mean enough to keep you going in case you both lose your jobs. If you don't have a separate rainy day fund you don't have $3,000 to invest. Got one, Jane?"

"Actually, we do, Fred, but it's more of a rainy day *plan* rather than a pile of money. We've got another $1,600 in the savings account we don't normally touch. Probably we should put it away as a certificate of deposit we can't easily get to. You know, to put the $1,600 beyond the bounds of easy temptation. It's enough to pay our rent a couple of months. We've got a lot of food in the house so we won't starve. We've also got two credit cards that we use but pay off each month. In a pinch I think we could run each of them up to their $5,000 limits. So that's $11,600 we would have access to, so I think we could make it."

Jane continued. "It's really better than that. First of all, we both have steady jobs now and I can't believe we'd lose both of them in the same week. If either of us did lose our job we'd probably get at least a couple of weeks severance pay. It's never taken either one of us more than a week to find a job."

"Wait a minute," Joe protested, "seems to me it took you about four weeks to get your present job after you quit your last one. And I don't remember any severance pay either."

"I knew you were going to bring that up as soon as I said it. That was entirely different. We didn't really have any responsibilities so I pampered myself a bit. But when I decided it was time to get back to work I found my present job in four days. If we had a child or an investment, I would have gotten a new job in a flash. No question about it."

"Stop! Time out!" cried Fred, dampening the rising heat with downward motions of his half outstretched arms. "I get the idea. You've got a plan and a lot of confidence in yourselves and a little rainy day money. That, plus your budgeting, will probably get you through. I mean that. The fact that you budget means you're aware of the comings and goings of your money. The majority of people don't seem to be aware of where their money goes with any degree of accuracy. If you're budgeting, it probably means you have reserves for such things as car breakdowns and holiday gifts."

"Well, you know," said Jane quietly, "we do. And it proves the value of budgeting. Why, our friends the Repaskys are a good couple to know in so many ways but they seem to be unaware that Christmas is coming until they suddenly find out they're into Christmas shopping again. Then Mitzy Repasky does a song and dance about how commercial everything has become and how they don't have the money for gifts and how they're going to end up maxing their plastic and won't get things paid off until August. I could scream when she starts that stuff. I say to her, 'Look, Mitzy, you knew last Christmas that Christmas would be coming again in 365 days.' So I say, 'Mitzi, why can't you figure out how much you can spend for Christmas then divide by twelve and put that much aside every month? Then come Christmas, you could pay cash for all your presents.' Well, Mitzi looked at me as if I was absolutely nuts. She said that kind of thing couldn't work for them. They needed every cent just as soon as it came in. They couldn't possibly have money building up in an account while they had bills to pay. I gave up."

"There are an awful lot of Mitzis in the world, Jane, so don't let it worry you," offered Wendy. "Fred and I have met a lot of them. We don't think anyone can make it big financially if they don't have a good sense of the comings and goings of their money. Usually it requires formal budgeting. You can struggle by without budgeting, but we highly recommend it."

Fred took the floor. "Enough general talk. I want to tell you two specifically what you ought to be doing to get where you want to be. Where you want to be is financially independent at an early retirement age. Let's say by age 55. That's it. Your specific goal is to have, let's say, a million dollars by age 55. Oh yes, and let's say you want at least $100,000 income for personal use each year. If you have a million dollar net worth by 55, and 100 thou personal income each year, you'll be in a position to do or have all the things on the list Joe and I created. Are you with me?"

Joe and Jane bobbed their heads vigorously and about in unison indicating their assent. They were eager to hear the specifics of Fred's approach. Joe was already thinking about his million.

Fred went on. "Good. First, keep on with your budgeting. You need a planning budget and a means of keeping track of your actual performance. Refine as necessary. For instance your planning budget should cover all the income you expect to take in during the next twelve months. Figure it month by month on a spreadsheet. You'll need a separate spreadsheet, blank except for the headings, on which to write in your *actual* income and expenses.

"You don't need a computer to do spreadsheets. You can simply rule some columns on a lined piece of paper. Have the left column be a list of all the budget items, then twelve columns for months, then a totals column at the right."

"Fred, you're micromanaging again. Jane knows what a budget is," said Wendy.

"Oh please, Wendy, I know she does!" complained Fred. "But I don't know how detailed it is or if it's just a budget for the year. As a start, under the heading 'income' they need to have a row for Joe's gross income, a row for Jane's, a row for rental income and a row for other income. Plus a row for monthly income total."

At the mention of rental income and other income (whatever that was) as part of their budget, Jane and Joe twisted in their chairs and nodded to each other. This was more like it, was their attitude.

"Now, I realize you're an experienced budgeter, Jane, but just bear with me a little longer. I want to make sure you understand the minimum information your budget should have. It can be expanded later. For example, I envision you sometime adding additional income rows to handle income from your different properties."

Joe and Jane again jiggled in their seats, nodded and smiled at each other.

Fred went on. "As expenses, you need your major household expense categories and a subtotal for household. Next, to prepare for your rental activities, will come rental property expenses and another subtotal. At this stage, as rental expenses put down taxes, insurance, utilities, routine maintenance, advertising, miscellaneous and debt service. Then put in a total for all expenses, both household and rental. Can you see where this is going?"

Jane nodded.

"Okay," Fred said, "put in another row now to show the surplus or loss for the month. Simply subtract total expense from total income. The point is, for planning purposes, you would like each month to show a surplus, even if it's a small one. Governments seem to plan to operate at a loss; that's how come we've got a huge national debt. Families should balance their budgets month by month. They shouldn't plan to operate at a loss."

"Yeah, but Fred," questioned Joe. "What if it turns out you have more month left at the end of your money?"

"I know very well it happens, Joe, but it certainly shouldn't be planned that way. If it turns out that way during the planning process, shift some expenses to a month where more income is forecast. Right away you'll see one of the many, many benefits of budgeting. If a short month turns up while you're planning it makes you very conscious of a weak point in your financial plan. Plan around it and you'll know well before the actual weak-money month arrives that here comes a time to be extra careful with funds.

"Nevertheless, the unexpected still happens. Budgeting won't prevent gremlins from screwing up well-laid plans. You could still have more month left at the end of your money."

"Now, let me first tell you about the way I handle reserve accounts. You may think my way is too tedious for you, so later, if you want, I can give you a shortcut way."

"For reserve accounts such as for holiday gift buying and car repairs as Jane mentioned, set up a reserves page ruled into month columns. Each reserve item needs three rows labeled 'in,' 'out' and 'total.' It's probably obvious the 'in' row is for entering the amount actually being put into the reserve account for the month. It should match the amount on your planning budget—you know, one twelfth of the item's estimated yearly total.

"The second row is for entry of the 'out' amounts, if any, you actually take out of the different reserve accounts each month. The third row would carry the running cumulative total for the reserve item. Make the cumulative total calculation once you've recorded the actual ins and outs. It's a simple calculation. Just add the 'in' amount to the previous month's end total and subtract the 'out' amount. The result will be your new reserve balance for that item.

"Do the same thing for each reserve item. At any time, you can add the balances for all of your reserve accounts to determine how much you should be holding as total reserves. Subtract the grand total of all reserve amounts from the total of your actual savings and see how much is left over. Excess over reserves represents surplus and could be the amount available for investment. But let me get back to the surplus business a little bit later.

"Overall, the matter of handling reserves is pretty easy. Of course, whether you have just two or as many as eight reserve items on paper, all reserves, plus your rainy day money, would be stored in a single bank account. Some people set up a separate bank account for reserves to keep them separate from their regular checking and savings accounts. It really depends on how big your reserves are and how much self-control or discipline you have."

Joe looked puzzled. He cocked his head and bunched his eyebrows.

Jane saw his look and so explained. "Joe, we've had some trouble with this so let me go over it. First, let me tell Wendy and Fred that we have two bank accounts; one is a checking account and one is a savings account. Joe's checks always go into checking, less the amount we think we'll need in cash until his next paycheck. We pay most of our household expenses, by check, from that account.

"Most of my paycheck also goes into checking but part goes into our savings account. We get a pitifully small amount of interest on our savings, but it's good to have our money divided.

"Right now we've got about $4,600 in our savings account." She raised her hand to stifle the comment she could see was about to come out of Joe. "Now, Joe, look at this. She then took an envelope from her purse and jotted the following on its back:

Spendable Savings		$ 3,000
Rainy Day Fund		1,000
Reserves		
For car repairs	300	
Christmas fund	<u>300</u>	
		<u>$ 600</u>
		$ 4,600

"Joe," said Jane patiently. "We can't touch our reserves until our car breaks down again, or it's after Thanksgiving and we go Christmas shopping."

Joe slipped in a comment. "Amazing! Why didn't you explain that before?" Sometimes, where details about finances were concerned, Joe just didn't seem to get it.

"Joe, I've gone over this stuff many times with you. If you've got it now, it's the very first time. In the past when you've seen that we have, say $2,700 in our savings account, right away you were talking about how we could spend $2,700! In the past, whenever we built up any savings—let alone reserves—you almost felt it was your duty to spend it all. We can't do that, Joe."

Jane was warming up to her subject. She wasn't normally a nag about things but sometimes Joe's financial nonchalance exasperated her. "Look, Joe, we can only spend $3,000, not $4,600. Also, we want to invest the $3,000 and get a payback not just blow it on some toy. Your buddy Marty Repasky, as you know, would spend the $3,000 in a heartbeat on something like a used jet ski. Then, for sure he would misuse the darn thing, and it would sink in a deep-water channel off the coast. Bye-bye, $3,000. Forever. Joe, I don't want that to be us."

"Bravo, Jane!" cried Wendy with a whoop and a few claps. "You tell 'em, girl. I don't know how many times I've heard stories—and Fred has too—about how the husband, or the wife, just can't keep their paws off what should be family savings. Maybe it's because, as they say, opposites attract, but there always seems to be one member of a couple who is concerned about saving money and the other who wants to spend it. Some people just don't seem to get it. You've got to save and accumulate to get anything really worthwhile. Your stories about your friends Mitzi and Marty crack me up.

"I know couples just like them, or at least we did. Oh, they're probably still around but we don't seem to associate with them anymore. Our paths just never cross. Two different worlds kind of thing. But the couple I'm thinking of spent everything they got as soon as they got it. Both worked. Good jobs. Always complained they never had any money, but they kept buying things. Useless things to tell the truth. It was weird. And Mitzi's attitude towards Christmas spending . . . well, that was my old friend all over. So, Joe, are you sure you understand it?"

"Yes, ma'am!" said Joe with a wide grin. "We've got $4,600 to spend on Christmas presents providing it's not raining and the car is still chugging."

The others stared at him, horrified. Wide-eyed Wendy raised her fingers to her upper lip to shield her half-opened mouth.

"Just kidding," Joe said sheepishly. "I meant $300."

The others finally exhaled heavily and relaxed. But they were shaken.

"Let's get on with it," declared Fred. "Glad you two see the importance of budgeting. You must also master the simple concept of reserve accounts, and I think you pretty well have. Well, at least Jane has!" he added with a chuckle.

"Set up a reserve account to provide for any large pay-out which you know will occur except you don't know when. Setting aside for Christmas is another good example. Setting aside for car repairs is another one.

"I know most people would find this discussion boring, but as far as I'm concerned, using reserve accounts is about the only way people who weren't born with a silver spoon, or who got a big inheritance or who have a sugar daddy will make it. If you don't have reserve accounts in addition to us-ing a planning budget, you'll almost always be defeated in your attempts to make it big financially. Overly simple finan-cial planning can be torn apart by the unexpected. Or even by major expenses that are absolutely foreseeable. Case in point is your friends the Repaskys who, you say, don't set aside for Christmas and seem unaware it's even coming until they hear the Salvation Army ringing bells."

"As usual, Fred has made things too black and white," interjected Wendy. "Truth is, if you make a lot of money over a long period of time, and you're just naturally frugal, and if you make wise investments from time to time, I think you can make it anyway. In fact, during our earlier years, when we didn't have much money and before Fred got a bee in his bon-net, we got along just fine without all this budgeting and re-serves business. Those things aren't absolutely necessary and Fred knows it!"

Fred was a little annoyed as he responded. "Yes, in our earlier years we got by okay . . . but we sure weren't going anywhere financially. That is, until I got that bee in my bon-net!

"The fact is, Wendy, probably all you can claim about people who make it without financial planning is that they don't budget on a formalized basis. That is, they don't write it all down. But, if they make lots of money for a long time, and if they're frugal, and if they consistently make wise investments, they probably do all the things I say to do except they do them mentally. Or maybe they just figure things out on paper once in a while then throw their notes away. They wouldn't use needed money frivolously like the Repaskys blowing the family savings on a leaky jet ski.

"Most people have a far better chance of achieving financial independence by following tried and true methods, especially if they're starting with average or lower incomes. Oh, once you're sitting on a big pile of treasure you can relax in terms of formalized budgeting, although I never have. Younger people, who are struggling as young people are supposed to struggle and have dreams of making it big, can certainly benefit from formalized budgeting and reserves.

"Wendy's earlier statement brought up another aspect that is absolutely critical," added Fred. "Her hypothetical non-budgeting successful couple was frugal. Frugal is a key word. Means lots of things. Sure it means being value conscious and not wasting money, but I think of it mainly as living within your means. That's a key to becoming wealthy. Whatever amount of money you take in as a family, you must, must, must spend less than that on living expenses and pleasures.

"You've always got to have money left over. Every month. And that becomes the money you invest and that's how you accumulate wealth. If you don't believe me, go to a bookstore and you'll see a zillion books on how to get yourself out of financial trouble. The key thing is to live within your means. So many people live beyond their means even if they have huge salaries or professional incomes. They use credit for living expenses and pleasures. They pay exorbitant amounts of interest to finance their credit card buying. People who live beyond their means are not frugal people.

"They may have a lot of things and live in high style but probably don't have a lot of wealth. Certainly they don't have the net worth that should go with the high living they do. As a result, their financial well-being is very precarious. If something happens to their income stream they're in real trouble."

Fred continued: "When I talk to you about making it big financially, I mean in a solid, sustainable way. I mean high net worth and not simply a lot of spending. I mean a high enough net worth and income to allow you to retire at age 55 with financial peace of mind. I don't want you two to be worried that three or four months of illness is going to put you in the poorhouse."

"Are you finished, honey? Let's have lunch!" Wendy pleaded.

"Just a minute, please," objected Fred. "I've put off telling Joe and Jane a vital bit of information. I'm hungry, too, but let me get this bit out before I forget it. I'm getting older, you know. Got to get my advice while you can!"

The others, who had pushed back their chairs and had been rising out of them, plunked down again. Wendy let out a sigh and an "Oh, Fred!"

Fred glowered at Wendy but resumed addressing the Andersons. "I'll be brief, but this is important. Joe and Jane, I want you to put into your budget to pay yourselves first. I want you to budget 10% of your total monthly income into an investment reserve as if it were a monthly expense. I want you to treat it as an absolute priority. You have to think of it as something you must set aside come hell or high water."

The Andersons shrank a bit under Fred's flat gaze that bored right into them. His voice also captured them with its intensity. They knew he meant business.

Fred continued: "Plan to pay 10% to yourselves right off the top by putting it into investment reserves. Off the top means from gross income, not just your take-home pay. This is going to hurt you in the short run but you must, must, must do it for the sake of the long run. You will become wealthy if you do this . . . so long as you play your other cards right as well.

"Shift your other budget items around to make room for the top 10% to yourselves. Cut back in other areas. Become as frugal as you need to be, the 10% is vitally important. You'll be amazed at how fast your investment pot grows once you start.

"You say you've got $3,000 you think of as investment money. You say that some months your nest egg grows and sometimes it shrinks. One of you once told me together you make about $46,000 a year. I'm telling you right now, this time next year you must have at least another $4,600—10% of your gross—added to your $3,000. A year from now you should have not less than $7,600 available for investment.

"You might have to trim Christmas and vacation spending, but you must do whatever it takes to set aside 10% of your gross. But don't cut other reserve accounts off entirely. You'll still have to maintain your rainy day fund and car repair reserves and so forth.

"Once you get your budget worked out so things are working smoothly, I have a strong feeling you'll end up with monthly surpluses. Tight budgeting tends to cause surpluses.

"Now, let's go to lunch, I'm starved!" Chairs started to be pushed back again.

"Not so fast, Fred," Joe called out. Everyone froze. "You promised to tell us a shortcut way to handle reserves. You know, for those of us not so inclined to handle a whole bunch of reserve accounts. I see the point of them, but frankly I'm not like you. I'm afraid I might start an elaborate reserve accounts system as you suggest but then get bogged down. Then I'd end up dropping the whole mess."

Fred broke out in a smile. Joe looked relieved because he had been worried he might offend his mentor.

"Oh yeah," Fred said. "Forgot. But you're right Joe. If something seems too tedious there is definitely a danger the whole concept would go down the toilet. I'd rather you take a shortcut than avoid reserves entirely. So here's what you and Jane could do. Make a list of all the unexpected expense and occasional big ticket items you think you'll be hit with sometime in the year. Prepare a list just one time each year and include such items as car repairs, insurance, gifts, vacations and so forth. Beside each, put the amount you think the item will cost. Be reasonable but go on the high side with your estimates. Total the listed amounts.

"Now, simply divide the total by twelve. The result is what you must put into a separate account each month as fresh reserves. Set up a new checking account at the bank and actually call it your reserves account. Use your $1,600 rainy day and reserves amount to start it off. Add the fresh reserves amount every month. When you run into an expense for an item on your list, just pay for it out of your reserves account. Simple.

"At the end of twelve months, if your original estimates were right on target, you would have paid out about the same amount as you put in. Only the rainy day fund amount would be sitting in the account intact. Simple.

"It's probably best to use your interest-bearing savings account to keep your investment money apart from temptation and everything else. Then you can easily watch it grow."

There was nodding of general assent as they pushed back their chairs for the third time. You could tell everyone was thinking about what Fred had just said. Would the Andersons do it or not? No decision was asked for or even expected at the moment. They needed time to discuss it between themselves and to think about all the concepts Fred had declared were important. For now, however, they were all going to lunch.

The Andersons still had no idea that they would be millionaires within 15 years.

They had learned, however, that already having a large sum of money was not essential to starting a wealth-building program. Whether they started with no savings at all or $3,000 really didn't matter in the long run. It was essential to live within the means of their present income and to be setting some money aside each month. Before establishing a fund for real estate investments, Fred had advised them to set up reserve funds for large sporadic expenses and for rainy days. Fred had also emphasized the value of budgeting, and suggested the target of setting aside 10% of their gross income as savings.

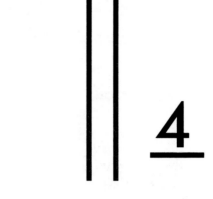

Keeping Score

After a week of agonizing, the Andersons reached the conclusion that trying to make it big would be worthwhile despite the need for belt tightening.

"The bottom line is," declared Joe as they settled into bed after a long day, "if we don't do something like the Madisons have done, we may not go anywhere. Oh, we can have a quiet, happy life for sure. But in the long run we may never get most of the things on our list of goals."

Most of the week was spent dissecting their budget and redoing it. They really didn't have an *e*laborate budget; it was mainly a matter of deciding what items to cut and by how much. They thought Fred was being too tough when he said pay your investment account 10% of your gross income each month. They wished he had said 10% of *t*ake-home pay, but he hadn't.

Once they got over their irritation with Fred and accepted the need for forced savings, they felt better. It initially occurred to Jane to just set aside 5%. Joe, anxious to become a millionaire, declared he was prepared to set aside 15%! A new round of squabbling ensued. Finally they compromised in the spirit of balance. They would tighten their belts for the cause but wouldn't give up all pleasures and decided to set aside the suggested 10%.

In addition, they decided to use the approach Fred suggested as simple for their reserves budgeting. It wasn't in them at this stage to use the more elaborate method Fred used for himself. Why not try the simple approach first? If it didn't work they could add refinements, or complexities, as needed.

Jane made a list of all the high-cost items they would have to contend with for the next twelve months. Besides gifts (for both Christmas and the half dozen or so birthday presents they usually bought), they listed car insurance, repairs and licenses, life insurance, uninsured medical and vacation expense. After considerable discussion, they put a dollar amount beside each item. For vacation they put down what they thought it would cost them to spend five days close to— but not on—the beach at a popular seaside area within four hours drive. It would be a modest vacation but it would be an away-from-home vacation. They would have fun and they would be practicing balance.

Jane totaled the listed amounts and divided by twelve. This became the reserve amount they would set aside each month to take care of big items when they became due. Since Joe had just received his monthly paycheck, they would open a new bank account starting it with their present $1,600 rainy-day and reserves money plus the first of their new monthly reserve amounts. Thereafter, any big items would be paid from this account. Hopefully, they would then be able to pay cash for such items. In fact, they would probably pay for most things by credit card then pay the credit card bill in full each month. This would give them convenience at the time of purchase, plus frequent flyer points from the credit card company and no interest charges.

Since they already had a savings account, they made sure it had their $3,000 investment nest egg amount plus an amount equaling one tenth of Joe's gross pay. It hurt to add the 10% but right away their investment nest egg jumped to $3,208. They were on their way! When Jane got her twice-a-month paychecks, she would be adding another $87.50 to their investment fund each time. Yes, it would hurt but it was still their money, and they were building for their future.

The Andersons still had a regular checking account for routine things and it was to receive the remainder of their take-home pay. It dismayed them that its balance would remain small. They could see that just about everything they put into it during a month would be paid back out within the next month. However, they consoled themselves with the comforting facts of a systematic reserves build up and a growing investment pot. They were pleased with themselves. They knew the Repaskys and the Archers didn't have anything like it. No wonder their friends probably weren't ever going to get anywhere. A pity, they thought!

At their next meeting with the Madisons, they excitedly told what accounts they had set up and how they had adjusted their budget to provide 10% of their gross income to their investment fund. They also told of their resolve to try hard for three years to get a wealth-building real estate program off the ground. If they didn't see strong indications the plan was working within three years they would re-think everything.

"Sounds like a good plan," said Fred to the complete relief of the Andersons. They figured he may think they weren't serious if they set a limit.

"You've got to have balance," declared Fred. "You're living in the present so you've got to have some fun in the present. Yes, it's important to sacrifice as need be for the future but not to the extent you make yourselves unhappy now. A three-year limit seems reasonable. Within that time you'll want to see good indications you're getting somewhere or you'll relax your austerity program and maybe do something else. Makes sense."

He continued. "There's an important reason why your self-imposed limit doesn't disturb me. Fact is, in three years you'll most certainly see yourselves traveling up the road to financial success. You'll see! If you don't see measurable progress it means you haven't been diligent enough. It will mean—barring a pile of plain old bad luck—you simply haven't been trying hard enough. That being the case, you ought to get out. Why would you not try hard enough? Simply because you're not motivated enough. Simple.

"Doesn't worry me, though. From what I've seen and heard over the last couple of months, you are motivated. You can be hard workers. You're diligent people and seem to be honest. You seem to be able to grasp important concepts quick enough, too. Bottom line is, I think you'll do very, very well and you'll easily be able to see it within three years."

The Andersons looked pleased. Fred had their attention so he went on: "Here comes an important concept and instruction.

This one is not optional. Joe, Jane, I consider it mandatory that you do what I'm about to say. It will be your means of measuring your success—or lack of it."

The Andersons sat up a little straighter and looked intently at Fred.

Fred posed a question: "What is a millionaire?" Without waiting for anyone else to respond, he answered himself. "Good question. Some people think a millionaire is a person who acts like a millionaire, however millionaires act, or looks like a millionaire, however they are supposed to look, or spends like a millionaire, however they are supposed to spend. I'm telling you the presumed, stereotypical millionaire is an illusion. Excluding wealthy celebrities or sports stars or the occasional showoff, most millionaires do not stand out as different from anyone else. The typical millionaire is not ostentatious, and does not dress, act or ride around in an extravagant manner.

"According to an excellent book I really enjoyed reading called *The Millionaire Next Door*, anyone in any established middle class or higher neighborhood may be a millionaire. You just can't tell by looking at them or how they live. You certainly can't tell by their spending habits. In fact, the book points out that flamboyant spending and a high-living, ostentatious style frequently just indicate someone living at the edge of—or beyond—their income means. High income by itself does not mean a person is wealthy. It may just mean a lot of money passes through their hands. If they spend as much as they get they aren't necessarily wealthy.

"The truest measure of the wealth of a person, or family, is net worth. Net worth is determined by subtracting the total of all financial liabilities from the total of financial assets." Fred used a felt-tip pen to boldly write the following formula on a sheet of paper:

Assets minus *Liabilities* equals *Net Worth*

Then Fred went on: "To be a millionaire, a person's assets must be at least a million dollars higher than their liabilities. It's that simple.

"Now, a person with a big house, big car, fancy clothes and extravagant spending habits could have a million dollars or more in assets. They could just as well have almost a million dollars in liabilities and thus have a low net worth. They wouldn't be millionaires regardless of how much high income money passes through their hands.

"It is, of course, possible to have a negative net worth. Many young people have a negative net worth. In fact, it is virtually the normal condition of someone just starting into the workforce. Even college graduates starting into highly paid new professions are likely to have negative net worth for a while. The reason? Student loans and credit card debt. The new grad may owe thousands and have very few tangible assets.

"It's also possible to be a temporary or fleeting millionaire. How? Well, let's suppose you receive a million dollar inheritance or win a million dollar lottery. Within hours of receiving it you're likely to start spending it. Unless you invest a good portion of it astutely, it will gradually—maybe rapidly—dwindle away. You could drop back below the millionaire level very quickly.

"When I talk about *you*, the Andersons, working toward becoming millionaires, please understand me as meaning working toward becoming sustainable millionaires. This means your goal is not only to have a net worth of at least a million dollars, but also a sustainable or ongoing income that will allow you to remain at not less than the one million net worth level indefinitely.

"How much income you will need without tapping into your principal is a function of your spending habits. In other words, your lifestyle. Some millionaires spend a lot, but not usually extravagantly, and some spend very little. It's largely a matter of age and life-long habits. If someone has been frugal all their life and partly through being frugal became a millionaire, they are unlikely to suddenly become high-rolling big spenders.

"To have something tangible to focus on, let's assume that to be sustainable millionaires you two will have to have an annual income of at least $100,000 for your personal use. Consider this one of the Anderson goals."

Fred then told the Andersons they should calculate their net worth as of the moment when they first decided to try to make it big financially. This would be their starting point, their benchmark, their ground zero. They should write down the figures formally, date the record and keep it in a special folder or binder.

Further, Fred said, anyone striving to become a millionaire should re-calculate his or her net worth regularly. Obviously it should be done at the end of each year, meaning as of December 31st. It could also be done mid-year, meaning as of June 30th. Fred explained it also made sense to redo the calculations soon after each property acquisition. Every net worth record should be dated and kept.

"Why so frequently?" Joe asked.

"Because," Fred replied, "regular re-calculation of net worth is the best means by far of keeping track of your progress up the wealth ladder. You can easily compare your current status with net worth of one, two or ten years previous. You can determine your percentage of increase over previous periods. Given a little history, you have the basis of determining your trend, which hopefully is upward, and even project two to five periods into the future. It's wise to make projections and to keep track of the percentages of increase you presumed. Why? You will find it very interesting, over time, to compare your actual performance with your projections. Not only will it be interesting, it will be instructive and allow you to get better and better in your projections.

"Who cares?" Fred asked rhetorically. "Well, you, Joe and Jane, as aspiring millionaires, should and will care once you're doing it regularly. It will be a most powerful motivator. You will actually be able to see and measure the results of your efforts. You will start getting excited about the progress you're making because you'll see it. You'll be spurred on towards greater and smarter efforts. You will see more easily how to increase assets and diminish liabilities thereby increasing your net worth.

"Eventually, you should be able to determine with some accuracy—certainly to within six months—when you will become a millionaire. Once you've reached millionaire status, you'll be hooked and will probably continue the technique through achieving your second million and beyond. Gee, two million net worth! That means you would be a multi-millionaire! Has a nice ring to it, don't you think?"

Wendy felt compelled to speak. "Fred calls them net worth statements but to most everyone else they are known as balance sheets. And another thing, I don't think all millionaires prepare balance sheets every six months and whenever they buy a property. Fred sometimes overdoes things."

"Wendy, my love," Fred said sweetly. "You may be correct, but maybe not. I've a feeling those who become millionaires the hard way become very conscious of how they're doing financially. They calculate statements of net worth regularly, precisely to see how they are doing. Not only that, anyone involved with real estate ends up in bed with lenders. Lenders invariably want balance sheets and profit and loss statements, too, for that matter. So, it's partly have-to and partly want-to.

"I'm telling Joe and Jane, and anyone else striving for financial independence, that regularly preparing statements of net worth, as a means of gauging performance over time, is one of the smartest things they can do. And it's simple to do. Also, once you've done it a few times and start to see yourself moving up the ladder, it's inspiring and fun. It's a means of keeping score."

Fred warmed up to his point. "Why do golfers keep track of their strokes? Keeping score wouldn't seem to have direct bearing on how good you are as a golfer, but it has a major effect. Perhaps your score gets into your brain and your brain keeps figuring out how you can be a better golfer. Causes you to become more focused maybe. Even if you're playing by yourself, it seems to be a human tendency to want to improve over your past performance.

"Not only that, obviously your performance can get better by trying to beat the performance of others. It's called competing. Competition causes you to try to excel. So, think of the process of becoming wealthy as a game. Then think of a net worth statement as your scorecard. Want competitors? Think of the entire country as playing against you. If that notion seems too far-fetched, you can at least think of competing against your friends, the Archers and the Repaskys. Only problem is, they don't know they're in a contest! Plus, based on what you have said about them, I'm already convinced you're going to win!"

Joe responded. "Oh, we're with you, Fred. We like the idea of knowing how we're doing. Plus, and this is bottom-line stuff, if you're our financial doctor, why wouldn't we follow your prescriptions? Since you've done what we want to do, why wouldn't we follow your advice? Are you with me, Jane?"

"Exactly!" replied Jane. "It doesn't make sense for us to do it our way, so to speak, when our way hasn't gotten us anywhere. Actually, if we don't follow Fred's advice, I'm not sure we'll get anywhere on our own. So yes! Absolutely! We'll start doing net worth statements. But I don't think our first one is going to look very good. It'll probably be negative."

"Negative net worth is all right at this time, Jane," Fred said. "We're going to establish your starting point. Sort of like your score for your very first round of golf before you take lessons. It will only be bad if your net worth remains negative after you've taken our lessons and put things into practice. Why don't we go ahead and get started? Let Wendy and me help you prepare your starting net worth statement. No need to be bashful, we know your financial condition isn't the best. That's why you're here. Come on now, tell the doctor!"

It wasn't hard for the Andersons, with help from the Madisons, to come up with the following as their starting net worth and income statements. They reflected their financial position at mid-point of the current year, which is when the Andersons started thinking about trying to make it big financially. The starting year was to be considered wealth-building year number one. The Andersons were starting to hope they could be millionaires within 25 wealth-building years.

Joe figured out this would mean somewhere around his 55th birthday. Doesn't sound too bad, he thought.

Joe & Jane Anderson Net Worth Statement
June 30, Wealth-Building Year #1

ASSETS:

Household furnishings	$ 3,000
Joe's car	6,200
Jane's car	8,800
Cash in bank	4,600
Total Assets	$ 22,600

LIABILITIES:

Installment loan on TV	$ 400
Anderson credit card debt	300
Loan on Joe's car	4,700
Loan on Jane's car	7,400
Total Liabilities	$ 12,800
NET WORTH (Assets - Liabilities)	$ 9,800

Income Projection Statement
June 30, Wealth-Building Year #1

Joe's gross annual salary	$ 25,000
Jane's gross annual salary	21,000
Total Anderson family gross income	$ 46,000
Planned set-aside for investments ($383.33/mo.)	4,600
Gross funds available for all else	$ 41,400/yr.

Wendy had pulled out some recent newspapers for the Andersons to scan the classified ads to get the typical price asked for their car makes, models and years. If they had been at home, Joe and Jane could have logged on to the Internet and found their car values on a site such as Kelly Blue Book, www.kbb.com. They used 90% of the typical newspaper price as their balance sheet values. After all, Fred had explained, the idea was just to get a reasonable, conservative value. Pinpoint accuracy wasn't important. However, it was important not to delude yourself—let alone anyone else—by using purposely inflated values.

The Andersons had no idea how much their home furnishings and personal items were worth. Wendy pointed out that their stuff was worth a lot more to them than anyone else. Valuations along the lines of garage sale prices were appropriate. They made a list of the major things they had in their apartment: living room set, almost new 32-inch TV, small dining room set, bedroom set, washer and dryer, microwave, his clothes, her clothes, a small amount of inexpensive jewelry, a few power tools and so forth. Beside each item they put a value representing what they thought they could buy it for at a garage sale or through a used furniture ad. In no case did they use a value higher than 50% of new item cost. Wendy had told them to be certain to include the value of any investment retirement account as one of their assets. However, the Andersons did not own an IRA.

Liabilities were easy to determine. Jane slipped home and looked at their payment records for their cars and the TV set. They had loan payment coupon books that showed balances owing after payments were made. She also looked up bank records to see how much they had in their accounts for the date of the net worth statement. Fred pointed out that if the loan information hadn't been handy, a quick call to their lenders would have gotten it.

Joe and Jane were surprised to see that they were worth almost $10,000. They had no idea they were worth that much; it seemed like a good sum to them. Of course, they hadn't thought about it before. They agreed it wasn't hard to calculate their net worth and saw it would be easy to update it every six months.

Then a cloud seemed to come over Joe. He gloomily commented that while a $10,000 net worth seemed surprisingly grand to them, it was a long, long way from $1,000,000.

"That it is," Fred affirmed. "You've got your work cut out for you, that's for sure. But don't worry. You two seem to have all the qualities needed for where you're going. We'll guide you toward becoming millionaires."

Once they were alone again, Joe and Jane reviewed what they had recently learned. They now knew what was meant by the term sustainable millionaire. It meant a person whose assets exceeded liabilities by at least $1,000,000 and who also had a personal-use income of at least $100,000 each and every year. They also had learned how to periodically prepare income and net worth statements as a way to keep score or keep track of their wealth-building progress.

5

What Type of Rental to Buy

Fred explained to Joe and Jane that before considering particular properties to buy, it was important for them to consider the rental market as a whole and where they, as landlords, wished to fit within it. First, they needed to find out the most common monthly rental amounts for their city. Rental rates would vary a great deal, from low for shabby houses in deteriorating areas to high for palatial places in prestigious neighborhoods. They needed to determine the range of rental amounts and get a sense of what are the most common amounts.

Fred suggested they check the Sunday classified ads for unfurnished apartments, duplexes, townhouses and single-family houses for rental amounts. They could also get free rental guides from racks just inside the front doors of many supermarkets. They would see photos of the larger apartment complexes and lists of rents, sizes and apartment features. Naturally they could call the numbers listed on for rent signs sitting in front of any property in any area which appealed to them and simply ask for information.

What the Andersons were to determine was the range of rents for, say, one-, two- and three-bedroom unfurnished apartments, townhouses, duplexes and houses. Besides the range of prices, they had to determine the most common prices.

"For example," Wendy said. "Your research may reveal one-bedroom unfurnished apartments rent from $250 to $800 a month. Further, the most common rent paid for one bedrooms is $400 to

$450. Similarly, two-bedroom apartments may be available at anywhere from $325 to $925 with $475 to $550 being most common.

"Townhouses, duplexes and single-family detached houses generally will be a little more than apartments. Naturally a third bedroom in any building costs even more.

"You know," Wendy went on, "Rents vary a great deal in different parts of the country. The prices I just mentioned are about right for this area right now but wouldn't be valid for Manhattan or San Francisco. Anyone in those or any other areas would have to do their own research if they were thinking about becoming landlords.

Fred jumped in: "Techniques and approaches I will recommend you use are price-proof. You see, I'll express all of the buying decisions and the analyses and the returns sought in terms of percentages. Relationships remain the same regardless of price and time. If rents are high, costs are likely to be proportionately high as well. It doesn't matter since the key to value still is annual cash-on-cash return expressed as a percentage. Likewise, if I was making recommendations to you years from now, when you'll laugh looking back at the low rents which prevail today, the approaches and percentages recommended will still be valid.

"Think of the total population of renters in the city—perhaps 25 to 35% of the total population—as forming a pyramid. At the broad base of the pyramid are the many people, perhaps thousands, who can afford the lowest rents; at the pyramid's apex is the single person who can afford the highest rent in the city. Using the examples Wendy came up with, base of the pyramid rents are $250 for a one-bedroom apartment and $325 for a two-bedroom. Top rents at the apex or pinnacle of the pyramid are $800 for a one-bedroom to $925 for two bedrooms.

"There are problems with catering to either the base-of-the-pyramid-people or the pinnacle person. Let me explain. Base-of-the-pyramid people can include persons with unstable incomes, rent payment problems, bad credit and behaviors that make them undesirable as tenants. The behavior problems we're talking about are those that interfere with the rights of other tenants or neighbors such as too much noise, regularly parking improperly and not adhering to stipulations in leases.

"You can, or at least try to, determine if a prospective

tenant is undesirable in terms of behavior by checking with his previous landlords. Don't limit your reference checking to the prospect's current landlord. Check out the information the prospect puts on the application they sign and submit.

"You can, or at least try to, determine the applicant's credit history by doing a credit check through the local credit bureau. And you can try to determine if a person has stable income by checking with the employer they've listed on their signed application.

"I'm saying 'at least try to' in recognition of the fact that some prospective tenants will lie on their applications. Can you believe that? It's true. For example, they may give the name and telephone number of a friend or relative as their previous landlord. You'll get nothing but glowing tales about your applicant. And there are plenty of evasions possible to prevent you from getting valid credit bureau information."

Since it seemed Fred was finished telling them about base-of-the-pyramid renters, Joe decided to make a comment and ask a question.

"I've heard," Joe said, "you can make a lot more money concentrating on the lower class rentals. For example, they don't pay much rent, so they don't expect much in return. If something breaks down, you don't really have to do anything about it. Even if they press you on fixing something you can point out how little they're paying for rent and that you can't afford to pay for repairs. What do you think, Fred?"

"Good grief, Joe, whoever told you that was the way to be a landlord ought to be arrested! At the very least that person ought to be in some other business. It's people like whomever you talked to who give the rental industry a bad name. Sounds like a slumlord type.

"Owning and operating residential rental property should be—and with most landlords is—an honest, honorable business. Landlords supply a basic service. Providing accommodations is fulfilling the basic human need for shelter. Shelter ranks just after food and clothing as a primary necessity. Plain old decency demands that when you rent a place, regardless of how humble, it should have the basics and everything should work properly. If anything provided doesn't work, or breaks down, it's the landlord's obligation to fix it at the landlord's expense. Plus the landlord should make a reasonable effort to have the repair made promptly. In my mind there is no question of the landlord's obligation. Laws in most states back up this position.

"Naturally if the tenant's actions—or actions of the tenant's guests—cause a breakdown or damage, the tenant is legally required to pay for repairs. That is, whenever it's not simply a matter of normal wear and tear or age that causes the breakdown. I've charged tenants when my plumber has told me the clogged toilet was full of chicken bones or a toy, for example."

Fred continued: "In return, the landlord has a right to expect the tenant to fulfill his obligations. In simple terms that means the tenant has to pay the rent in full, on time and without demand, plus abide by the terms of the rental agreement.

"Granted, there is a wide range of quality in rentals. The most basic units don't have very much and they don't cost very much. It's affordable housing, let's say. Nevertheless, a minimum standard ought to be maintained by the landlord. That includes fixing any of the basic things and equipment promptly and at the landlord's expense. Of course, over the years Wendy and I have run into all sorts of tenants. Quite frankly, some were demanding and lousy. Terrible people. Completely unreasonable in their demands. We've had locks smashed or windows broken because the tenant lost her key. For sure, not all tenants are saints. When it's clear the tenant caused the problem we charge them for the repair without question.

"Let me put it this way for you. When Wendy or I encounter one of our tenants in a supermarket, we want there to be friendly greetings from all parties. We don't want to have to avoid eye contact or go down a different aisle to hide from them. We don't want to feel guilty, and we don't. Our attitude about problems reported by our tenants starts with the knowledge that every business that ever was has problems. Secondly, we assume the tenant—our customer—doesn't want to have to contend with the problem situation any more than we want to hear about it. Next, we know very few problems fix themselves, so we accept that we, as landlords, will have to intervene at some level. Finally, realizing the problem needs attention, our practice is to try to get the situation corrected as fast as possible. And we do get things fixed rapidly most times. Lots of times we've completely amazed our tenants at how fast we provide attention. We've gotten many, many compliments from tenants in this regard and you know they talk among themselves. We think it helps keep our rentals full."

Wendy jumped in: "Yes, I absolutely think it does. Instead of having residents who are festering about a problem the blankety-blank landlord won't fix, we've got contented tenants singing our praises. And it doesn't cost us a penny more to provide good service. However, we don't pay for premium services from repairmen. That is, unless it was an extreme emergency, we would never pay overtime or weekend rates to get something fixed. Our tenants know that and understand. They do know we'll make every *reasonable* effort to get them fixed up as soon as practical. Most residents who know their needs are taken seriously and whose problems are handled quickly don't object to paying fair rent. Plus, they'll pay in full and on time. Fred and I have been operating this way for years and we believe we have lower vacancy figures than any landlord we know. So, it doesn't just make us feel good, it pays!"

Fred summed up: "It's a matter of conducting your business in an honest, ethical way. Give good value and you'll get a good return. Treat your tenants, meaning your customers, in the same way you'd want to be treated if your roles were reversed. It works for us."

Joe and Jane seemed satisfied so Fred continued talking about the range of rental properties and renters.

Concerning top-of-the-pyramid rentals, he told them the biggest problem is the lack of people able or willing to pay top dollar. If there's an acute scarcity of such applicants at the particular time an expensive rental is available, it remains empty. While the gorgeous prestige rental sits empty, their lender will still be expecting a little something month after month.

"The pinnacle renter," added Wendy, "paying you more, naturally expects more from you. They may be particularly finicky and demanding."

Fred and Wendy's years of experience had molded them toward the middle of the rental pyramid regarding the type of rentals they would own and the type of renters they would seek. Therefore, they recommended that the Andersons only purchase the most common, middle-of-the-road rentals in the most sought-after rental areas. Using the price examples given previously, the Madisons recommended to the Andersons that they think of owning only apartments which would—in good rentable condition—command $400 to $475 for a one bedroom and $475 to $575 for two bedrooms.

Wendy pointed out that such middle-of-the-road rents would not likely be found in large complexes that offer lots of amenities. There would be no swimming pool, no weight room, no tanning booths and no keg parties put on by the management. This was just as well, she said, because the Andersons, and any other new landlords, were better off starting with small, bread and butter type properties that had the basics and could be offered in a clean, neat, attractive condition. Amenities were expensive. A swimming pool, for example, was particularly costly to maintain and to insure even if few used it. The more amenities, the higher the rent had to be. Moving up the rental pyramid meant fewer potential renters.

The best rental areas, the Madisons explained, may or may not be the areas most sought after by owner-occupant types. Certainly, the best rental areas are not going to be the areas of prestige housing. Good areas for middle range renters were usually close to mass transit lines, fairly close to malls or shopping centers and fairly convenient to the city's current center of activity.

Fred decided clarification was necessary. "The city's center of activity may not be its physical center or its traditional center. For whatever reasons, the city may have developed, or is developing, in a lopsided manner. Since for years the city has been growing mainly in the southwest, don't buy a rental property in the northeast! Of course it will be cheaper to buy in the northeast but rents and the property's continuing value, including its ultimate resale, will always be lower. It may always perform lower than you'd hoped because, being well away from the centers of activity, it's hard to rent. Hard to rent means higher vacancy and lower than normal rents when occupied.

The Madisons advised strongly against buying, for rental purposes, any property that is remote, close to an undesirable feature, such as a salvage yard, or quite unusual or hard to find even if fairly central. Think of the preferences of the middle-of-the-road renter. If it's very difficult for a prospect to even find a vacant rental there's more likelihood it will stay vacant. While every dwelling may appeal to someone, after all someone did build it in the first place, you hurt yourself as a landlord if you narrow your field of potential renters to only those who like the bizarre.

"Buying the cheapest building can be a false economy," Fred said. "It may be the cheapest because it's in an obscure, hard to find location and therefore is an undesirable rental. Don't buy rental property simply because it is cheap. You must only buy desirable, well-located properties. Purchase on the basis of something being a reasonable-to-good deal not simply because it's low cost."

"Well, Fred, you've certainly got me convinced and Jane, too, I'm sure," exclaimed Joe. "We'll try to become landlords of only middle-tier properties and cater to middle-of-the-road renters. We'll only seek orthodox looking buildings in locations convenient for the renter, not far from what the renter would consider the city's center of activity. Have I got it right?"

"You have," chuckled Fred, "now let me tell you guys a few more things to keep in mind."

"First, only offer apartments unfurnished. Since sometime in the 1970s, furnished units can be found mostly as transient rentals where the occupancy is not expected to exceed six months. Some states require landlords to apply and collect sales tax to any rental if the initial term is less than six months. To avoid the administrative headache of collecting and reporting sales tax, apartment owners normally won't write a lease for less than six or seven months.

"Furnished boarding houses and rooms for rent offerings still exist because there is still a need for such accommodations. Perhaps the space needs of the occupant are very small, perhaps the need for a sleeping room is temporary, perhaps the occupants are persons of modest means. A significant need for furnished, shorter-term rental units exists but they tend to be small units, with one exception. The exception is the corporate rental. Companies sometimes have a need to temporarily house key employees for several months while a special project is being completed. The company may prefer to provide a large, fully-furnished rental apartment rather than require their employees to stay in hotels. In such cases the company is the lessee and in turn it has its employees actually use the facility. This type of specialty rental is not for the novice landlord.

"Once a full bedroom, separate from living room and kitchen, comes into the picture," stressed Fred, "the landlord should not provide furniture. If they do they will attract the type of renter who travels light and rapidly. While furnished apartments *may* rent very quickly to a transient type person, the transient can move out just as quickly, perhaps with a piece of the apartment's furniture and perhaps without paying some of the rent. Landlords are better served by having stable renters with lots of their own furniture who will not move without a compelling reason.

Fred strongly recommended buying used rentals over new ones. In addition, he noted that the novice landlord should not be the builder or developer of new rental units. Why? Because building and developing are highly specialized endeavors in themselves and not all who try such endeavors do it successfully or profitably. To also expect to be a successful developer and landlord for the first time is tempting the fates too much.

Wendy added: "Nothing is as appealing as a brand new rental unit except a well-maintained, sparkling clean, used unit. New units cost more because they are built using current high prices for materials, labor and land. Naturally, if a rental property costs more, higher rents must be obtained to provide adequate profits. The higher the rent, the higher the landlord must reach up the pyramid of renters."

"Except for the fact that new construction comes with warranties," expounded Fred, "buying used rental properties makes better economic sense in the same way that buying a used car is better than buying the latest model. The prestige obtained through buying brand new is costly and fleeting. Used rental units are usually full or mostly full when you buy them. This gives you the tremendous advantage of having proof positive of what revenues can be expected. It should also be possible to determine with fair certainty what expenses will be. You also know who your established neighbors are and the overall condition of the area. Novice landlords should buy and operate several used properties before they even consider purchasing brand new units. Our own conclusion is that we will always buy used."

The mentors and protégés then discussed the types of properties to be considered. They started with consideration of the single-family, detached house. It is the easiest residential rental to buy, and there are more properties of this type to choose from than any other type. The three-bedroom/two-bath variety is best because it is the most desired configuration. It is also the most popular arrangement for those who wish to buy and occupy a house of their own. Fred advised that even though the Andersons were after a rental property they must be mindful of ease of resale should that be necessary or desired.

"A small to medium-sized house is best for rentals since that's what the majority of house renters want or can afford. Many new landlords start with a house as their first rental. Sometimes they have lived in the house and when they move to bigger quarters for themselves they keep their previous house for use as a rental. Or they have inherited a house and decide to use it as a rental rather than sell it.

"One reason new landlords start with a house is they feel they know something about houses. Therefore, especially if they have lived in it, they feel it will be manageable. They know any problems the property has. Another main reason for starting with a house is its affordability. Logic suggests it is easier to buy a single house than a property with multiple units, even a duplex. But it's not necessarily so. A moderately priced, single-family house may have about the same cash requirement as a modest duplex. However, the duplex with two units may provide better profitability than the single house.

"Some landlords buy one rental house, like it, operate it successfully, meaning profitably, then buy a second. Then they buy a third, a fourth and so on. Whenever they have extra funds and can find a good deal, they buy another rental house! Some specialize in buying repossessions from the U.S. Department of Housing and Urban Development (HUD) or the Department of Veterans Affairs (VA). Some keep acquiring repossessed townhouses. I know landlords who have acquired 14 houses, 22 houses, even 32 houses, one at a time. They do well financially but each landlord has admitted to being run ragged handling his or her portfolio.

"Invariably the houses are located on different streets and sometimes in different parts of town. Most times the design of each house is different and each has special quirks. All windows may be of different sizes; you can't assume what works in one dwelling will work in another or even fit. Because of different configurations and sizes, all rents may be different, although similar. At some point, for a variety of reasons, it is better for a landlord to convert from single houses to multi-family properties."

Fred and Wendy then assured the Andersons there was absolutely nothing wrong with starting a career as a landlord with a single-family rental house. A single rental house was far better than no rental property at all. And, it might be all the beginner can afford. One has to start somewhere.

Fred further explained that if a rental house was good, a duplex was even better and a lot better than two single-family rental houses. Likewise a triplex was better than three single rental houses. A quadraplex, with four dwelling units under one roof, was better than four single-family houses or two duplexes. Fred said even if the Andersons started with one or more single houses, as soon as practical they should dispose of them in favor of multi-family units.

"Fred, what were your first and second rental properties?" Joe asked.

"Fair question, Joe," Fred responded. "My first buy was a duplex. My second buy was another duplex. My third buy was a triplex. My fourth buy was a 17-unit property, but I still had the two duplexes and the triplex. It all worked out okay but it could have been better in many respects. I was certainly busy since I still had a full-time traveling job. Luckily, Wendy was a solid supporter and handled things admirably whenever I was out of town.

"If I knew then what I know now I would have traded in the smaller units and applied the proceeds towards the larger property. I want you guys to benefit from the knowledge I acquired while learning what I shouldn't do.

"I'll explain. Just consider a duplex compared to two single houses. With the two houses you've probably got two locations to go to show or service your rentals. You've got two roofs, two yards, eight exterior walls and so forth. Unless the houses were built by the same builder at about the same time, you're likely to have two different brands for every piece of equipment and every appliance. With the duplex you go to one location only for servicing and showing. You've got just one building to look after. What you learn about problems or repairs or appliances in one of the units may well be helpful in dealing with the same situation should it arise on the other side.

"You should see my point more dramatically when you compare four single-family houses—probably of four different designs and located on four different streets—to one quadraplex. Logically, the quadraplex is the way to go.

"Regarding management, the multi-unit building is also clearly the way to go as well. So much easier to go to only one location. Even for rent ads in the newspaper are easier. One address only. Want to put out a for rent sign? Only one is needed for a multi-unit.

"You're safer financially with a multi-unit. If you have a single-family unit and it's vacant, you're 100% empty! What a vacancy factor! Of course, your mortgage marches on as if you're 100% full. Hopefully your single unit will not stay vacant too long. While it's empty, however, you're dead in the water.

"With a duplex, chances are only one unit will be vacant at a time. That's 50% vacant or, as optimists would say, 50% full. With a quadraplex, again it is probable that only one unit will be vacant at one time. If that's so, your vacancy is only 25%, which leaves you with 75% of your normal revenue to handle . . . what?" Fred looked at Joe.

"Your mortgage."

"Because it what?" Fred looked at Jane.

"Marches on."

"Correct! Don't let me scare you with these high vacancy percentages. I used them to illustrate my point. While it is true an empty rent house is 100% vacant, if you are a competent landlord it won't stay vacant very long. As a beginner, let's suppose it takes you four weeks after one tenant moves out to have it fixed up, cleaned, advertised and re-rented. Such a turnover shouldn't happen more than once a year. If so, you will have lost revenue for four weeks out of the 52 potential rental weeks in a year. Your vacancy rate would therefore be 4 divided by 52 or 7.7% for the year. A lot better than the 100% temporary vacancy rate.

"When a vacancy rate is quoted, it is normally expressed as a percentage per year. Not only that, it is usually calculated based upon the percentage of potential revenue actually lost. Here's an example. Suppose potential rent from your rent house was $500 per month or $6,000 per year and you lost $400 rent due to turnover. The calculation for vacancy loss generally would be $400 divided by $6,000, or 6.7%. However, if any part of the departing tenant's deposit is retained, it is commonly applied as revenue brought in by that unit. So, if you kept $100 of the departed tenant's deposit you, in effect, lost only $300 from that unit—$300 divided by $6,000 gives you 5% as a vacancy factor.

"It doesn't much matter which variation of vacancy factor you use so long as within your rentals you remain honest and consistent with yourself year after year. Keeping track of vacancies makes good sense as a way to measure your own performance. If it keeps going up, you need to find out why and make changes if necessary. You can't delude yourself by always blaming vacancy on a slow rental market. The top performer gets her rentals rented despite a slow market.

"I mentioned in my earlier example that it took four weeks for the beginning landlord to get his house re-rented once a tenant departed. The four weeks part is something the beginner would have to work on. Let's say it took him ten days to get the house de-trashed, painted inside, cleaned and ready for new occupancy. Ten days for a beginner would not be unusual. Many beginners don't fully grasp the money they're losing and take their own sweet time getting their apartments ready. It's their attitude: It's our rental after all, isn't it? Fair enough, just as long as they realize it's also *their* profits they're losing! Because, as they dawdle, what else is happening, Joe?"

"Their mortgage is marching on!"

"Correct!

"If you're geared up for it, anticipating the move out and on the ball, even a unit left in the worst possible condition should be made ready for rental again in no more than three working days."

Jane spoke up. "Would you mind telling us what your vacancy rate has been?" She looked at Fred then toward Wendy.

"Not at all," Wendy responded. "Over the last eight years or so, as far as I can recall, we've always been under 3% vacancy and most years under 2%. Most landlords consider 5% or lower as being very good. Most large complexes have between 5 to 10% vacancy, unless they're in an especially hot rental area. For the small landlord, I think it's the personal touch and involvement that makes the difference. We think an owner operating his own rentals is going to remain much closer to the situation than, say, a new employee at a large complex or a rental management firm. Not that employees can't be terrific, mind you. It's just not quite the same if they're not dealing with their own money.

"If it's your profit at stake, you learn to pay attention and do it right. Plus, you should screen prospects carefully so you've got a better chance of getting good residents. Good, middle-of-the-road residents who are responsible citizens will take care of your place. It's where they live and a decent tenant will look after it just as though they owned the place. And if you treat them right in terms of responding quickly to their problems and complaints, they'll stay with you longer and treat you right when they leave."

"Amen," added Fred. "Let me go on about the overall financial advantage of a single, multi-family building such as a quadraplex over a multitude of single-family houses. I don't care what town you live in, the following relationships will hold true. The numbers will be different, but the relationships will hold.

"Think about revenue generated by your assets. If you pay $50,000 for a rental house, you're probably going to take in something like $500 a month in rent. So, if you bought four such houses, your assets would be four times $50,000 or $200,000. Your monthly rental revenue would be four times $500, or $2,000. Agreed?"

"Agreed."

"Well, a quadraplex of the same quality and condition as the four houses that generate $2,000 a month rent would only cost you about $160,000. If you can generate the same revenue by investing $40,000 less, clearly the quadraplex generates revenue much more efficiently. On top of that, as we discussed before, the quadraplex can be managed more efficiently than four separate buildings. Your profitability will be better with the quadraplex too, because of just one small yard to contend with instead of four, one roof instead of four and so on.

"But I'm not selling quadraplexes. I'm simply trying to illustrate the advantages of a multi-family building over separate, single-unit buildings. A duplex will perform better than two single houses, and a single eight unit will perform better than two quadraplexes. I want you to understand that even if you start your rental portfolio with single houses, townhouses, or even a duplex or two, once you're ready to get bigger you ought to get rid of the small units in favor of multi-family buildings. Regarding liquidity, quadraplexes are about as easy to sell as single-family rent houses or duplexes. Of course there are more potential buyers for houses, but there are still more than enough for well-located quads. If you go above 20 units in one building it will be harder to sell because there are many fewer buyers. But there are enough, so I wouldn't worry about it. Once you're a successful landlord operating 20 or more units, it's unlikely you will be overly concerned about liquidity."

Joe summed it up. "Fred, we appreciate your advice as to what type of rentals we ought to have. Your description of the pyramids of rentals and renters has helped a lot. Plus, you've made a strong case for multi-family buildings as opposed to having a whole bunch of single rental houses. But our bottom line is: What can we afford? Sure, it would be nice to have a six-unit building, but we're not even certain about being able to get one unit. We don't want to disappoint you, but reality is reality." Joe looked at Jane. Jane solemnly nodded in agreement.

"You're absolutely right, Joe!" Fred came back. Don't forget I said a duplex was better than two rent houses, but one rent house was better than owning no rentals at all. Yes, we realize affordability is the big issue here. And yes, reality is reality. But be optimistic, please. You're supposed to still be saving your initial investment pot. Time for you guys to begin seriously looking around. My recommendation to you for your first buy is to look at everything currently on the market from single houses through quadraplexes. You might get lucky. You might find the bargain of the century."

Once alone again with Jane, Joe went over Fred's

explanations as to why they should buy only properties with dwelling units renting at the middle of the range of rents for their city. They reviewed why units commanding the highest rents and lowest rents are to be avoided. Also, which neighborhoods and locations are best for rentals. And, although they might buy a single-family house or duplex as their first rental, they had learned they should upgrade to larger, multi-family properties as soon as practical.

PART 2: NECESSARY KNOWLEDGE

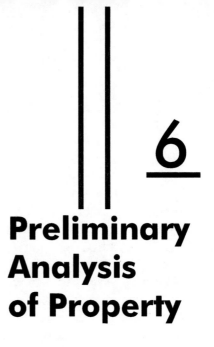

6

Preliminary Analysis of Property

	Gross Potential Income
Less	Vacancy Loss
Equals	*Net Effective Income*
Less	Operating Expenses
Equals	*Net Operating Income*
Less	Debt Service
Equals	*Cash Flow*

Two months passed before the Andersons again sat with the Madisons to discuss their wealth-building plan. Joe and Jane described their progress. They were funding their reserves account out of each paycheck received and reserves were building nicely. Now, theoretically, any anticipated large expense plus inevitable car repairs could be paid in cash from reserves.

They complained, however, about how hard it was to cut monthly spending enough to put 10% of their gross income into their investment fund. Nevertheless, they were doing it and their nest egg was growing steadily. They were pleased to see themselves as getting somewhere so were anxious to take the next step—to actually look for a property to buy.

Fred told them that even though they didn't have enough money to start investing, there was no harm in looking for investment possibilities. "In fact," he said, "it would be a good idea to do so to keep up your interest in buying properties and to see what kinds of things come on the market.

"Look at newspaper classifieds under the headings: 'Income Property for Sale,' 'Duplexes for Sale,' 'Triplexes for Sale,' 'Quadraplexes for Sale,' and of course 'Houses for Sale.' And, consider any of the multi-family places offered under the 'Investment Property' heading. There'll be many more houses than multi-family properties on the market so consider any of the less expensive three-bedroom/two-bath listings in areas you feel would be good for rentals.

"Look especially for key words that might indicate a property needing sweat equity. For example, the terms handyman special and fixer-upper suggest below-market prices for someone willing to put in some work. Don't be surprised at understatement in ads. The term needs work might really mean it needs to be demolished and new topsoil brought in. Be on the lookout for anything which seems to need just superficial or cosmetic improvements."

Jane asked if they should contact realtors. Fred, who was a broker with an active license, said, "Certainly. Real estate agents are there," he explained, "to provide a useful service— and to make their living while doing it. Agents know they can't sell anything if they never tell anyone about what they're trying to sell. Therefore, they're happy to give information to whoever calls. But be fair and let whoever you talk to know that you're just starting to look and aren't quite ready to buy."

The Andersons were legitimate buyers. It was only uncertain as to when they would make a purchase. But that would be true even if they had a couple of hundred thousand dollars cash in their pockets. They would still have to look around to find something that interested them and it would take time.

Fred advised them to tell any agent they talked to that at this stage they were just gathering information and preferred not to work exclusively with any one agent. However, if the agent came up with anything new or additional, he or she should not hesitate to contact them. Fred explained that this approach gave a fair chance to all agents but didn't give any of them the false impression of exclusive dealings.

"Be absolutely fair," Fred cautioned, "with any agent you start working with on any particular property. If an agent gives you information on a particular property and subsequently shows you through it, you should continue dealing with the same agent if you have continuing interest in the offering. Definitely do not use the services of one agent for all the preliminaries then switch to another for submitting an offer to purchase. It just isn't fair."

Fred went on to relate how he, as an agent, had been victim of a prospect who used his services to search the market, find suitable properties, show them and provide essential data. Once the prospect had zeroed in on a particular property, he advised Fred by telephone one morning that his aunt—an agent with another agency—was going to be submitting his offer to the seller that day. Fred was astounded! He would be cut out completely from any payment for his efforts. The property was not his listing and he would not be the selling agent either if he didn't prepare and submit the offer! Fred knew he was the procuring cause, meaning he was instrumental in a continuing, uninterrupted manner to the prospect's decision to go for this particular property. When he pointed this out to the aunt, she blithely informed Fred that if the offer didn't come from her, there would be no offer . . . period. She declared she was her nephew's real estate advisor and he would do whatever she suggested. "My advice to you, Mr. Madison, is to get over it," she said to Fred.

So Fred lost out after investing considerable time and effort in the prospect. Accordingly, he advised the Andersons not to switch agents in mid-stream if one had put in time and effort on their behalf. On the other hand, Fred advised against sticking with agents who didn't seem to know what they were doing. He told them they may encounter agents who had experience only in selling houses to owner-occupants. It wouldn't take even the novice Andersons long to discover that such an agent's knowledge of the ins and outs of the rental business was purely superficial. The agent wouldn't really understand what information the Andersons needed or why. Worse, the Andersons would get no help from such an agent in analyzing the subject property."

Fred said: "If you find you're dealing with an unknowledgeable agent on a property in which you might have serious interest, you should politely tell the agent why you do not feel comfortable continuing to work with him or her. The agent probably would already feel beyond the depth of his or her expertise and might suggest another agent or his or her own broker."

As the Andersons investigated more and more properties and perhaps even bought some, they would undoubtedly encounter some very competent real estate sales agents. Once they found a highly competent, highly ethical agent who they felt comfortable working with, they could consider using him or her regularly as a buyer's agent. A buyer's agent works primarily on behalf of the buyer and announces so on first contact with the seller or any other real estate agent involved with the subject property. The declared buyer's agent was free to vigorously delve into any aspect of the property that may be relevant to the buyers. He could also conduct negotiations representing only the interests of the buyers.

Traditionally, real estate agents have represented sellers and owed allegiance to them in an effort to get the highest sales price possible. Now, Fred explained, it was common to have single agency agents who represented either the seller or the buyer. A buyer's agent, for example, worked towards getting the lowest possible purchase price for his clients. Naturally it is vital for any agent to declare at first significant contact whose interests he represents. All agents have a legal duty for fair, honest dealings with all parties.

"Nationwide," said Fred, "there is also a trend towards transactional agents who facilitate real estate transactions but are not strictly on the side of either buyer or seller.

"Once you've got the experience and competence to feel confident in pursuing your own interests in purchases, a transactional agent would be fine. Until then it would be beneficial for you to work with a buyer's agent if you can find a good one. Until you find a good one it is probably best to tell any agent you talk to that you prefer not to be officially represented by an agent for the time being."

Fred finally got into the basic information the Andersons were to obtain on any property they wished to seriously consider buying.

To begin with, he said, they needed asking price, size in square feet, configuration of each unit (number of bedrooms, bathrooms, etc.), when built, actual rent obtained from each unit and taxes. Also, who (tenant or landlord) paid for each utility, how much each cost if landlord paid and any special costs and/or restrictions that might be related to an owner's association.

Jane asked, "Shouldn't we be going through these buildings to see what they're like inside?"

"Not at this point," Fred replied. "Oh, you should drive by and around any property you think you might be interested in but don't plan to go inside before you do an analysis of the figures. You don't want to waste your time or bother any tenants with a walk-through inspection since analysis may indicate it's a property not worth trying to pursue. To a degree, it's a which comes first the chicken or the egg kind of proposition. Experience tells me it's much easier to do a lot of analyses than a lot of physical inspections. Inspections, other than drive-bys, should be done only for those properties whose figures indicate that they may be winners."

Fred told them they should try to get as fine a breakdown of operating costs as possible from the seller. However, anyone planning to buy rental property should prepare their own list of operational costs and their own estimates of expense amounts. The buyer's list of costs should then be checked against the list provided by the seller. A cross-check of list items had to be done. There may be items on one list that were not on the other. If so, it was important to find out why. Whatever the reason, the prospective buyer needed to know the details since they could have a bearing on valuation of the property. The prospective buyer's job at this stage was to gather all the data possible in order to evaluate the deal.

"For example," Fred said, "when considering a duplex, suppose you put yardwork and a dollar estimate on *your* list of expected costs. To your surprise, the seller's list doesn't mention yardwork. Upon questioning, you find that one of his two tenants cuts the grass around both sides of the duplex. The seller says yardwork doesn't cost him anything. However, with further questioning you discover the seller has, in fact, provided a lawnmower for the tenant who cuts the grass. The seller says he didn't actually give the lawnmower to the tenant; it belongs to the property. You realize immediately the cost of any lawnmower repair will *also* belong to the property. Delving further, you find out that the cooperative tenant pays $40 less rent per month than the other tenant because the seller gives him a year-round break on rent for tending the yards. Was the seller's list of costs truthful? To an extent yes, but there should have been a footnote explaining the yardwork arrangement. Did the seller's list give all the info needed to evaluate the property? No."

Fred pointed out he did all his own rental yardwork for at least five years.

He addressed the young couple: "Initially at least, you might plan to operate as I did because you would prefer to get the extra $40 a month rent from the tenant who was cutting the grass, but you would have to check the lease. For the current lease term, the seller may have stipulated the $40 monthly discount on the lease or show only the net rent payable. You, as a new owner, would be obligated to honor existing leases."

Fred gave the Andersons another example. "When considering a quadraplex, you list electricity and an amount as one of the expected operational costs then find the seller's list of costs doesn't mention utilities. The seller says units are separately metered and tenants are responsible for paying for utilities they use. Seems okay, but you ask who pays for the parking lot lights. The seller claims he forgot about them. It turns out the landlord, in fact, does pay for security lights but says it's *only* $15 a month. You delve further and find, as expected, the landlord also pays for utilities and a turn-on fee if electricity or water is needed for apartment fix-up between tenants. The seller then says it only happens a couple of times each year and just for two or three days at a time. However, the cost is about $40 each time considering the turn-on fee and utility minimum charges. In summary, the seller has understated—misrepresented is possibly too harsh a word—his costs by $180 a year for the security lights plus $80 a year for apartment cleanup utilities. Makes you wary about all the data the seller has given you. That's the advantage of cross-checking your list against the seller's list."

Wendy expanded on the theme. "A seller, on the other hand, may list a cost not on your list. The seller might list a quarterly homeowner's association fee or the monthly cost of a dumpster shared with an adjacent property. When this happens, thank the seller profusely for letting you know about costs for which you, as owner, would be liable. Put such items on your standard operating cost list ready for evaluation of the next property."

"Joe and Jane," Fred intoned, "if you two buy a property without learning of unmentioned costs before closing, you can object and cry foul after the closing, but it won't do you any good. You see, buyers are supposed to exercise due diligence in evaluations of properties they are thinking of purchasing. The existence of a dumpster on the property line and the absence of individual garbage cans on the subject property should cause a diligent prospective buyer to ask who pays for garbage removal.

"When considering a larger property, or one offered by an owner of lots of properties, you may discover a cost that you, as owners, wouldn't be subject to. On three properties I bought there were operational expenses listed which related to particular accounting methods of the owner/sellers. The charges were overheads applied to each property operated by the large owner. One was for computer costs. The company's central office housed a central computer and staff while individual properties just had a personal computer used by the manager. However, the total computer system-related cost—including central office staff cost—was spread among all rental properties. Each property paid a portion of the total based on its revenue contribution to total, company-wide revenue."

The other costs Fred ran into were a maintenance staff charge and a headquarters overhead charge. Both were charges levied by large owner organizations to their individual rental properties. The accounting practice of the large landlords having central offices was to apply all costs to revenue producing units on the basis of pro rata shares. Nothing wrong with that, but a small landlord does not have central office or headquarters overhead costs. One of the advantages of being a small landlord is inexpensive office operating costs.

Fred went on: "Of course, there is the potential problem of accuracy both in the figures supplied by the seller and in your own estimates. The more experience you have, the better your own estimates will become. Gradually you'll come to rely almost entirely on your figures for the biggest variable costs such as supplies, repairs, yardwork and utilities. It's easy to determine what last year's taxes were and the local tax assessor will give you a very good estimate of the current year's taxes. Call your insurance agent or several agents to get the cost of insurance based on the current value of improvements on the property. Accept the seller's figure for insurance cost with a grain of salt. It may be correct for the seller but it is unlikely you'll enjoy the same premium amount. It's no surprise that your agent is going to quote current rates and use a higher property valuation than on the seller's policy.

"Look with caution at figures supplied by the seller. While most sellers will give you accurate data, there is incentive for cooking the books. Sellers naturally want the numbers to show their property is the buy of the century. Unfortunately, a few owners succumb to temptation and adjust or omit figures.

"The revenue and vacancy loss area is notorious for being adjusted on fact sheets handed out by some sellers. Revenue will be maximized with vacancy minimized. It's best to develop your own figures for these areas. Fortunately, it's not too difficult to construct your own reasonably accurate income figures. Start with the current rent roll of the subject property. The rent roll is simply a list of current tenants along with the amount of monthly rent they pay, plus their security deposits. Ask for copies of the current leases although you may not get them unless you request them within a formal offer you make.

"First match the rent amounts payable according to the leases against the rent roll. Bring any discrepancies to the attention of the seller. If rent roll rents don't match lease amounts, ask to see the documentation which explains the differences.

"Once current rents have been verified, do the multiplication to determine the gross potential monthly and yearly rents. It is called potential because it's the amount of rent you would get if the units remained at the same rates and fully occupied and fully paid. Of course, tenant turnover and vacancy will reduce potential rent to a net income level. You'll get better at estimating vacancy rates with experience but, as a beginning landlord, at least 5% and as much as 10% vacancy should be assumed. Never use zero as a vacancy factor even if the seller insists that her units always stay rented. At best such a claim means the units are relatively easy for the current owner to rent using the current owner's prospect-screening techniques, which may be virtually non-existent.

"Also, be very careful if you are considering any property where at least half the clientele is, or may be, students. Regardless of how good your student tenants are, there is an excellent chance some will leave your rental at the end of their study year regardless of when the lease term ends. Many colleges end their academic years between mid-April and mid-May. Some student tenants who signed twelve month leases the previous August may 'blue sky it' at the end of May. That means they take off flying into the blue sky for home two to three months before their official lease term is up. While you will retain their security deposit and may endure a frustrating session in small claims court, you essentially have two months vacancy facing you. Most returning students won't be available to re-rent your unit until late July.

"Students by the thousands rent apartments and it can be very profitable for landlords. However, if it's likely that students will be a significant percentage of the tenants of any property you are considering, be sure to boost the vacancy factor you use in your evaluation. If a unit is vacant 2 months out of 12, its vacancy rate is 2/12ths or 16.5%. Hopefully, you'll have a multi-family property as opposed to a single unit house and most of your students will not take to the blue skies come late May. Plan to use at least 10% as a vacancy factor if a high percentage of the apartments are or will be rented to students."

Fred told the Andersons that for the most part he and Wendy avoided student rentals although they did have a few students as tenants. They reasoned it was best to leave to student rental specialists the potential high vacancy problems and aggravations inherent in dealing with young people who had just left home for the first time.

Fred further said that even though he and Wendy had a long track record of enjoying vacancy rates under 3%, he still used 5 to 7.5% when evaluating a new property. He said he sized up property condition and made a subjective judgment of the current manager's efficiency in deciding which vacancy rate to use. Poor property condition and/or a poor manager meant the 7.5% rate would be used. Fred figured less stable tenants would go into a property in poor condition or would be allowed in by a poor manager. If they bought the poor property, Fred figured it would take Wendy and him six to twelve months to turn the property around to make it a good performer. In that period, all undesirable tenants—disruptive, slow pay or no pay types—would be flushed out. Overall property curb appeal would be dressed up as well and units improved as vacancies occurred. With proper screening of the better prospects attracted to a better property, the Madisons would gradually achieve a low vacancy rate.

Whichever method is used to compute a vacancy factor percentage, it is the percentage, Fred explained, that gross potential rent is reduced by to obtain net effective income.

Joe, looking a little lost, interjected, "You've told us so much I think I'm getting confused. Just what do we need to do to analyze a property we become interested in?"

"Guess I did get carried away, Joe! I've gone on and on, I admit. But you need to keep in mind all the items I mentioned when you get seriously interested in purchasing something. Let me kind of summarize and write it down for you."

Fred took out a piece of lined paper and drew a couple of lines to create inch-wide columns by the right side. He headed the columns "Per Month" and "Per Year."

"Notice the month and year columns," Fred pointed out to Joe and Jane. "I believe it helps you visualize if you develop your figures for both periods. Some cost elements, such as taxes and insurance, are normally thought of in terms of a year. So write them down in the Per Year column. Other items such as rents are normally thought of in terms of per month so write the rent amount initially in the Per Month column. Once you've got every item and figure listed in the most appropriate column, do conversions so each item is expressed in both monthly and yearly amounts. There's nothing to it. Either multiply or divide by twelve."

Fred made up some realistic figures for a quadraplex. He chose to have each of the four rental units rent for $525 per month. Fred's paper looked like this:

PRELIMINARY ANALYSIS CHART (excluding debt service)

	PER MONTH	PER YEAR
Gross Potential Income—4 X $525	2,100	25,200
Vacancy Loss Factor—7.0%	147	1,764
Other Income	0	0
Net Effective Income	1,953	23,436
OPERATING EXPENSES		
Taxes	217	2,604
Insurance	55	660
Contracted Repairs	90	1,080
Supplies	60	720
Utilities (Tenants pay regular utilities)	7	84
Yardwork (Do self)	0	0
Management (Do self)	0	0
Advertising	6	72
Miscellaneous	10	120
TOTAL OPERATING EXPENSES	445	5,340
NET OPERATING INCOME	1,508	18,096
DEBT SERVICE (Principal and Interest)		
CASH FLOW (Spendable by Owner)		

"That doesn't look too bad," said Joe. "We get over $18,000 a year profit! Not bad at all!"

"Good grief, Joe! *You* don't get to keep the $18,096 listed as net operating profit! You'll have a mortgage to pay off! See, I've left space for entering debt service expense. That means your loan payments. Put that figure in and subtract to get something called cash flow. Cash flow is what you guys get to spend on yourselves.

"This little format fits all sizes of properties. Use it for a one-unit house or a 150-unit complex. For the big properties you will have sources of other income such as laundry income or vending machine income. Plus, you will have other expense items such as swimming pool upkeep or security services or goodwill parties."

"Well, what about debt service?" queried Jane. "How about putting in a realistic example figure there so Joe and I can see what the bottom line would look like."

"Can do, Jane. You know there are lots of considerations and decisions to make concerning how your new rental property is going to be financed. Let's say you negotiated the price of the quadraplex down from an asking price of $159,000 to a purchase price of $155,000. You somehow come up with a 10% down payment of $15,500. Your primary lender, a mortgage company, is willing to give you an 80% loan and will hold a first mortgage. Your elderly seller, who plans to simply retire and travel, is willing to loan you 10% of the price and hold a second mortgage. Considering both the primary lender's and the seller's involvement, you're getting 90% financing, which is not bad at all. Now don't get excited, this is still hypothetical, but it is a realistic financing plan."

Fred continued: "Let's suppose your lender gives you an 8.5% interest rate loan. It's a one-year adjustable type, which, incidentally, is what I favor personally. It amortizes over 30 years and for the first year at least, the combined principal and interest payment will be $938 per month. Let's say the sellers agreed to 7% fixed-rate interest and require you to pay $110 a month including principal and interest. They also want a balloon payment of all remaining principal seven years after the sale/purchase is closed. Between your two lenders you guys will have to fork over $1,048 a month or $12,576 a year.

"Your cash flow in this example would be $5,520 a year or $460 a month. Here, let me fill in the chart." The revised chart:

PRELIMINARY ANALYSIS CHART (excluding debt service)

	PER MONTH	PER YEAR
Gross Potential Income—4 X $525	2,100	25,200
Vacancy Loss Factor—7.0%	147	1,764
Other Income	0	0
Net Effective Income	1,953	23,436
OPERATING EXPENSES		
Taxes	217	2,604
Insurance	55	660
Contracted Repairs	90	1,080
Supplies	60	720
Utilities (Tenants pay regular utilities)	7	84
Yardwork (Do self)	0	0
Management (Do self)	0	0
Advertising	6	72
Miscellaneous	10	120
TOTAL OPERATING EXPENSES	445	5,340
NET OPERATING INCOME	1,508	18,096
DEBT SERVICE (Principal and Interest)	1,048	12,576
CASH FLOW (Spendable by Owner)	460	5,520

"You must make up a chart like this for every property you're possibly interested in. They're not hard to put together and you learn a lot by going through the motions. And, you may see some very interesting things when you compare any analysis chart you've prepared against a data sheet given to you by the seller or the seller's agent. A lot of sins of omission are made. Frequently, some kind of expense gets left out by the seller making the bottom line look better. Inadvertently, of course! Sometimes you may find a sin of commission where the expense item is given but grossly understated. Or the revenue is overstated—another sin of commission."

"Buyers must do their own evaluations—or analyses—to determine the likely profitability of any property. Ultimately, the goal is to determine if the asking price is fair. Most likely it's too high. But, Joe and Jane, don't be alarmed. Most sellers seem to overprice their offerings, sometimes by a little and sometimes by a lot. Most sellers feel a buyer is not going to offer the asking price even if it is fair. They anticipate every buyer will figure in a discount and offer less than asking price. Other sellers may honestly feel their property is worth their asking price even if everyone else considers it's worth a lesser amount.

"The more properties you consider, the wiser you'll get. Analyze any properties that seem appealing to you as possible rentals. You'll be surprised, as you analyze, to see the wide variation in cash flows. What at first glance may seem the buy of the century may turn out to be a real loser, once you analyze. Do enough analysis work and you'll get to know which situations make sense."

Fred cautioned the Andersons. "The chart we just constructed is a necessary first step but we're still a ways away from determining profitability or fair price. For example, price is obviously going to affect profitability because it relates so closely to down payment and debt service. The lower the down payment, the higher the profitability is likely to be but not necessarily so."

"Why's that?"

"Low down payments cause bigger loans, and bigger loans—as a percentage of purchase price—frequently command higher interest rates for the lender. If you're paying higher interest, your profitability will be lower. Also, sometimes a low down payment will cause closing costs to be higher. The points or fees you pay to get the larger loan may be higher. And of course, there's private mortgage insurance, called PMI. PMI is frequently required if your down payment is less than 20% of the purchase price. It adds the rough equivalent of about one third of 1% of the loan interest rate as a monthly expense. So, considering higher interest rates, higher closing costs and the possibility of having to pay monthly PMI, low down payments can reduce profitability somewhat."

"I see," said Joe. "Does that mean you favor high down payments?"

"Not at all. In fact, as a generality I favor as low a down payment as you can get away with, applying common sense of course. Especially when you're younger and in the acquisition stage of your life you should use as much real estate leverage as possible. High use of leverage means low down payments which means some costs will be higher. However, the advantages of high leverage can be so enormous they can overshadow the few higher expenses you may run into."

"But what if you have only a small nest egg?" ventured Jane. "We don't have much choice as to high or low down payment. It has to be low. As low as they go!"

"Many people don't have any choice if they want a property. Their budgets only allow for a tiny down payment. So what if some costs are higher? *Owning the property is the thing!* If young people want to get in the rental real estate game at all, they'll most likely have to go for low downs. In my opinion, it would be a bad mistake for a young couple to wait until they have saved enough to make a conventional 20% down payment. For one thing, they may never be able to save a full 20% plus closing costs so they won't get to play in the game at all. Secondly, while they're saving—possibly for years—property values will keep creeping up. Their target will be on the move! Far better to buy a rental property as soon as possible, providing it's going to be profitable."

Wendy jumped into the discussion: "Okay, Fred, you've made that point. How about telling Joe and Jane about closing costs and calculating profitability. Before they nod off, that is."

"Oh yeah, closing costs. Can't forget those! Closing costs are such things as points, meaning the up-front cost of getting a loan, survey cost, state taxes on documents and the cost of title insurance. As I've told you already, when a seller or agent says you only need 10% to buy a property, they're referring strictly to the down payment itself. They assume everyone knows closing costs will add another 2 to 5% of the purchase price as a cash requirement. So the 10% cash requirement they easily tossed out to get your attention could easily end up meaning 14%. Not a difference to be sneezed at if you're on a tight budget."

"Any way to avoid the extra cash for closing costs, Fred?" Joe asked. "We'll have a hard time raising the basic 10% let alone 14."

"Understood, Joe, and yes, there is a way. You may be able to negotiate with the seller for the seller to pay the closing costs for you to conserve your cash."

"Why would the seller do that?"

"Primarily to help you buy what he's trying to sell. If the seller sensed, after you've negotiated the price, that the only thing stopping you from buying his property is your shortage of cash, he may very well agree to pay your closing costs. At least he would for a price. He may want to increase the agreed upon sale/purchase price by the amount of closing costs he is going to pay. If he was going to pay $4,000 in closing costs for you he would increase the previously negotiated price by $4,000."

"In that case, would you still do the deal Fred?"

"Certainly. If I were the seller I'd do it to make the sale and because it really doesn't cost me anything. As the buyer, I'd go for it in order to acquire the property when I didn't have enough cash. Of course, I would understand I'm really paying for it through a higher mortgage, resulting from the $4,000 higher price. But so what? The slightly higher mortgage payment would be more than offset by the advantage of using greater leverage. You see, in essence I would have financed my closing costs."

"I'll bet real estate agents like that kind of final arrangement," declared Jane. "They would already have figured their commission on what everyone thought was the final price and then the price jumps by four grand. More commission!"

"It generally doesn't work that way, my friend. It typically comes about when a stalemate occurs. Buyer, seller and all realtors involved want the sale/purchase and the buyer simply doesn't have enough cash. So, everything stops. Beads of sweat appear on the foreheads of the realtors as they see their commissions—already mentally spent—going up in smoke. The seller thinks with dismay that he's going to have to start all over again with another prospect. Suddenly, the concept of the seller paying closing costs is introduced and everyone can see that the deal can go on. The realtors gladly agree to freeze their commissions as based on the originally agreed price. They get no commission on the $4,000 price increase. But they're happy. Their forehead sweat dries up."

"So, Fred," ventured Jane, "as long as we master the Preliminary Analysis Chart you drew up for us, are you saying we can evaluate any residential rental property? Didn't you say we could use essentially the same chart for anything from a one-family house to a 150-unit apartment complex? Oh yes, remembering, of course, to factor in debt service!"

"Yes and no," replied Fred. "*Yes* the chart is relevant with small modifications to that range of sizes. But *no*, the chart by itself doesn't give you all the answers you need to make a proper decision on a property. Note that I've called it a preliminary analysis chart. It's a necessary step but only a first step."

"That chart seemed pretty thorough to me!" exclaimed Joe. "Are you telling me we've got to go further? Aren't we overdoing things here?"

Wendy responded: "Fred and I have gone through this preliminary analysis business many times for our own purchases so I know this is just the first step. I also know you've then got to consider how you're going to finance the purchase and costs involved with that. And don't forget, you've got to make an evaluation of the physical aspects of the property. So all in all there's a fair distance still to go in the evaluation process. Isn't that right, Fred?"

"Yes, indeed. Don't plan on jumping the gun, Joe. If you buy anything without a thorough analysis you're going to end up paying more than you should for it in more ways than you can think of. Just be a little patient. I'll go over all the other steps. Then I'll tie everything together and you'll see the logic of it and the value of the approach."

Later, back at their apartment, the Andersons discussed what they had just learned from the Madisons. They now knew how to locate possible rental properties to buy and what basic information had to be collected. And, they knew now why given income and expense figures were to be used cautiously. If they doubted given figures they were to adjust them towards being conservatively reasonable. They also now knew how to develop a simple preliminary analysis chart and a reasonably accurate cash flow forecast.

7

Physical Evaluation of the Property

On a pleasant Sunday afternoon, the Andersons and the Madisons were once again seated on the Madisons' front deck. Fred had already started talking to the young couple about his favorite topic—rental real estate.

"Don't buy anything sight unseen," Fred warned. "Of course you wouldn't, you say, but people do it all the time on Internet auctions—sometimes without even seeing a picture. Even if you see a photo, please realize it's easier than ever before to alter a picture! In the past there were plenty of cases of trusting souls investing in Florida or Arizona land without walking on it. Too frequently the land they bought turned out to be virtually worthless. 'Trust me,' hucksters say. Don't.

"You must perform due diligence when evaluating residential rental property. You must see it and touch it. Walk on it, into it and around it. You must see inside all rooms and, if possible, above and below them, before closing. Due diligence means you must investigate all aspects of whatever you're considering buying in a meticulous, careful manner as any aware, reasonable person would in view of the magnitude of the issue.

"Let's say you've been attracted to the neighborhood and the street on which the prospective rental property lies. Let's say you've already got the basic data by telephone, fax, mail or through visiting with a friendly realtor. You've done the preliminary analysis chart as described previously and based on the resulting numbers you're somewhat interested. I've told you before that I advocate doing a paperwork analysis first, to see if there are good financial possibilities, before doing a physical evaluation other than a simple drive-by.

"One way to start the due diligence process would be to drive to the prospective neighborhood on routes you think prospective tenants would travel. See anything that would cause a prospect to turn around and leave you waiting for a no-show? No-shows happen with a surprising frequency. In part it's because a prospect may call all appealing ads then set out to see each. If the prospect finds just what they want, their searching ends immediately. Some prospects do not have enough manners to then cancel other appointments they've made.

"Another major reason for no-shows is that the prospect gets to your property early, doesn't like it or the route to it and drives by it without stopping. Doesn't matter how nice the apartment is inside or what a great value it is. If it doesn't have curb appeal—that's the quick view from the curb—or route appeal, you'll have trouble renting it.

"Curb appeal can often be improved, but you can't do much about route appeal or the appeal of a rental's immediate neighbors.

"Evaluate the drive-up in the eyes of the prospect. If unappealing, can you improve things at reasonable cost? If not, drop the property from further consideration, regardless of what a bargain it may seem to be! Now, you can start to guess why such a property may be priced low.

"As you drive around the adjacent blocks at least twice, evaluate the tone of the neighborhood. Is it clearly a college student area? Perhaps there are lots of student-type cars parked helter-skelter, even on lawns. Or is it a family neighborhood with lots of kid-toys in evidence? Does it appear to be a well-kept area? Are some properties clearly being neglected? Is the area going downhill?

"Regardless of the average values of neighborhood properties, you should be after an area that looks neat and orderly. It doesn't matter if the buildings are modest and it doesn't matter if the area is mature or even old. It's how it has been kept up that is important. If you want good tenants, your rentals need to be in a convenient, non-trashy area. Overall, the tone of the neighborhood should be pleasing to you. Maybe it has some flaws, but if it has very many flaws, buy somewhere else. Follow your intuition. If you don't have a good feeling about the prospective rental neighborhood go elsewhere. If you're not comfortable with the area it is unlikely you'll ever be happy owning there, and your rental experience will suffer accordingly."

As Fred paused to sip a little iced tea, Wendy picked up the conversation. "As we've suggested previously, if the prospective rental is distant from your town's direction of growth or any of its natural centers of activity, you don't want to own it unless it's got convenient mass-transit access. Look for something closer. You could run yourself ragged trying to rent an apartment in a remote area that most people don't even want to drive to or walk to let alone live in. Use common sense. Size up an area and its location through the eyes of prospective renters. Assume the property you are considering suddenly becomes totally empty. How much trouble would you have getting possible renters just to come to see it?

"Once you're satisfied that the area is acceptable—maybe not perfect but at least acceptable—stop in front of the property and slowly walk around it. Walk around it twice—once clockwise and once counterclockwise. You'll see much more if you change perspectives. Examine the building carefully as you circle it.

"What are you looking for? You're just gathering general impressions at this point, but try to see beyond the merely cosmetic. If the building is surrounded by unkempt vegetation and is badly in need of paint, make a mental note but try to look deeper. More importantly, is the masonry badly cracked? Is the siding rotted or pulling away from the walls? Are there clear signs of water damage? Is there a bad erosion problem or evidence of rain water ponding by the building? Does it look like any part of the building is subject to flooding? Does the building appear to be structurally sound? Make notes of these types of problems.

"If there appear to be major problems that clearly will be costly to remedy, as a novice you ought to stop considering the property. Of course, you may not be able to tell what is a major problem and what is not. If you're in doubt about problems you noted, but are otherwise interested in the property, consult someone who really knows. Be wary of free advice from well-intentioned but non-experts such as brothers-in-law! By the way, some wood rot, water damage and surface cracking in masonry are normal and not necessarily costly to fix. Keep in mind it's unlikely you'll find a used building in perfect shape. Think used car rather than new car.

"If there are porches, exterior stairs, railings or balconies, get on them. Jump lightly on porches or balconies to see how much 'give' there is. Give railings and supports a good shake. Does exterior flooring appear deteriorated or rotted?"

Wendy paused, glanced at Fred and raised her eyebrows. She was questioning whether he wished to add anything to her remarks. He did. "Stand back—even across the street—to look at the roof," Fred stated. "Use binoculars if you have them. Does the roof look sound or badly deteriorated? If it's shingled, are the shingles lying flat or are they curled? Do all the surface granules of shingles appear to be wearing off? Do there appear to be unusual bumps, ridges or dips in the roof's surface? You're probably not an experienced roofer, but you're just trying to ascertain possible trouble spots at this point.

"Now go inside. At this stage you don't need to go inside each unit nor spend more than ten minutes in each apartment you enter. Keep it simple, keep it brief. Tenants don't like to be bothered, and you may be intimidated if they're watching while you inspect. Two solutions: don't bother all tenants and inspect when tenants are not likely to be home. Of course, the seller, manager or realtor should pre-arrange all viewings. Besides not being courteous, in your area it may well be illegal to go in unannounced or without prior permission. While leases generally give landlords the right to show apartments to inspectors or prospective buyers, advance notification is still generally required. Usually the person who will show the property will talk to affected tenants the day before your intended visit or leave them a written or recorded message explaining the upcoming walk-through."

After explaining physical inspections for some time, Fred asked the Andersons if they had questions.

Joe asked, "Fred, why wouldn't you inspect all the units before you buy?"

"You certainly would before you buy, Joe, but I've found it's not necessary at this pre-offer stage. You might not be making an offer, in fact. At this stage you're trying to decide if you like the property enough to give it the full treatment. Of course, if the property has only one, two or three units, you might as well take a quick look in each. But if it's a quadraplex, just look at two units at this point. In general, while you're in the pre-offer mode, take quick looks in about half the total number of units. If there is more than one floor to the building, be sure to inspect a mixture of upper and lower units."

"So, eventually we must inspect all units before we buy," Jane recapitulated. "It's just that you feel we don't need to take the time or bother at this early stage. Is that what you mean, Fred?"

"Precisely. Considering you may end up looking at a dozen or more properties before you find one you want to try to purchase, you don't need exhaustive inspections too soon.

"Now, any offer you submit must include a clause whereby you get a limited time to conduct any or all inspections you want, including the inside of all rooms. Plus, you must make it a contingency clause, meaning giving you the right to back out of the contract if you are unsatisfied with the results of your inspections. Beyond that, your offer also must have a clause giving you the right to a final inspection of the property's systems—electrical, mechanical, plumbing, heat and air—a short time before your scheduled closing. So you get another shot at it. And, if you find anything wrong, have the contract say the seller must fix it at his expense.

"Right now I'm trying to tell you how to evaluate a property in an overall sense. Just as one more step in the process of deciding whether or not to try to buy the property and how much to offer for it."

"Question!" Joe blurted out. "Fred, you keep jumping back and forth between 'offer' and 'contract.' Are we talking about the same thing here?"

"Yes, we are and no, we're not!" replied Fred with a smile. "Sorry to confuse you all! You see, when you initiate an offer to purchase something—anything for that matter—it continues to be called an 'offer' until it's accepted. During the period before it has been accepted—and therefore it is still an offer—the person making the offer can withdraw it. No questions asked. As long as the offer remains on the table—not accepted and not withdrawn—it legally continues to be known as an offer. Course, offers usually contain a time clause so if nothing happens within, say, five working days, the offer becomes null and void.

"If the offer is accepted, which in real estate is by the seller signing the offer and the prospective buyer being so informed, the offer legally becomes a contract. A contract cannot be terminated except by mutual agreement, by effect of a conditional clause within the contract or by closing of the sale."

"But what if the seller counteroffers our offer?" questioned Joe.

"If the seller changes any part of your offer and sends it back to you, it legally becomes his or her offer to you. It's still an offer, but it's the seller's offer. Same rules apply. You can accept, thereby changing his offer to a contract, reject it or modify it. If you modify it, then it again becomes your offer back to the seller. Got that?"

"Yeah," and "Think so," responded Joe and Jane.

"Good," said Fred. "Then let me proceed with telling you what to look for when you first go inside a rental property you're considering buying."

Fred did just that: "The first look is to get overall impressions. In an overall sense, are the units in excellent shape, average shape or tragic shape? The more rental units you look at, the better your judgment will become. Before looking at used rentals on the market, visit some brand new units, if possible, to refresh your mind as to what new, fresh and clean look and smell like. Obviously, used rentals are not going to be as impressive as new but they could be close. At the bad end of the range are older, mildewed, poorly maintained units. Most rentals for sale will fall between the extremes. That's okay. You're buying used property, not new.

"Look at the walls and ceilings. Are there signs of rot or separations at joints or corners indicating settling and possible structural damage? Are there water stains and/or blistering of interior paint indicating water leaks? If so, have the leaks been repaired, or are they still active?

"Look at the appliances. Do they appear shabby and

dated? With a little cleaning could they appear fresh and appealing to a prospective renter? What about the flooring—
carpet, wood, vinyl or other? Will it need immediate replacement or are there at least several years of life left in it?

"Although you are not visiting to inspect the housekeeping of the existing tenants, you won't be able to avoid forming
impressions about the residents. These can be very revealing.
Expect a range of housekeeping and degree of furnishings.
Not everyone has a full set of tasteful furnishings and not everyone keeps their home spotless. Expect it, and for the most
part, live with it. However, if most units are very poorly furnished and the housekeeping is almost all bad, you have to
evaluate the property downward accordingly.

"Make mental notes of defects of all kinds as you make your
escorted tour through the units, but jot down your impressions
as soon as possible afterwards to avoid forgetting something.

"Certainly make note of anything, inside or out, that
appears faulty but which is beyond your personal competence
to evaluate. Examples might be shabby-looking, noisy A/C
compressors or rust-stained water heaters. In these cases, if it
gets that far, special mention of the potential defects ought to
be made in the offer.

"Some portions of the property may be inaccessible during the informal inspection. Examples include attics and crawl
spaces. Don't worry about these areas at the pre-offer stage,
unless you have some evidence that significant damage or defects may be found there. Otherwise, plan to include these
areas in your detailed inspections to be conducted once your
offer, if there is one, has been accepted. Further, any orthodox
lender you use will require an inspection by a licensed professional for wood destroying organisms. These inspections include examination for dry rot and termites. If there are
problems, lenders require that they be fixed and the property
re-inspected by the same company to obtain a 'clear' report. If
you have special concerns about an attic or crawl space, you
can specifically direct the termite inspector, which is what most
people call the exterminator or pest control specialist who
makes such inspections, to inspect these areas closely. You'll
have more influence over the inspector if you, as buyer, pay
for the inspection, but sellers typically pay for it."

"I've heard that buyers usually pay for termite inspections, not the seller," commented Jane.

"It's a negotiable item," Fred explained. "Which party usually pays probably depends on the tradition in the area. We advocate the buyer paying, but sellers often want to get an inspection done just before or just after they put their property on the market. They want to find out the extent of any problems they may have. They may suspect or even know for a fact that they have problems. They might very well get everything fixed before offering the property for sale. Then they can wave a 'clear' termite report in front of any prospect."

"One thing, though," Wendy added, "if you as buyers pay for the termite inspection, or any other inspection for that matter, be sure to add the cost of it into your analysis. Any money you spend related to the cost of buying a property is a cost of acquisition."

"Thanks, Wendy, I should have mentioned that," Fred said while nodding. He then went on: "The desired outcome of a pre-offer inspection is for you to get a gut feeling about the property. Do you feel good about it or bad or somewhere in between? If you feel bad about it, it's probably best to not give the property further consideration, at least for the time being. Never say never. After you've done a similar evaluation of everything else on the market, you may find the current subject is the best of a bad bunch and may wish to reconsider it.

"If your overall impression has been neutral to good, examine your notes closely. Make a list of the things you feel must be done almost immediately in order to bring the property to acceptable status. Then, check with knowledgeable people to get rough ideas about how much the immediate repairs might cost. But remember, you're not going to be trying to bring the property back to like-new condition. Never forget: you are looking at used cars not new cars. A used car doesn't need to have new tires and new upholstery to work well. First time rental property buyers sometimes get the wrong idea about what conditions are normal and acceptable to most renters. If they are fastidious about their personal residence they may think all renters are equally fussy. Not so. The standard for units ready to rent should be apartments that are very clean, no damage, everything working that is supposed to work and with an overall appearance pleasing to prospective renters.

"The apartments may not be especially pleasing in appearance to you or to your wealthy spinster Aunt Pettibone, but neither you nor Miss Pettibone is a prospective renter, so your points of view are not appropriate. Put yourself in the shoes of the people who would be likely renters. Try to envision the property and the apartment interiors through their eyes.

"Be careful too about deciding what must be improved or replaced immediately. Let's say you think the carpet needs to be replaced in one apartment. If the apartment is occupied, there's no immediacy about it unless you have knowledge that the existing tenant is about to move out. You must, of course, honor existing leases. If the lease doesn't expire until after you buy the building, the existing tenants may, at that time, renew or be willing to remain on a month-to-month basis. It is a fact that even month-to-month tenants may stay for years. Now consider, if they are not complaining and you feel the rent they are paying is adequate and they are not planning to move, why would you replace the carpet? The time for improvements, upgrades, and the like is when there is a move out. Once an apartment is vacated, fix it up as necessary, establish a new higher rent, then re-rent it.

"Using your notes and memory after physically evaluating both sides of a duplex, your fix-up list might look like this." Fred drew a simple chart:

Unit A

Needs new stove/oven	$300
Carpet poor	700 when vacant

Unit B

Needs 3 mini-blinds	75 install self
Replace bathroom sink	120 incl. labor
Replace disposal	135 incl. labor

Exterior

Cleanup shrubbery, yard	200 or do self
Total	$ 1,530

Fred continued: "If this list constituted all of the major items you noticed on a pre-offer evaluation, the property would seem pretty good. Of course, more faulty items may be discovered during a detailed inspection after the contract is signed. $1,530 is the cost to hire people to do all items immediately. Only $830 needs to be spent to get everything in order right away since the carpet shouldn't be replaced while the apartment is occupied. As the new owner, you could handle the shrubbery and yardwork, so only $630 cash needs to be spent. If you are moderately handy, you could save about another $140 labor by installing the new sink and disposal yourself. Doing so would reduce the cash requirement to $490. Not too bad at all! But, remember ... we're still at the pre-offer stage! In this case, you can probably negotiate the asking price down to offset the cost of the faults you discovered in your quick physical evaluation.

"The approach I just described," said Fred, "is how you would evaluate any property regardless of size. Naturally it gets more complicated as the number of units in the property increases, or, as the complexity of the property increases, such as when it has a swimming pool, an elevator or a central boiler instead of individual water heaters for each apartment. It's further complicated if you become suspicious of major structural, foundation or roof problems or problems you can't evaluate easily yourself. Should you hire experts at this stage? No. You are still at the pre-offer stage and you may never agree on a contract. Don't hire anyone yet, but if you think the property is otherwise promising, it may be wise to get the free informal opinion of a roofer, air conditioning expert, or other expert if you suspect significant problems. Only do this if you're pretty certain of submitting an offer. Don't waste an expert's time if an expert opinion is not needed. Besides, experts won't be free repeatedly if they don't get some chargeable business out of you once in a while.

"Remember to keep all your notes about the real and suspected faults of any property you inspect. Should you get to the offer stage you can formally include the suspicious items in the offer even if you haven't got an expert's opinion of the costs to correct them."

Joe and Jane now knew that for any property which interested them it was necessary to investigate the neighborhood, routes to the property and the property itself, both inside and out. The Madisons had outlined to them the importance of preliminary pre-offer inspections and final inspections. They now had a good idea as to when to consult experts. They knew they should develop a list and costs of fix-up items to be handled immediately after closing for any property they considered buying.

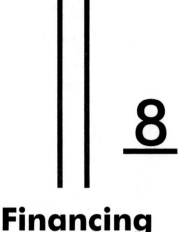

8

Financing

"Financing rental properties is a big subject," Fred said while seated at the Madisons' kitchen table. The Andersons were over for another session with their mentors. They had driven by some properties for sale to get a general idea of what was on the market, but when they looked at the asking prices, they worried that it would take years to save enough to finance their first property. When they told Fred of their concerns, he assured them that a lesson on creative financing would allay many of their fears. "I'd like to be able to give you one neat concrete example of financing that wraps it all up but I just can't do it. The subject is too broad. You'll just have to bear with me as I work through it. Stop me when you feel the need for a break.

"Except in tight economic times," Fred continued, "there are lots of sources of financing for small rental properties. Don't feel restricted to the banks where you have your checking and savings accounts. Approach any and all places that lend money. Look into credit unions. Contact other banks and savings and loan institutions. Contact mortgage brokers.

"Our local newspaper runs a list of mortgage lenders on a weekly basis and shows the basic terms of loan programs they offer. Two things to remember are: one, not all lenders available to you are in the newspaper's list, and two, not all lending programs will be listed.

"If you want to see what's offered all over the country, you can search for mortgages on the Internet. Some websites give you the basics on literally hundreds of mortgage loan alternatives. As time passes, the Internet will play an increasingly important role in creation of new mortgages, but I believe a good many people will always want to sit down face to face with a local person. Besides, not everyone has Internet access. For those who want to use it, it's a great way to see what's available and to see the variety of offerings.

"But here, let me show you what's in our newspaper," he said and flipped through a nearby stack of papers to retrieve the "Homes" section of the previous Sunday's issue. He riffled through the pages, then noisily pulled out page six. As he unfolded it and laid it out in front of them he continued: "Looks like 18 to 20 lenders are listed here and each has two to four loan programs described. This seems like plenty of lenders, but in fact, if you didn't want to or couldn't do business with any of these, you could easily find five or ten more who didn't bother to get themselves on the paper's list. Plus, every lender may have a dozen different loan programs available even though they only feature two to four here. I'm telling you this so you won't get discouraged if you don't see good financing possibilities straight away. Be prepared to contact a number of lenders and ask them about their loan programs for financing investment properties. Most loans listed in the newspaper will be for owner-occupied single family residences. You'll have to contact lenders directly to see what's available for rental property."

"You mean we really shouldn't bother with the newspaper mortgage information?"

"No, Jane, the newspaper is a good starting point. Study the lenders and what they're offering. Probably they're listing their best programs. You'll be able to see who is most aggressive, meaning who offers the lowest rates and best terms. Pick out perhaps the half dozen lenders who appear to offer the most consumer friendly rates and plan to call each one. But be careful! What appears at first glance to be the best program is not necessarily the best. To give an obvious example, as beginners you might assume the lowest rate indicates the best loan. It ain't necessarily so! Notice right beside the interest rate they give what are called points. As used here, a point means 1% of the value of the loan and to you it's a cost of getting the loan. Usually beside the lowest interest rates you'll find the highest point rates. Very simply, the lower the interest rate, the higher the cost of getting the loan is likely to be."

"Wow!" exclaimed Joe. "These listings show from zero points to three and a half points! I'll go for zero points."

"Wait a minute, honey," cried Jane. "To pay zero points the chart shows you'll end up paying the highest interest rate. I'd want to go for the lowest interest rate, wouldn't I, Fred?"

"Let me answer," Wendy ventured. "It's a matter of evaluating all offerings in terms of which provides the best cash-on-cash return on investment. So when you do your final analysis in the buy or not decision, you'll need to plug in different combinations of interest rates and points to see which give you the best bottom line. Points add to your investment acquisition cost, meaning the cash you need to get into the investment. If your cash supply is skimpy, you're not going to be able to pay many points. If you don't pay points you're going to end up paying a higher interest rate. However, since your cash investment is less, you may end up with a better return on cash investment even though your mortgage payment is higher because of a higher interest rate. You've just got to figure it out on paper. You've got to do any analysis several ways. By the way, the lenders say you can always trade points for rate. They mean if a lower interest rate is important to you, you can get it by paying more points."

"Well said, Wendy," Fred said admiringly. "You've captured an important concept in a nutshell. Just a couple more things about points then we'll move on. First of all, lenders use two terms, loan discount points and loan origination fees, which amount to the same thing to borrowers. Both may be applied by the lender, so be sure to ask if they do. Both work the same way. Both are expressed as points and each point means 1% of the value of the loan you seek. Both are a cost to you of getting the loan. Both represent up-front cash. Just be careful about getting excited when a lender says zero points. Quickly ask if that means zero discount points and zero origination fee. As often as not the lender will say something like: 'Oh, of course we always have to have our one-point loan origination fee.' Watch them. Some lenders are tricky.

"Secondly, for investment property loans, lenders almost always want one-half a point or more in addition to the points required for owner-occupied dwelling loans. For example, if a lender quotes one point for a home loan, the lender will want one and a half points or more for a rental property loan. The interest rate usually will be higher, too, by a half a percent or more. Their rationale is that loans for rental property are riskier than home loans, and they're probably correct. Suppose you have two loans, one on your own home and one on a rental house, and you became disabled. If the disability causes such severe financial difficulties that you must default on one of the loans, which one will it be? Probably you'll let the rental property loan go down the toilet since most people will do anything to save their own homes. It makes sense unless the rental is so profitable it's the one thing keeping you afloat financially.

"Points, by the way, generally constitute the largest of the acquisition expenses known as closing costs.

"You know, to this point we've been talking about orthodox, primary lenders who do the bulk of rental real estate financing. However, in your quest to get the best possible loan terms and use the smallest amount of cash to acquire a property, don't overlook other sources of financing. Do you have a wealthy relative or friend? You shouldn't really be looking for or counting on gifts from relatives or friends, but they might help you out if they're approached properly. If you want a loan, offer your wealthy friend about the same terms you find you'll have to pay an orthodox lender. And be prepared to justify your request by having a proper analysis or business plan that shows you'll be able to pay back the borrowed money and still make a profit. Be prepared to properly collateralize the loan by having a formal loan agreement backed by a recorded mortgage on the property. By collateralizing I mean putting up something of value as security for the lender against the funds you borrow. If you don't pay back as agreed, the lender can take your collateral. The collateral in the case of rental property investing is the property itself.

"A wealthy friend who's convinced you'll pay back a loan may cut you some slack compared to an orthodox lender. Besides giving you an interest rate slightly lower than the going open-market rate, the friend won't ask you for loan points or an origination fee. Just as important, if not more so, the friend may be a little more tolerant of any spots on your credit history or if you have no credit history. A skimpy or troubled credit history might very well cause an orthodox lender to tell you to go see someone else. But don't abuse your friendships. If you have a bad credit record, clean it up before you ask any friend or relative for money. Prove you are responsible and know how to manage money. Pay off any bad debts that show up on your credit report. If you can't prove you can properly manage your money and can't prove you always make good on your debts, you've got no business asking anyone for a loan."

"Uh, Fred," interrupted Joe in a quiet voice. "We don't have any rich relatives. As for our credit history, well, it wasn't great, but we've cleaned it up. Just after we got married we found we could get a copy of our credit reports from the local credit bureau. Good thing we did, because we discovered I had three old items that showed balances owing. Not big amounts but the companies had turned them over to collection agencies. Actually, they were debts of mine before I even met Jane. We sure were shocked when we saw them on my credit report. Frankly, I had forgotten all about them. In any event, it took a lot of calling, but I finally settled with the collection agencies and they got the credit bureau to make the records show zero balances owing. I hope lenders will look kindly on you if you have finally paid off everything and the incidents were not recent. What do you think?"

"Joe, many lenders, but not all, will be understanding if you've paid off any bad entries and have been clean, that is, without any new bad entries, for the last two to three years. It kind of relates to how anxious they are to put new loans on their books. They might want you to pay a higher interest rate because you are still somewhat of a bad risk in their eyes.

"I can't emphasize enough how important it is to maintain a spotless credit history. Bad items stay on your credit report for seven years. You were very wise to settle those old debts and have zero balances put onto your record. With a bad credit report, you'll never be able to borrow any significant amount unless you pay extra high interest rates. Not only that, Wendy and I and others won't even rent apartments to people with bad credit reports. Right, Wendy?"

Wendy was pleased to jump in. "Absolutely correct! We check the credit reports of everyone who wants to rent one of our apartments. In fact, sometimes when we say to a prospect, 'How's your credit, because we will be checking with the bureau,' they hem and haw then back out the door. They say they want to think more about whether they want the apartment and, of course, we never hear from them again. Just as well, too."

Wendy continued: "Our thinking is that if someone walks away from, say, a $200 jewelry store debt or from $150 still owing on a TV, why would we entrust them with even a one-bedroom apartment worth $40,000? If they've ducked out on small debts before, why wouldn't it occur to us that they may neglect to pay the last month's rent when they eventually want to move on?

"And you know, it's conceivable that a store could re-possess an unpaid-for ring or a TV set. If they could track them down, it's conceivable the stores could sell the used ring and TV to recoup some of their loss. Just like they repossess and resell cars. But guess what? In our business we're actually renting time when we rent an apartment. We can't go back and re-rent October if a tenant skips out late in October without paying. The time is lost. It's outright theft. Luckily we have very little of that kind of thing, because we try to screen prospects carefully. Checking credit helps us a lot. The bad guys end up renting apartments where they don't check credit. Others get the problems we side-step."

"Well thanks, Wendy," said Fred with a chuckle. "You've terrorized our young friends. They'll never want to go into the rental business now!"

Jane came to Wendy's defense. "Oh, not at all, Fred. Wendy's just telling it like it is, and we appreciate it. No need to protect us from problems; every business has some. Besides, Wendy also told us how you guys avoid taking bad actors. You use the local credit bureau to check out all prospective tenants. That sounds like the way to go."

"We find that it works," responded Fred as he nodded. "Our batting average is not 1000 when it comes to screening prospects, but it's pretty high. We've ended up with some pretty nice people in our places. We've had very few bad apples but we have had some." He turned to Joe. "Joe, even if you don't have any wealthy relatives it doesn't mean you necessarily have to stick to orthodox lenders like banks, S&L's and mortgage companies for all funds. Think about the seller as a financier, at least for part of what you need. Surprised? Well, you'd be surprised at how often it happens in the field of rental property.

"Just think of Wendy and me, for example, or any apartment owner our age or older. Maybe even younger. If we were going to sell some of our apartments, we might very well help the buyer finance our own sale. Why? Well, let's suppose we don't have a need for all of the money we'd get if our equity in the property was totally cashed out. If we weren't about to buy anything else we would be looking for a suitable place to invest the cash proceeds of the sale. What could be better than taking a mortgage on the property we're selling? We could get a good interest rate, have good collateral and help ourselves get the price we want on our sale. We would be making it easier for the buyer to buy our place. Nothing wrong with that. As a matter of fact, we've had half a dozen or so second mortgages and never had a problem with any of them.

"However, we wouldn't want to be the buyer's primary financier even if we owned the property we were selling free and clear. We're not really in the financing business. We might very well hold a second mortgage for 10% or up to 30% of the purchase price, but that's about it. Now, we probably wouldn't be seeking to hold a second mortgage, but we'd seriously consider doing so if asked and if it was important to closing the deal. The key thing is to be prepared to ask the seller. All she can say is one of three things: yes, no, or hell no! There's so much to be gained if the seller is willing to participate in the financing. To the extent that the seller will help you, you just need that much less from the primary lender.

"Here's an example of what I'm talking about. Suppose you find a property that seems perfect but have only enough cash for a 10% down payment. Also, you've checked around and find the best you can get out of a primary lender is a loan for 80% of the purchase price. What to do?"

Both Andersons hunched their shoulders and drooped the corners of their mouths. They didn't know. They only saw the hypothetical buyer needed another 10% in cash.

Fred saw they didn't have a clue so he continued. "The likely answer is to ask the seller if he'll hold a second mortgage in order to sell the property. The seller will ask what you have in mind. You then describe how you have 10% cash and will try to get a 75% primary loan and you would like the seller to hold a second mortgage amounting to 15% of the price. After a bit of negotiation the seller might very well go for it. It won't work all the time but will frequently enough. For the most part primary lenders will go along with the plan, too, since their risk exposure is now based on a 75% of value loan not an 80% one. Just by asking, the buyer can be well on the way to buying a property for just 10% down. The seller may be somewhat firmer on his asking price if he's going to be holding a second mortgage, but that's overshadowed by the advantages to the buyer.

"So, what must you ask the seller, Jane?" Fred queried.

"If he'll participate in the financing."

"In order to do what?"

"Make the sale to you."

"Excellent!"

"Let me tell you one final way to get cash money to buy real estate. This one will probably shock you. Most people would probably think it's heresy but I don't. I've done it, in fact."

The Andersons leaned forward to hear about the scandalous method. Wendy looked a little apprehensive. She wondered what Fred could be thinking.

Fred paused for effect then went on.

"If you have an investment retirement account, or IRA, you can cash it in. I know there are some drawbacks, and I realize the employer's contribution, if you're lucky enough to have that kind of plan, is generous and valuable. I also realize that contributions are from pre-tax earnings and interest gained is not subject to taxes until you retire. And yes, I do realize any withdrawals from an IRA before you're 59 and a half are subject to a 10% penalty plus your withdrawal is subject to income tax."

Jane was nodding her head in agreement; she knew all of these things.

"Years ago," Fred said, "while I was still a salaried worker-bee, I had an IRA just as I've described. Then I got interested in the possibilities of rental real estate. I made the plunge and bought our first duplex. Then a second. Everything went well. I could see we were on our way. When I wanted to get another property—a triplex—I didn't have enough cash for the down payment.

"My projections, all done with pencil and paper because personal computers hadn't yet become popular, were probably a bit grandiose. Nevertheless, I believed in them and they showed me a way to retire. My projections required me to keep getting more property, improving it, selling it at the right time and so forth. Actually it was a primitive version of the plan I'm gradually outlining for you guys. It became obvious to me that the way to make money was to own rental property rather than to continue forever working for someone else. I calculated that I could retire early if I had enough rental property. Accordingly, I cashed in my IRA and presto, I was able to get the triplex. One more step on the ladder upwards."

"Gosh, Fred," said Jane softly, "I don't know if we'll ever have the confidence you had back then. The thought of cashing in an IRA kind of scares me. Everybody says it's what to have."

"Now wait, Jane, I'm not twisting your arm to cash in your IRA," Fred smiled. "Didn't even know whether you had one or not, but if you do it's a source of acquisition funds close at hand. I wouldn't expect anyone to do anything so rash as to cash in an IRA or a 401(k) until they prove to themselves, through actual experience, that they can grow much more wealth through rentals than they ever will through IRAs. Even considering employer contributions. Just keep the idea in your bag of tricks until you have the confidence and the need for cash for a property you really want bad. Then maybe you'll be bolder than you think you are."

"Let me say something here," Wendy interrupted, while turning her gaze from Fred to Joe, and then settling on Jane.

"Sure."

"Thank you. In case you didn't know, Fred *did* leave his salaried job and *did* retire for the first time on his 40th birthday.

His projections were good enough. His ideas worked. Just keep that in mind."

"Nevertheless," protested Fred, "my retirement didn't last. Within three years I was bored to death so I had to start doing something else. But enough about me. Let's go on to something else. But first, let's all take a little break." And they did.

Wendy pulled out an album of photos of properties the Madisons had owned over the years. The Andersons were impressed and somewhat envious. They would like to own one rental property let alone an album full.

Twenty minutes later, Fred waded into another matter. "The term of the loan is an important consideration, and for a beginning real estate investor, it's a no-brainer question. Always, always, always go for the longest term you can get. Go for thirty years, not twenty, fifteen or ten. Yes, I know in the long run you'll pay more interest, but it's still by far the best strategy for the beginner who is in the acquisition mode. Young or middle-aged people who are starting a rental real estate portfolio are clearly in the acquisition mode. What I mean is they're trying to buy, acquire and control as much property as possible. That's how they'll build real estate wealth the fastest. As they get beyond middle age, most real estate investors go into a consolidation mode. In this mode they won't acquire anything additional but will strengthen their positions in what they already own in terms of property quality and financing. Finally, once most real estate investors get to retirement age, they evolve from consolidation mode to payoff mode. At this point in their lives they may devote a lot of their extra money—beyond the amount needed for a comfortable if not luxurious living—to paying down mortgage loan amounts.

"At this stage, you should consider yourselves as being in the acquisition mode. You want to acquire as much real estate as you can. In order to be able to buy the most property, you must first go for the lowest amount of cash you can initially put into a property, and secondly go for the lowest monthly loan payment. To get the lowest payment for any given interest rate, you must go for the longest possible payoff term. That's 30 years generally, but I've heard of 40-year loans for some owner-occupied properties. If you personally dwell in one of the four units of a quadraplex apartment building, you may be able to get a 40-year loan. Take it if you can get it."

"Excuse me, Fred," Jane said timidly. "This might make you mad, but Marty Repasky sort of told us the opposite just the other day. He said that if he ever scraped up the money to buy a rental he would use all his profits to pay off his mortgage as fast as possible. He would only take a 15-year mortgage and try to pay it off in ten years in order to own the rental free and clear. He said he'd be damned if he'd pay the loan sharks any more interest than he absolutely had to. Marty was pretty adamant about it, I can tell you."

Fred smiled. "There certainly are plenty of people like Marty, Jane, but they'll never build much wealth in real estate. His ideas are fatally flawed regarding wealth accumulating. Oh, if Marty were 75 years old and only talking about his personal residence, I might agree with him. Elderly people get a lot of peace of mind out of owning their own home free and clear. That's understandable. They don't want any risk of losing their home. But that's not what to do if you're in the acquisition mode for rental property. If Marty starts with the shortest term loan, makes the highest mortgage payment he can afford and uses all his profits to pay off his loan even more quickly, I can almost guarantee the first rental he buys will be his last.

"Marty probably will never have the financial capacity to buy a second rental because he will never build up enough cash to acquire more property. Maybe he will twelve or fourteen years down the line, but by that time he's more likely to finally reward himself for his long-term sacrificing.

"His whole attitude is wrong as well. The folks who do the bulk of rental real estate financing shouldn't be thought of as loan sharks. They provide a valuable commodity—money —and are entitled to a fair interest rate in return.

"Anyone wanting to get beyond the bottom rung on the wealth ladder through real estate investing must plan to use OPM which stands for other people's money. There's no way around it if you start with virtually no funds as in your case. Nothing wrong with borrowing bundles of money and paying fair interest rates, providing the property you buy will safely pay the mortgage, plus maintenance, plus a decent profit to yourselves. If you buy properly—and I'm going to guide you as to what's proper—the loan will get paid off in due course with no particular worry on your part. So what if the loan isn't paid off for 30 years? If you make a good profit for all of those 30 years and your property is going up in value all the time, why worry about early payoffs?"

"Your strategy must be to minimize initial down payments and loan payments—through stretched out terms—in order to be able to accumulate cash for additional purchases and have the capacity to service additional loans. The more profit producing property you have, the wealthier you're going to become. And that's your objective, isn't it?" He looked over his glasses at both Joe and Jane.

"Yes, sir!" snapped Joe.

"I agree!" added Jane.

"Quite frankly," Fred resumed. "It sounds to me as if your friend Marty knows very little about what it takes to accumulate wealth. Lots of people are like him, however. In fact, it sometimes seems to me the majority of people don't have a clue about how to go about becoming wealthy.

"A variation of Marty's thinking, which I've heard numerous times from prospective buyers who came to me as a broker, goes like this. They say that whatever amount of money they have, they want to put it into a rental property to get the smallest loan necessary. That's the exact opposite of what I plan to tell them! So, I ask if they had $150,000 and a good quadraplex worth $150,000 came along, would they buy it outright to own it free and clear? Surprisingly, a number of them have said yes, although they've already told me they wanted to get wealthy. Then I explain why their intuitive way is not the best way considering their ultimate goal of wealth.

"I explain it to them this way. By the way, in this example I'm going to ignore closing costs to simplify things and to emphasize my main point. Okay? I say to the prospective buyers: suppose you put your $150,000 into one quadraplex, improve it and raise rents so it goes up in value 10% in two years. That's a value increase of $15,000 which seems impressive. Then the quad would be worth $165,000. They happily agree. So I tell them their appreciation return is $15,000 on a $150,000 investment or 10% over two years. They have to agree again, but they do so more slowly. Then I tell them 10% over two years is just 5% per year. Again, they have to agree, but by now they're definitely hesitant. Five percent return is pitiful if you've got $150,000 cash to play with. Then, I tell them I've got a better approach to recommend to them. They're all ears by this time.

"I tell them if they ever get hold of $150,000 cash they should try to buy five quads using $30,000 as a down payment for each. Once again I'm ignoring closing costs to simplify and make a point. If they put $30,000 down on each, they'll have five $120,000 mortgages. But their $600,000 total debt will be supported by their $750,000 in properties. Now let appreciation work its magic. Let's say they make the same kind of improvements as before. In two years each of the five properties goes up 10% to $165,000 each, same as the single quad did. But, because they've got five quads, their gain would be five times $15,000, or $75,000 total. $75,000 gain on a $150,000 investment is 50% in two years! That's 25% per year. They always get the point."

"Wow!" exclaimed Joe. "Twenty-five percent versus 5%, that's amazing. But they have to make payments on $600,000 worth of loans, right?"

"Right you are, Joe. But also remember they had month-by-month profit from five buildings all the while. Yes, they make less profit on each mortgaged building than from the one with no mortgage, but having five buildings more than makes up for it. In addition, they were paying off loan principal on each of the loans. Assuming an 8.75% interest rate, after two years they would owe only about $591,000, so that's an extra $9,000 equity for them. Analyze it anyway you want to, if you have a pile of cash and your goal is to become wealthy, buy as much property as you can. Don't be tempted by the notion of owning one property free and clear. Understand?"

"Absolutely!" the Andersons chimed in together.

"Although the seller may be willing to participate in financing through holding a second mortgage of 10 to 20%, the seller won't be interested in giving you 30 years to repay the loan. You, of course, would like to take that long in order to keep your payments low. The answer is to ask the seller to let you figure out a payment you both can live with while telling her you'll pay off in full in ten years. In other words, offer the seller a 'balloon payment' mortgage. With a balloon mortgage, you might make low payments as if based on an amortization—meaning full payoff—in 30 years. Then after ten years of low payments, the balloon bursts and you must pay the seller whatever principal remains on the note. Balloons can work very well for the acquisition minded investor and for the seller as well. In negotiating the second mortgage, try to put off the balloon burst as long as possible. Try for ten years but seven or even five years is acceptable. Do not agree to a burst in less than five years; the blasting fuse is too short."

"But, Fred," protested Jane, "how do we know if we'll be able to save enough cash to pay off the balloon when it bursts, even if it takes ten years?"

"Fair question, Jane, but as a practical matter you don't have to worry—at this time—about a balloon which isn't going to burst for another five, seven or ten years. You concern yourself with it only in the twelve months preceding the big bang. Even then, notice I said concern yourself not worry yourself. The reason is there are lots of things that can happen between now and then.

"For one thing, you might re-sell or trade the property for any number of reasons and in doing so, all notes including the balloon will get paid off early. Five years, let alone ten, is a long time. Think back to where you were and what you were doing ten years ago. Jane, I think you would have just attended your high school prom. Doesn't that seem like ages ago?"

Jane rolled her eyes heavenward, thinking of how far she'd come in ten years.

"If you still own the property, there's an excellent chance you will have wanted to refinance it. You might very well want to do so even if you didn't have a second mortgage. Don't forget the property is going to be worth a lot more so refinancing may make a great deal of sense, and the balloon mortgage would be paid off in the process. You might refinance in the last half of the ninth year simply to knock out the balloon."

"Then, of course, you can always ask if the mortgage holder really wants to be paid off as scheduled. Don't laugh. The mortgage holder may very well be willing to let your loan ride if your payment history has been good. As a matter of fact, Wendy and I were holding one second mortgage and our payer ended up asking us three times to extend the due date. We agreed each time. Each time we let it go for two more years. Why? Because when the balloon dates were getting close, we didn't really have any better place to put the money. At the time, we would have had to either pay down another mortgage, buy another property, or buy a certificate of deposit.

"The interest rate we were getting from the second mortgage was better than we'd get from either a new CD or through paying down any of the mortgage loans we owed. And we didn't want another property at those times. It made the best sense to send a letter agreeing to the requested extensions. For the third of the three requests we required the payee to first pay down the second mortgage's principal by $5,000, and then extended the term. Naturally, we had our authorizations formally recorded—at the payee's expense—so it could never be argued that we granted extensions freely or that we verbally said five years instead of two. It always pays to do business in a businesslike way and to be careful.

"All in all, there's a whole bunch of things that can be done concerning payoff of the balloon without using your own saved cash. I'd recommend using your fresh cash to buy yet another property, if possible, and handle the balloon in some other manner.

"The next big question concerning financing that should occur to you is: Should you take an adjustable-rate loan or a fixed-rate loan?"

"Fixed rate!" said Joe.

"Yeah, fixed, of course," said Jane.

"Sorry, guys," responded Fred as he slowly shook his head. "Always consider fixed-rate loans, but, for the most part for rental property, adjustable-rate loans will turn out to be better for you."

"How come?"

"To begin with, if you can get a loan for 8% or less fixed interest for a rental property investment, jump on it. In recent years when financing money has been plentiful, fixed rates of between 6.0 and 8% have been common enough for owner-occupied, primary residences. But remember I told you that lenders generally want one-half to a full point more interest for rental properties. Thus, unless you're going to be occupying one unit in your rental property as your prime residence, a fixed rate of 8.5 or 9% or higher is the lowest fixed rate you're likely to get. Quite possibly you'll be asked for 9.5 to 10% by lenders who aren't eager to make investment property loans."

Fred explained that adjustable-rate mortgage (ARM) loans always start out at a lower interest rate than a fixed-rate loan of the same size taken out at the same time. For a period of time, usually one year but sometimes for three or five years, an adjustable loan's rate is fixed. Toward the end of each fixed period—usually 45 days before an anniversary of the loan— the lender reviews the loan's index and margin to see if the rate should be adjusted.

"All ARM loans have an associated index and a margin, or add-on amount, set in the loan agreement. For loans under a million dollars, the most frequently used index is the U. S. Treasury bill adjusted one-year rate, known as the T-bill rate. This index is published regularly on the business pages of newspapers. In recent years it has fluctuated between 2 and 6.5%. Typical loan agreements specify that an add-on margin of 2 to 3.5 points is to be applied to the index to determine the effective interest rate which you must pay. The effective rate is normally rounded off to the next highest one-eighth of a point.

"For example," Fred went on, "an ARM loan for rental property might specify the T-bill rate as an index and a margin of 3 points. If, 45 days before your loan's anniversary date, the T-bill index is 5.5, your margin of three points will be added to obtain an effective interest rate for you of 8.5%. You'll be notified that 8.5% is the rate which will become effective upon the first-of-a-month closest after the anniversary of your loan. Your loan payment due one month after that will be for principal and interest at the new rate. You don't have to calculate a thing. The law requires the lender to keep you well informed about any adjustment.

"The lender will calculate a new payment for you—if the index has changed sufficiently from the year before to warrant a change—based on the principal you still owe and the years remaining on the note. For example, if you started with a $130,000, thirty year, one year adjustable loan, after three years or 36 months of payments, you may have paid the principal down to $126,800. Your new payment, starting with month 37, would be calculated based upon $126,800 owed, with 27 years remaining to pay it off at your new interest rate.

"Don't accept an ARM unless it has limits on how much of an adjustment can be made in one year and how much of an adjustment can be made over the life of the loan. These important features are known as the one-year cap and the lifetime cap. Typically the one-year cap or limit would be one or two points, meaning 1 or 2% interest. Lifetime caps usually are five to six points or percent. These are important protections for the borrower. They create ceilings on the interest rate you can be charged. For example, if you started with a 7.75% initial rate, the maximum rate you would ever have to pay would be 12.75% if the loan had a five-point lifetime cap.

"Some ARMs have floors as well as caps that place a limit on how low the interest rate can go. Object to any adjustable-rate loan with a floor unless the floor stipulated is at least one interest percent lower than the loan's initial rate. If you have to accept the lender's ability to raise rates if the base rises, it seems to me you should be able to benefit if the base drops below the point at which you took the loan.

"In general—and you must shop around—ARMs for investment properties can be had for 1.5 to 2.5 interest points *lower* than a fixed-rate loan for the same amount. These initial ARM rates are sometimes called teaser rates in that they are artificially low in order to entice you into taking one. In many cases, they are a good deal and you should seriously consider taking one. A real life scenario example is a fixed-rate loan offered at 9.75% and an ARM offered at 7.75%. You check and find the T-bill base is currently 6.00 while the margin offered with the ARM is 2.75. You add the base and margin together and find the true ARM rate should be 8.75%. 'Aha,' you say to yourself. 'The 7.75% is a teaser rate; the lender is trying to seduce me.' You know the lender will adjust your rate one year later and if the T-bill base remains the same, you'll be required to pay the true interest rate of 8.75%! Keep your wits about you . . . probably you will have to pay 8.75%, but that's still a full point under the fixed 9.75%!

"Think about it some more. Throughout the first year of the loan, under the 7.75% ARM you would pay two full interest points less than under the 9.75% fixed rate. On a $100,000 loan, the monthly payment is $859.15 for the 9.75% interest rate but just $716.41 for the 7.75% rate. The difference amounts to about $1,713 in savings for the year, or enough to reimburse you for a healthy chunk of the loan's closing costs.

"Admittedly, the teaser rate will disappear for the second year of ARM payments, but if the T-bill base remains the same, the interest rate will just go to 8.75%. A monthly payment of $786.70 then would be required, which is still $72.45 a month less than the 9.75% fixed-rate payment. It would amount to a savings for the second year of $869.40, which is more than enough to pay for one month's mortgage payment. Most people would love to save, by any means, enough to offset even one of their mortgage payments.

"The big question, of course, is whether the T-bill rate will remain the same at 6.00 as used for our example. Probably it will be different. However, it could be lower than 6.00 just as well as higher! If it's lower, your monthly payment will be adjusted accordingly. Suppose the base went to 5.75. If it did, your second year interest rate would be calculated at 5.75 base plus 2.75 margin for an effective interest rate of 8.50%. This would give a monthly loan payment $90.24 lower than the fixed-rate payment for an annual savings of $1,082.84.

"The T-bill rate would have to increase a full point, from 6.00 to 7.00 for the ARM rate to reach the fixed-rate interest of 9.75%. Could it do that? Yes, and in fact it could exceed it either by the start of year two or a later year. Your interest increases would be moderated by the annual caps and ultimately the lifetime rate but there's no doubt the rate could eventually exceed the fixed interest rate. However, could and will are two different things.

"A fixed interest rate loan means the initial interest rate you negotiate will prevail over the entire life of the loan. The monthly payment will never change. In that sense, a fixed-rate loan is comforting. You know whatever you agree to pay per month at the start of the loan will remain in effect until the loan is fully paid off. Fixed rates are comforting but having such comfort can cost you a bundle.

"My experience," Fred continued, "having had at least two dozen rental property ARM loans between the years 1981 and 2002, is that ARMs saved me a ton of money. Base rates fluctuated regularly over this period but went down as often as up. My monthly payments therefore were increased some years but decreased others. Only for brief periods were my interest rates the same as or higher than the fixed interest rates I could have opted for when my various loans originated. For the most part, my ARM rates were consistently and significantly lower than the fixed rates I was offered. I'm convinced I made the right choices."

Joe asked, "What about interest rates for the future?"

"It's a bit of a gamble," Fred responded, "but for the foreseeable future, rates are expected to remain fairly stable and relatively low. As the Federal Reserve Bank adjusts its requirements, rates will go up and rates will go down. Any real estate investor should remain conscious about which way interest rates are headed for the long run. Fluctuations throughout a year or even from one year to the next should not cause much of a problem. The prognosis for low inflation and therefore stable, relatively low interest rates in the U.S. is good over the next ten years. These are positive influences regarding mortgage interest rates. But there is no absolute certainty.

"Two other aspects of ARMs and one about the size of a loan need to be discussed. As previously mentioned, anyone middle age or younger who is trying to become wealthy through rental real estate investing should be in the acquisition mode. In this mode, to maximize the amount of property you can buy and control, you should try to minimize the amount of cash you use to acquire any particular property. Obviously, this strategy means you should go for as big a loan as possible on any new property. An unfortunate fact of life, however, comes into play if your down payment is less than 20% of the total purchase price of the property. Less than 20% down means you're seeking a loan in excess of 80% of purchase price. When this happens, primary lenders and their underwriters feel they must have extra protection for themselves. The protection they generally want is called private mortgage insurance, or PMI, with the policy premiums paid for by you. PMI benefits the lender only, not you. The lender will be paid off in full should you default on your loan.

"PMI costs from 3 to 7% of the monthly mortgage principal and interest payment and is paid as an add-on to the mortgage payment. For example, if the basic principal and interest payment is $1,000 a month, PMI may cost $30 to $70 additional. So, should you ever try for a loan greater than 80% from a primary lender since doing so may very well force you to pay PMI? Yes, by all means! Keep your eyes on the goal of acquiring as much property as possible, using as little of your own cash as possible. Do so and your cash-on-cash returns on investment will be maximized despite the extra cost of PMI. Don't wait to accumulate a full 20% simply to avoid PMI. Rather than wait while you muster cash, for the same money try to buy two properties with only 10% down each even if you are forced to pay PMI on each loan. Don't forget, if you get some seller financing so the primary lender doesn't put up more than 80%, you can avoid PMI altogether.

"Once your equity in a property exceeds 20%—through general appreciation or fix-up by you—you can ask the lender to drop any PMI you're paying. They'll drop it, providing you get an appraisal that proves their loan's balance is less than 80% of the property's current value. Call your lender first to tell them what you want to do. They'll tell you which appraisers are on their approved list. The cost of the appraisal should be offset by your PMI savings within a year.

"Regarding ARMs, the fear of borrowers is that the economy will go bad and interest rates will suddenly soar. Older investors and homeowners remember how adjustable loan rates crept into the high teens in the late 1970s. Adjustment caps, introduced in 1980, have greatly reduced that danger. Annual adjustment caps prevent the lifetime cap from being achieved in less than four years from the time rates start to rise. Lifetime caps, even if reached, prevent interest rates from becoming unbearably high although rental property profits clearly would be reduced. Historically, interest rates have not remained excessively high for more than a year or two. As the period of extra high rates passes, adjustable loan rates drop rapidly. By the way, if the economy is really so bad that inflation and interest rates are rising rapidly, rental property owners will be busy raising rents. There won't be a direct correlation, but rent increases are likely to be able to offset increases in mortgage payments.

"The second aspect about ARMs has to do with the ability to reduce an ARM's monthly payment by paying down the loan principal early. My theory is that there are good years for buying property, good years for selling it and good years for doing neither. However, even during times when it's not good to buy, you may still be accumulating cash for investment purposes. What should you do with it if there are no good buying opportunities?

"Well, you could use some cash to make a lump payment to reduce the principal of any mortgage loan you have. Paying down loan principal will save you a lot of interest, whether your loan is a fixed rate or an ARM. But, is your monthly payment affected? With the fixed-rate loan the answer is a resounding no. With a fixed-rate loan, you will reduce the remaining term of the loan from, say, 26 to 23 years but your monthly mortgage payment will remain constant. The benefit of the principal pay down will not be felt for years. On the other hand, if you make an extra lump payment against the principal of an ARM, the reduced principal will be considered when the next rate calculation is made. At that time, the loan's base, margin, remaining principal and remaining years will all be considered. If the base remains the same, the calculation that will determine your monthly payment must be reduced. Thus, within months you'll enjoy tangible benefits from your principal pay down. Plus, you'll still save considerable interest as you would have with the fixed-rate loan. If you choose to make a sizeable, once-a-year pay down of ARM principal, make it about 60 days before a loan anniversary, since adjustment calculations are generally performed 45 days before anniversaries."

Joe spoke up. "Fred, you sound pretty convincing about the advantages of ARMs for rental property financing. We'll be sure to look into them carefully when it's our time to buy."

"Good man, Joe," Fred responded brightly. "For rental properties ARMs are likely to be your best bet unless what?"

"Unless we can get an investment property loan at a fixed rate of 8% or less!" Jane answered.

"What a woman!" declared an admiring Fred. "I can tell you two are going to become millionaires."

Jane blushed a little and Joe grinned broadly as they savored Fred's praise.

The long session on financing ended. The Andersons went home. The next day, by themselves, Joe and Jane reviewed what Fred had told them. They now had a working knowledge about where to go to get financing for residential rentals and some things about seller financing. They had a new respect for the importance of a good credit rating. They understood the need for low down payments to maximize leverage if they planned to acquire a portfolio of rental properties. They had learned why long amortization periods are best. Also, why adjustable-rate loans are better, most times, than fixed-rate loans for rental properties.

$$9$$

Closing Costs

A few days after the long session on financing, which took place at the Madisons' home, the Andersons hosted a further information meeting at their apartment. Jane had invited Fred and Wendy for coffee and dessert. Once the plates were cleared away, Fred started in on his subject for the evening.

"Discount points and origination fees," Fred told the Andersons, "are likely to be the most costly items considered as a closing cost. The down payment itself, which must also be paid at closing, is generally bigger but is not considered as a closing cost in normal usage of the term.

"The next highest closing cost is title insurance. There are two main types of title insurance, mortgagee's and owner's. The mortgagee is the lender, and mortgagee insurance strictly protects the lender. Lenders require you to get mortgagee insurance to protect them. You as the borrower or mortgagor simply get to pay the title insurance premium. It's a one-time cost payable at closing.

"Owner's insurance protects you, or at least your equity at time of closing, and again you get to pay the one-time premium. You don't have to take owner's title insurance. You may not want to if, at time of closing, your equity in the property is minimal and you are confident about the chain of previous ownership.

"Title insurance protects you in case there is a defect in the property title conveyed to you at closing. It doesn't happen often, because closing agents check for defects and correct known or discovered defects before closing. However, it occasionally does happen due to human error or a defect that was impossible to detect in advance. Suppose you bought property that was on the market due to a divorce or from an estate. Although all property claims of the estate heirs and the divorced couple should have been settled, a missing heir might suddenly appear or the ex-husband or ex-wife might claim they were cheated. A dark, gray cloud forms above the title; someone may be saying they still have an interest in the property you just bought! Your blood pressure may start to rise.

"When a title cloud appears, the closing agent, which will be either a law firm or a title company, tries to resolve the issue. Prior to closing, the agent works to get the title perfected, as they say. Should a problem arise after closing, title insurance pays for defense of the title to get the defect resolved. Either the law firm or a title company will have issued the title insurance only after checking the courthouse records to see who was the recorded legal owner of the property and who had recorded claims against it. Record searches cover at least the last 30 years in an unbroken chain of ownership and frequently much longer. If a cloud arises, it may be because the closing agent made a mistake, or the claimant is mistaken, or the claimant is able to prove his case. After closing, the title insurance company is responsible for obtaining resolution of disputes. Occasionally, the property is taken back or a money settlement is made. The mortgagee, or lender, loses no money because mortgagee title insurance covers potential loss. Neither do you, if you have owner's title insurance, to the extent of your equity at time of closing.

"To put things into perspective," Fred went on, "I have never been part of an after-closing title dispute on any property I've ever owned. In addition, in the 150 to 200 or so closings I've been personally involved in as a real estate salesman and then broker, I've never heard of any of the buyers later becoming involved in a title dispute. Nevertheless, lenders require you to pay for a title insurance policy for them. But you don't really have to buy it for them if you don't want to. Of course, they don't have to give you the loan you need either. Never forget the adage: 'He who has the gold sets the rules.'

"Should you buy owner's title insurance since it's optional? In most cases, yes. The risk may be small but the consequences great. Can you afford to lose the cash you put into a new property? Your equity may not be much but it probably represents a lot of effort on your part to get it together. A verity of life is that carrying an umbrella seems to decrease the chances of rain. Not carrying one seems to do the opposite. Insurance also may be subject to unfathomable mystical probability rules. People hate to pay insurance premiums but they're mighty glad they did when something bad happens. I don't like to buy insurance any more than anyone else but was glad I had windstorm insurance when a rare Florida tornado destroyed a beach house I owned.

"If you decide to buy owner's title insurance, buy it at closing and get the special lower premium that prevails when there's a simultaneous issue with mortgagee insurance. Title insurance rates are generally set by state laws. Typically, a sliding scale is used so the cost of the premium is based on the size of your loan. The owner's insurance premium, being based on your equity, takes into account the total cost of the property less the amount of the loan. An example of title insurance base cost, assuming simultaneous coverage on both types of insurance for a $160,000 property with a $128,000 loan, is $740. You can just contact a title company or real estate attorney to get a quick quote on any purchase you're considering.

"Besides base rates, work fees, endorsements and riders may be added to provide extra protection for special circumstances of your purchase and extra profit to the issuer. For example, there may be extra-cost endorsements for buying a multi-family building, buying into a planned unit development, known as a PUD, obtaining an ARM or buying a condominium. Endorsements cost $25 to $50 apiece."

"Where do you get title insurance?" asked Jane.

Fred answered: "Through title insurance companies or attorneys who also do closings of property sales/purchases. Where you get it really depends upon where or who you want to do your closing. If you decide to use an attorney, it's best to choose one who regularly handles real estate matters. Some specialize in real estate transactions. Title companies are specialists and frequently are headed by an attorney or have one or more on their staff. Check with your lender before choosing a title company; your lender may have a list of approved companies but the choice is yours. I've experienced closings with both attorneys and title companies. Most times everything worked out without a hitch but I've seen both types of closers make mistakes which had to be corrected on the spot.

"For routine property purchases when no party—buyer, seller or lender —foresees a problem, I think title companies and attorneys can do equally well. If the deal is known to be complicated, or if significant problems are foreseen by any party, I would go with an experienced real estate attorney."

"Which costs more, Fred?" asked Joe.

"In a general sense, they cost about the same. Both vendors gain from selling you mortgagee insurance, maybe an owner's policy as well and perhaps some endorsements. Both attorneys and title companies seem to come up with fees such as document preparation, xxx search or review or underwriting fee, but these are not necessarily unfair. Total charges from a busy title company and a busy, experienced real estate attorney will be competitive when competition exists.

"The next highest closing costs are taxes imposed by your state. In Florida, for example, to generate revenue, the state imposes intangible taxes and documentary taxes on the total value of the loan and mortgage involved. Together, they currently amount to 55 cents per $100 of the loan involved. Considering the $128,000 mortgage loan on the $160,000 property mentioned above, Florida's intangible taxes and documentary taxes would be .55 times 1,280, or $704. Nothing can be done about state taxes. You just have to pay them.

"Joe and Jane, you should want, and your lenders will require, a formal appraisal of the property you are considering buying. Plus, you should specify a contingency clause in any purchase offer you submit to the effect that if appraisal valuation doesn't equal the purchase price you can cancel the contract. In actual practice you'll end up re-negotiating the purchase price if such a thing happens. An appraisal for a four-unit or smaller property will be $250 to $450 and, for small properties, it's usually paid as part of the up-front application fee. Narrative appraisals on larger properties can cost from $600 to $3,600. Any loan your lender commits to is going to be contingent upon an acceptable appraisal, meaning an appraised value that is determined to be at least as high as the purchase price. For example, while you might apply for a loan equaling 80% of the purchase price, the lender is likely to commit to 80% of the purchase price or appraisal, whichever is lower. Such a stipulation is to the advantage of both the lender and you. If the appraisal comes in low, meaning lower than the contract price you've agreed to, you won't get the loan you expected and will be able to get out of the contract or renegotiate price.

"By the way, it's usual for a lender to charge an application fee that must be paid before the loan processing procedure is commenced, other than giving you a good faith estimate of costs. Typically, part of the application fee is used to obtain a credit report on you and part is for the property appraisal. If the loan doesn't go through, the application fee is not returned since it has been used or committed.

"Your lender will require, and you should too, a survey of the property you're buying. The title company will want to look at it as well, before closing, to see if there are any encroachments from your property onto a neighbor's property or vice versa. If there are, they'll have to be dealt with before closing. They may have to be excluded from coverage by the title insurance. Whether or not the property is in a flood plain ought to show on the survey as well. Also, the survey will show all easements for utilities and other things. The title company, you and your lender will all have to be happy with the survey before you would want to close the deal."

Fred continued: "Either the buyer or seller can pay for the survey; it's a matter of negotiation. I, as a buyer, prefer to pay for it so I can select the surveyors and deal directly with them, especially if the survey reveals a surprise. On one property I was considering buying, the survey revealed that the neighbors were using part of the property as their driveway! When confronted, the shocked neighbors got their own survey. To their dismay, both surveys showed the neighbors were in fact encroaching on the property for sale.

"I realized I'd be paying taxes on the nine foot strip of land the elderly neighbors had, apparently innocently, been using for years. Further, if I knowingly allowed the usage to continue without protest, the neighbors might be able to eventually claim it as theirs. I put the closing on hold until a solution could be reached.

"Selling the strip to the neighbors was a possibility, but they didn't seem to have a lot of funds. Besides, it would diminish the size of the property I was looking at. While the strip wasn't essential in the short run I reasoned I might eventually benefit from having as large a piece of property as possible.

"Finally," Fred said, "I reached an acceptable agreement with the elderly neighbors with whom I preferred to have a cordial relationship. The neighbors signed a document acknowledging their use of the driveway strip which they didn't own. In the document I agreed to let them continue to use the land, at no charge, for as long as they both lived in their house. However, the agreement was to be reviewed every three years and could be cancelled on 90 days notice. On this basis the purchase closed. If I chose to resell the property, I have a way out of the agreement should a new buyer want full use of all the land. And, if the aging neighbors move, I probably would erect a fence on the property line and thus take possession of the driveway strip. Then the issue could be resolved permanently.

"Surveys cost $225 to $350 for a simple property up to the size suitable for a quadraplex and can cost up to $1,500 for a moderate sized but complicated property.

"Another closing cost is that your lender will want a credit report on you to check upon your creditworthiness. Even if you have reviewed your report recently and have a copy you're willing to give to your lender, they will want to obtain their own directly from the credit bureau. This is to avoid any tampering by any interested party, including you. Usually the $50 to $60 cost of a credit report is covered by your application fee.

"Once the closing is complete, the closing agent will have certain documents formally recorded at the courthouse for the county in which the property is located. Examples are the deed and the mortgage or mortgages. The order of recording, incidentally, is what determines whether a mortgage is considered a first or second mortgage. Primary lenders insist their mortgage to be filed or recorded first in order to have first claim on the property in case you default.

"Courthouses charge by the page for whatever they record. Closing agents figure out in advance how many pages they will be taking to the courthouse and charge you accordingly at closing. Recording a typical set of documents will cost you, as buyer, less than $40.

"Other costs that may appear on your closing statements are document preparation charge at $100 to $150, flood zone certification at about $50, tax payment verification at $50 and underwriting fee at $100 to $250.

"Better plan on miscellaneous charges as well. Figure another $25. So," Fred stated, "using again the example of the $160,000 property purchased with a $128,000 mortgage and assuming one and one quarter total points, I would estimate closing costs at about $4,270. That amounts to 2.67% of the purchase price, which is within the normal range. Since an 80% loan was being obtained in this case, the total cash the buyers would be expected to bring to closing would be 22.67% of the purchase price. Actually, it would be 22.67% of $160,000 less the amount of earnest money deposit that was put up with the offer. Earnest money should have been held in a trust account then brought to the closing."

"Is down payment, less earnest money deposit, plus closing costs, all the cash money the buyers have to bring to a closing?" asked Jane.

"Probably not. Buyers are expected to pay for certain things known as prepaids although prepaids may be offset by prorations in the buyer's favor. Discussion of prepaids and prorations are only relevant if a closing is about to take place so let me defer discussion of them for now, Jane. I'll go over them carefully with you and Joe when the right time comes. That'll be once you have a specific property and closing date in mind. Okay?"

"Good idea, Fred," said Joe. "I think we've been hit with all we can absorb for this session."

Later, once the Madisons had gone home and the dishes washed, the Andersons reviewed what they had learned about the items which constitute closing costs and what are typical amounts. They were glad the Madisons had explained the various items and marveled that there are so many different ones. The largest closing costs are loan discount points and loan origination fees. The next highest were title insurance fees.

10

Completing
the Analysis

Joe and Jane drove by twelve prospective rental properties over the next six weeks. The twelve were the ones whose ads made them sound best and which seemed to be in reasonable areas of their city. They worked by themselves rather than with a realtor at this point. They reasoned that they should get a feel for what was available before asking a realtor to represent them. Fred had told them that some realtors were excellent and not to hesitate to work with one, providing he or she was known as good in the field of rental properties. It was the Andersons' intention to work with a realtor, probably on a buyer's broker basis, when the time was right. In their minds, however, the right time hadn't come. For one thing, they were still saving down payment money so they really weren't even close to being able to buy anything. Just as important, they wanted to work at their own pace until they got a feel for the market.

Fred had told the Andersons that active realtors hear about most of the best properties first, so it could be good to have one being vigilant on their behalf. The Andersons, who did not disagree with Fred, nevertheless decided to look by themselves for a while.

They learned about the twelve prospective rental properties by looking in the newspaper and in a couple of free realtor magazines picked up in the lobby of the supermarket. Jane found some properties by looking at a site like www.realtor.com. Seven of the properties were single-family houses that the advertisements indicated were perfect rental houses. Plus, there were three duplexes, one triplex and one quadraplex listed for sale.

In all cases Joe and Jane located the offerings on their city map and drove by each one. Actually they could tell from the map that they probably wouldn't be interested in seven of the twelve places simply because of where they were located. Five of the seven were either remote or not near any kind of city activity center. Two were in a bad area of town. However, Joe and Jane decided to drive by all twelve as part of their education process. It was a good idea.

Curb appeal of six of the properties was very low, at least to the Andersons' eyes. An offering that was remote looked quite good but Joe had some trouble finding it. Imagine! Not only was it remote from all city activity and from the Andersons' present apartment, it was hard to find! They remembered Fred's admonition to think of how a prospective renter would think. They could see Fred's point. It would be difficult to get a prospect to look at any vacancy in a remote location. If it was hard to show, it would be hard to rent, unless they lowered the rental rates to make it a real bargain. However, lowering the rent would work against their desire for profits. They would have to be able to purchase it at a bargain price to make it worth their while, but if they were able to buy it for a song, they may eventually have to sell it for a song. They decided to follow Fred's advice and leave the remote rental to someone else. They were learning.

The two properties in the bad area of town actually looked pretty good. One was a house and one was a triplex. Unfortunately, properties around the offerings were not in the same good condition. There were some real eyesores close by each. Again, they followed the Madisons' advice to try to look through the eyes of people who would be likely renters. In both cases they decided that even though they liked the prospective properties—at least from the outside—they wouldn't want to rent in the somewhat dumpy neighborhoods. Such a shame, they thought, that some uncaring property owners could adversely taint an entire neighborhood.

Two properties were in desirable rental areas but they were the structures in probably the worst condition on their streets. Joe and Jane figured the neighbors would love to have the properties bought by new owners and fixed up to the level of all the others. The Andersons decided to keep both places on their list of possibilities but weren't enthusiastic over the prospect of an extensive fix-up for their first venture.

One house, one duplex and a quadraplex seemed to be suitable in terms of initial curb appeal and neighborhood. Vegetation around the duplex was badly overgrown but they followed the Madisons' advice to look past the purely cosmetic. They felt a half day's effort by both of them could clean up all the vegetation and yard around the duplex. They decided these three properties would constitute their hot prospects list.

Before gathering information to do preliminary analyses of the hot prospects, the Andersons decided it was time to get more information from Fred and Wendy. Even though they weren't financially ready to buy, they had learned a thing or two about financing and now were familiar with closing costs. They were ready to find out how the preliminary analysis, physical evaluation, financing and closing costs tied together in helping to decide to buy or not. They felt it was time to learn how to complete the analysis.

Wendy greeted the Andersons warmly when they rang the Madisons' doorbell at 7:00 P.M. four days later. She had been expecting them. She questioned them about their hunt for rental properties until Fred arrived. Once Fred had been briefed and Joe said what he and Jane wanted to know next, Fred launched into a discussion about how the analysis would wrap everything together.

"Sounds like you guys have done some pretty useful legwork," said Fred. "Just like shopping for a new car. The more cars and the more dealerships you look at, the wiser you become. Look, look, look until you can hardly stand it anymore. You'll find you're noticing more and more details. Things you may have missed on your early drive-bys will start revealing themselves. You'll become more knowledgeable. You get smarter the more properties you look at. But on top of just looking, with rental properties you need to do a thorough analysis of the numbers.

"Let me give you a quick review first. The preliminary analysis we discussed previously focused on the income and operating costs of the property. The preliminary physical evaluation of the property should tell you, prior to submitting an offer, whether or not you wanted the property at all. And if you did like the property, to get some sense of what fix-up expense you would immediately encounter should you acquire it. You should remember you aren't buying a new car, so to speak, but a used car with flaws. You must be prepared to accept some flaws but you need to know what they are. In addition, during the pre-offer physical evaluation you should note anything that looks suspicious and potentially costly. Also note anything suspicious that is beyond your level of competency to evaluate. These notes should be kept until an offer is prepared—if one ever is—so they can be mentioned as contingency issues in the offer. Once your offer becomes a contract through acceptance by the seller, the contingencies would give you the right to have experts examine suspicious items to determine the cost to correct, if correcting were needed. If you didn't like the results of the inspections, you could ease out of the contract or possibly renegotiate it. Remember all this stuff, Joe? Jane?"

"Yeah, pretty much," responded Joe while glancing towards Jane for agreement. "Between the two of us we've got it for sure. Also, we made some notes after each of our previous discussions and we can review those."

Jane spoke up: "We certainly have taken things seriously. We want to become millionaires and think you can show us how. We've already learned a lot but we're anxious to learn how to tie everything together for the final analysis. Joe and I are determined to own rental property. But we want to 'buy right' as Fred has often said."

"Glad you feel that way, Jane. I think you guys are going along in the right way. I'm impressed you took the initiative to at least drive by some rentals for sale. You're ready for today's lesson, so let's get started."

Fred explained the place to start was with the asking price and what percentage of it they thought they could make as a down payment. He didn't mean they should plan to pay the asking price—probably they wouldn't—but it was the logical place to start. Subtracting down payment from price would show what amount had to be financed. The initial assumption should be that the entire loan necessary would be obtained from one primary lender. It might not be, but this was the place to start. He said he would use a $100,000 duplex as an easy example with a nice round number. He told them that while $100,000 could certainly buy a duplex in their city, it might not in some other areas of the country. But it really didn't matter, he said, since the example was meant to show the technique and relationships. Fred drew a chart as follows.

He explained the extra columns, which he headed Trial 2 and Trial 3, would be used as they tried various "what ifs."

Analysis Chart for Duplex Example			
	Asking Price	Trial 2	Trial 3
Price	$100,000		
Down Payment 10%	10,000		
To Be Financed 90%	90,000		

"Next," Fred explained, "you would use your research into mortgage loan rates and apply it to the amount to be financed to see what your monthly debt service payment would be. Debt service means how much you have to pay monthly to pay off the loan in full over its term plus the interest due. Let's suppose you find a lender who offers 90% loan-to-value (LTV) loans for investment properties at 8.5% interest. The loan is available to investors with 30-year amortization, 1.0 loan discount points and one-half a point as an origination fee. Total points to get the loan are thus 1.5. It will take 30 years to pay off the amount borrowed.

"To calculate for yourself the monthly principal and interest payment, you can look on the Internet at one of the many websites that offer mortgages and include a means of calculating payments. Of course, not everyone uses the Internet.

"For many years, I used an orange book of mortgage payment tables the size of a shirt pocket to calculate payments. Such books are still available at bookstores for under $10. They have different pages for all the typical interest rates from, say, 5 to 15%, in one-eighth of a point intervals. For loan amounts from $100 to $1,000 by hundreds, then from $1,000 to

$200,000 by first thousand dollar increments then $5,000 and finally $25,000 increments, payments are shown for loans with terms of one year through 30 years.

"The best thing to use by far, in my opinion, is a small calculator designed for real estate calculations. Calculating loan payments is a main function, but they also tell you how much interest and principal is paid in a particular year or how much interest has to be paid through a specified number of years, or how much principal will remain unpaid. Many other functions can be performed as well. Such calculators typically cost less than $40. Using one has clear advantages over both little orange books and the Internet. When you get into analyzing deals and different versions of deals, it's nice to be able to recalculate mortgage payments quickly. The calculator is the handiest means of doing 'what ifs' as you vary the price you'll offer, and amount of down payment and therefore the amount to be financed. But a calculator is not necessary and certainly a computer is not necessary. I've done hundreds of payment calculations during my early years just using my little orange book of payment tables. Now, my early years were before the Internet was envisioned. In fact, even before personal computers were anything but a novelty. But, if you have ready access to the Internet, by all means use it.

"In our example, the calculator indicates that the monthly principal and interest payment on a $90,000 ARM loan at 8.50% interest for 30 years is $692.02. Multiply the monthly payment by 12 to determine debt service for the first year of payments; it is $8,304.24. Pressing a couple more calculator buttons shows $7,623.90 in interest and $680.37 in principal would be paid over the first 12 months. Each of these facts will be used in our analysis.

"Now, let's see how much cash is required to acquire the property. At this point continue to assume that we'll be paying asking price and can get a 90% LTV loan. Now the chart can be completed to determine the cash needed to close. Ignore for the moment the matters of prepaids and prorations. We'll just include down payment plus typical closing costs. Once again extra columns are provided for second and third trials."

Analysis Chart of Cash Required to Close

	Asking Price	Trial 2	Trial 3
Down Payment	$10,000		
Points—1.5% of Loan Amount	1,350		
Mortgagee Title Insurance	520		
Owner's Title Insurance	105		
2 Endorsements	100		
Settlement Fee, Title Search, etc.	140		
State Taxes $.55 per 100 of loan	495		
Application/Appraisal	300		
Survey	225		
Credit Report	55		
Recording	25		
Tax Service Fee	50		
Flood Certification Fee	50		
Miscellaneous	0		
TOTAL CASH TO ACQUIRE	$13,445		

"Now," instructed Fred, "look at the preliminary analysis of the property."

Analysis of Income, Expenses and Cash Flow

	Trial 1		Trial 2		Trial 3	
	Mo.	Yr.	Mo.	Yr.	Mo.	Yr.
Gross Potential Income (2x575)	1,150	13,800				
Vacancy Loss Allowance 5.0%	58	696				
Net Effective Income	1,092	13,104				
Operating Expenses						
Taxes	117	1,404				
Insurance	28	336				
Repairs Done by Others	40	480				
Maintenance Supplies	27	324				
Utilities Paid by Landlord	3	36				
Yardwork (Do self)	0	0				
Advertising	3	36				
Miscellaneous	4	48				
Total Operating Expenses	222	2,664				
Net Operating Income	870	10,440				
Debt Service (P&I)	692	8,304				
Cash Flow Spendable	178	2,136				

"Notice the $692 per month used as the debt service payment. Remember this is the payment calculated for our $90,000 loan.

"Also notice that at the bottom of the year column, $2,136 shows as the cash flow from 12 months of operating this duplex. That's the profit for you as owners. The gravy. The spoils of the rental battle. The cash in pocket which can be spent with abandon! Actually, I hope some of it—perhaps $500—is set aside as ready reserves for maintenance. However, the bulk of it should be put into your investment money account in preparation for your next purchase."

Fred looked directly at Joe then Jane.

"Think about it," he challenged, "How will you get to put the $2,136 into your pockets?"

Fred waited a moment then answered his own question.

"You get it by investing $13,445 of your hard-earned and saved cash, that's how. Remember? Down payment plus closing costs totaled $13,445."

"So, calculate your cash-on-cash return. Divide 2,136 by 13,445 and multiply by 100 to get 15.89%. This percentage sure beats the perhaps 2% interest rate you would get from your savings account if you left your money there instead of buying the property. It also beats the 6.2% you might get by putting the $13,445 into a one-year certificate of deposit."

"Is 15.89% return on your cash enough if you invested it in our sample duplex?"

Again Fred answered his own question. "No."

He continued. "It's not enough if one-year CDs are paying 6.2%. Remember my 'three times current annual CD rate' guideline? To meet that minimum return you need 18.6% out of the duplex. As it stands, the deal should not be done. What to do?"

Without waiting for a response from the Andersons, Fred proceeded. "Well, there's not much you can do about the rents at this point. Even if you investigate and find the units are under-rented, meaning the present landlord is getting less rent than he or she should. Let's suppose you determine the apartments should be renting for $600 each, not $575. An extra $25 per month from each of the duplex's two units would mean $600 a year more gross income. An additional $570, the net after subtracting $30 vacancy allowance, would result in an annual cash flow of $2,706. Divide this number by your $13,445 cash investment and multiply by 100 to determine your cash-on-cash return; it would then be 20.13%. Very nice and above the 18.6% minimum return needed. So, should you proceed with the deal since you see, by raising the rents to normal market rates, you could get a good return?"

"No," Fred answered his own question again, then went on.

"You might want to feature improved future rents in your dreams but don't bring your dreams to the negotiating table. Absolutely don't negotiate based on what you could do! You must negotiate based on what the seller has done to this point. If raising rents is so simple, why didn't the seller do it? The answer to this question is probably apathy and/or unawareness on the part of the present owner. Presumably, the present landlord has tired of the property and has been thinking about selling for some time. She or he just hasn't kept up with current market conditions. You, on the other hand, as an eager prospective buyer with wealth in mind, must keep abreast of market conditions. You must keep your rents up to average market levels. You don't have to be a high-rent leader, but you must remain competitive. You certainly don't want to be renting under market.

"Even if you bought the duplex and closed tomorrow, you still may not be able to raise rents immediately. The main reason is likely to be existing leases that specify the rent is to be $575 a month. As a new owner you are, by law, required to honor existing valid leases until their specified terms end. What if there are no leases in effect? In that case, the tenants are considered to be on a month-to-month basis, and you could give them a rent increase notice legally. The minimum notice required, in the absence of a lease, is typically the normal length between rent payments."

Fred said, "I would advise against sending rent increase letters the day of closing for psychological reasons. It's in a new owner's interest to begin relations with newly acquired tenants on the right foot. Why antagonize them on day number one? It's better to take it easy in the first month while you learn about the property and its residents. In my opinion the earliest time to send a rent increase notice to a new property would be about the middle of the second month.

"Existing leases and the need for proper notice are just other reasons why boosting rents shouldn't be thought of as the way to make a prospective property's numbers work. The main reason is that you don't want to introduce what you could do if you were owner into any purchase negotiations. Keep your plans to yourself.

"If the operating costs are fairly represented, it would be unwise to consider that you could reduce expenses to improve profits thereby making the return better. Hopefully, you will be lucky and experience lower than normal operating costs during your first year of ownership, but don't count on it. On a single family house or a duplex, unlike much bigger properties, costs are not so high that a lot of trimming is possible. Not much can be done about taxes and insurance. Doing things yourself can significantly reduce repair costs, of course. Breakdowns are so erratic and variable in nature that you ought to plan to spend what history says has normally been required. Then, consider yourself fortunate if you experience a lower than average maintenance cost year.

"When analysis indicates your return on cash investment is too low and you can't boost profits by raising rents or lowering costs, the answer has to lie in lowering the purchase price, or the cost of debt service or both.

"This is how a proper analysis can help you determine how much should be paid for a property. The analysis will tell you how much the property is worth to you. It may be worth more to others—the seller, for example—but you are the important one.

"To achieve the desired minimum return, reduce the price in chunks and run the analysis with each reduction. Gradually, you'll arrive at the results you need. For our example duplex, let's see what happens if we drop the price by $10,000 and offer $90,000. This constitutes trial number 2 on our analysis chart."

Analysis Chart for Duplex Example

	Asking Price	Trial 2	Trial 3
Price	$100,00	90,000	
Down Payment 10%	10,000	9,000	
To Be Financed 90%	$90,000	81,000	

"Use your little mortgage payment table book or a calculator," Fred said, "to determine that the debt service on an 8.50%,
30-year loan for $81,000 is $622.82 per month. This is a reduction of $69.20 per month in debt service over the previous
amount of $692.02. Even more important, it's an increase in
monthly cash flow of $69.20, bringing it to $247.20. That's
$2,966.40 a year. Do analysis trial number 2."

Analysis of Income, Expenses and Cash Flow						
	Trial 1		Trial 2			
	Mo.	Yr.	Mo.	Yr.	Mo.	Yr.
Gross Potential Income						
(2x575)	1,150	13,800	1,150	13,800		
Vacancy Loss						
Allowance 5.0%	58	696	58	696		
Net Effective Income	1,092	13,104	1,092	13,104		
Operating Expenses						
Taxes	117	1,404	117	1,404		
Insurance	28	336	28	336		
Repairs Done by Others	40	480	40	480		
Maintenance Supplies	27	324	27	324		
Utilities Paid by Landlord	3	36	3	36		
Yardwork (Do self)	0	0		0		
Management (Do self)	0	0		0		
Advertising	3	36	3	36		
Miscellaneous	4	48	4	48		
Total Operating Expenses	222	2,664	222	2,664		
Net Operating Income	870	10,440	870	10,440		
Debt Service (P&I)	692	8,304	623	7,476		
Cash Flow Spendable	178	2,136	247	2,964		

"When we decided to offer only $90,000, we also reduced
our down payment to $9,000 and the amount to be financed
to $81,000. Our chart of cash required must therefore be
revised also."

Analysis Chart of Cash Required to Close

	Asking Price	Trial 2	Trial 3
Down Payment	10,000	9,000	
Points 1.5% of Loan Amount	1,350	1,215	
Mortgagee Title Insurance	520	505	
Owner's Title Insurance	105	95	
2 Endorsements	100	100	
Settlement Fee, Title Search, etc.	140	140	
State Taxes $.55 per 100 of loan	495	446	
Application/Appraisal	300	300	
Survey	225	225	
Credit Report	55	55	
Recording	25	25	
Tax Service Fee	50	50	
Flood Certification Fee	50	50	
Miscellaneous	30	30	
TOTAL CASH TO ACQUIRE	13,445	12,236	

"Now, Joe and Jane," explained Fred, "determine your revised return on cash investment. Divide the new annual cash flow of $2,964 by the $12,236 cash needed and multiply by 100."

"Wow! 24.22%! Great deal! Let's buy the place!" Joe exclaimed.

Fred cautioned. "Actually, not so fast. Yes, a $90,000 purchase price would make your investment return numbers sing, but the seller may object to the song. If his duplex was priced right to begin with, he is unlikely to accept a 10% reduction unless he is desperate to sell and his duplex has attracted little attention. Don't dismiss this notion; he may be desperate. Or he may have intentionally packed his price, meaning he priced it high in order to have a little wiggle room when dickering with potential buyers. However, unless he has done an analysis much the same as I advocate, or has paid for a thorough appraisal, he probably doesn't know the property's true value as an income property. You could plan to use $90,000 as your first offer. The seller could only say one of three things: yes, no or hell no. If he gives one of the last two refusals he is likely to accompany his response with a counteroffer."

"You should rework the analysis again to more precisely determine the maximum you should pay for the property. The maximum purchase price is where you achieve the minimum acceptable return on your cash investment. We set that figure at 18.6% which is three times the current one-year CD interest rate. Naturally, you would like to get a better return than your minimum. But you mustn't pay so much for the property that your return falls below the 18.6% minimum.

"Since paying full asking price of $100,000 would result in an almost 16% return, and a price of $90,000 would result in more than 24% return, it's a good guess that a price of about $96,500 would give a return of about 18.6%. Let's run the analysis again using a price of $96,500 as the third trial.

Analysis Chart for Duplex Example

	Asking Price	Trial 2	Trial 3
Price	$100,000	90,000	96,500
Down Payment 10%	10,000	9,000	9,650
To Be Financed 90%	90,000	81,000	86,850

"My calculator shows debt service on $86,850 at 8.50% would be $667.80 a month. This is about $24 less than the original $692.02 calculation. It adds $288 a year to the originally calculated annual cash flow bringing it to $2,424 as is shown when we complete trial number 3 on our analysis chart."

Analysis of Income, Expenses and Cash Flow

	Trial 1		Trial 2		Trial 3	
	Mo.	Yr.	Mo.	Yr.	Mo.	Yr.
Gross Potential Income (2x575)	1,150	13,800	1,150	13,800	1,150	13,800
Vacancy Loss Allowance 5.0%	58	696	58	696	58	696
Net Effective Income	1,092	13,104	1,092	13,104	1,092	13,104
Operating Expenses						
Taxes	117	1,404	117	1,404	117	1,404
Insurance	28	336	28	336	28	336
Repairs by Others	40	480	40	480	40	480
Maintenance Supplies	27	324	27	324	27	324
Landlord Paid Utilities	3	36	3	36	3	36
Yardwork (Do self)	0	0		0	0	0
Management (Do self)	0	0		0	0	0
Advertising	3	36	3	36	3	36
Miscellaneous	4	48	4	48	4	48
Total Operating Expenses	222	2,664	222	2,664	222	2,664
Net Operating Income	870	10,440	870	10,440	870	10,440
Debt Service (P&I)	692	8,304	623	7,476	668	8,016
Spendable Cash Flow	178	2,136	247	2,964	202	2,424

"Adding the third trial to our cash required chart shows:"

Analysis Chart for Cash Required to Close

	Asking Price	Trial 2	Trial 3
Down Payment	$10,000	$9,000	$9,650
Points 1.5% of Loan Amount	1,350	1,215	1,303
Mortgagee Title Insurance	520	505	515
Owner's Title Insurance	105	95	103
2 Endorsements	100	100	100
Settlement Fee, Title Search, etc.	140	140	140
State Taxes $.55 per 100 of loan	495	446	478
Application/Appraisal	300	300	300
Survey	225	225	225
Credit Report	55	55	55
Recording	25	25	25
Tax Service Fee	50	50	50
Flood Certification Fee	50	50	50
Miscellaneous	30	30	30
TOTAL CASH TO ACQUIRE	$13,445	$12,236	$13,024

"Divide the $2,424 return by the $13,024 and multiply by 100," Fred instructed, "to determine the return on cash investment is 18.61%. Right on the 18.60 target!

"The analysis, therefore, tells us we can pay a maximum price of $96,500 and still obtain the minimum cash-on-cash return. This price is 96.5% of what the seller is asking. Most sellers would accept it. Should you offer it?

"No," Fred immediately said in answer to his own rhetorical question. He then went on.

"For one thing, if $96,500 is the maximum you will pay for the property, because that's what your analysis says it's worth, you certainly wouldn't want to make that amount your first offer. It may very well be accepted! A better first offer would be the $90,000 we used for our second analysis trial. If the seller counters your offer at, say, $95,000, you might accept it if it looks like he has no bargaining tolerance left. But only go up to the maximum price you'll pay if the back-and-forth play forces you to do so. Don't let emotion and your ego cause you to pay more than the maximum value indicated by your analysis."

The Andersons nodded. Fred went on.

"Another reason for not proceeding too quickly with a $96,500 offer is that you haven't explored all financing possibilities. The ARM loan of 90% at 8.50% interest looks pretty good. However, it is not certain a primary lender will give you such financing on investment property without requiring PMI. Better check it out to be sure.

"Another financing possibility is to see if the seller would hold a second mortgage for 15% of the purchase price. Then you could obtain an ARM from a primary lender for 75% of the purchase price which most lenders certainly would be willing to do, even on investment properties. The total financed still would be 90% of the purchase price; you still must come up with a 10% down payment plus closing costs. For a second mortgage, offer the seller 7.5% fixed-rate interest with a 30-year amortization term but with a balloon at ten years."

Jane asked: "Tell us again why the seller would be willing to take the second mortgage?"

"Okay," responded Fred. "First, suggest it might be the only way you can buy his property. Second, tell him the 7.5%

fixed rate is 1.3% higher than he could currently get from investing in a one-year CD. Third, tell him you'll pay him at least $105 per month, or $1,260 a year, which is a few dollars more per month than it would take to amortize the loan over 30 years. Fourth, tell him that in ten years you'll pay him the more than $13,000 balance remaining. Use your real estate calculator to determine that the balloon payment will be $13,034 after 120 payments of $105 each. Fifth, tell him that if you default in your payments to him he would have the duplex as security collateral. Point out that if you didn't promptly make good on the payment default, he could start proceedings to get the duplex back.

"At this point the seller, unless he has an immediate need for all of his sale proceeds, should be fairly interested in the second mortgage possibility. He is likely to say something like: 'You mean you'll pay me at least $1,200 a year for ten years and then pay me a lump sum of over $13,000 more?' To which you'll respond, 'Yes.'

"Let's examine the effect of the two-mortgage approach on your return on cash investment," said Fred. "Assume you end up paying $96,500, which is the maximum trial number 3 of your first analysis indicated you should pay. Recall that your return in investment at this price was going to be 18.61%.

"Payment on the $72,375 loan, 75% of $96,500 purchase price, from the primary lender will be $556.50 a month. Payment on the seller's $14,475 second mortgage will be $101.21, but you'll pay $105. Your debt service will total $661.50. This is $6.50 a month less than the $668.00 payment to a single lender as calculated previously. Thus, your cash flow would go up 12 times $6.50 or $78.00 a year for a new annual total of $2,502 instead of $2,424.

"In addition, your cash required for closing would decrease by $217, because the primary lender's loan points would apply to a $14,475 smaller loan. Also, the cost of mortgagee title insurance would drop by about $50, again due to the smaller primary lender loan. Total cash required for closing would be reduced from $13,024 to $12,757.

"An annual cash flow of $2,502 from a $12,757 cash investment means a cash-on-cash return of 19.61%! Not too shabby compared to CD yields and savings account interest.

Clearly it would be worthwhile to try to convince the seller to hold a second mortgage."

Jane asked, "Should you increase your initial offer because you're going to ask the seller to hold a second mortgage?"

"No, Jane," replied Fred, who then went on. "Expect the seller to be a little more resolved to get the highest possible price. But do not, do not, do not ultimately pay more than the $96,500 the original analysis said it is worth."

"We wouldn't," said Jane.

"Absolutely not," emphasized Joe.

"Well, good for you guys!" Fred responded with a warm smile. "But don't just say that to please me. I want you to do it for yourselves. I want you to trust in the results of a proper analysis based on facts you gathered and that make you comfortable. Analyzing your annual cash return on the total amount of your cash is the best way to compare alternative investments.

"The analysis routine we just used is suitable for any size property from a one-unit rental house through to a 100-unit apartment complex. Probably beyond that even, but I don't have any direct experience buying or selling bigger properties.

"The only thing different as you go up in rental property size is the number of items on your list of income and expenses. Beyond that, the technique of analysis is exactly the same. Do a preliminary analysis, do a physical evaluation, then do a final analysis considering financing and all cash closing costs. Of course the numbers themselves will be bigger for a bigger property but don't let that throw you; the technique is the same. In all cases you determine the property's annual cash-on-cash return. Your goal is to maximize return and make sure it achieves the minimum you require. As you're well aware by now, the minimum return you must have—if you're going to manage the property yourself—is three times the current annual CD rate. Be prepared to do several trials of each analysis. Adjust price and financing as necessary to reach the return you want.

"Before making any offer, determine the maximum you can afford to pay for the property in order to achieve your return goal. Don't get emotional about a purchase, go by the numbers you calculated.

"There are a number of other ways to analyze properties but the cash-on-cash method is best for buyers, in my opinion."

Joe spoke up: "Fred, are you saying we can do a cash-on-cash analysis on any property we're thinking about? What happens if we do a physical evaluation and find costly repairs are needed immediately?"

"Very good question, Joe, with a simple answer. Suppose you were considering two duplexes identical in every aspect, except when you looked through them you found one had a vacant unit needing about $1,500 in repairs before it could be rented. In this case, you'd need more cash for the bad duplex than the other. That's obvious. Put the item, 'immediate repairs, $1,500,' at the bottom of your list of closing costs. Your total cash required to close will therefore be higher. Consequently, your cash-on-cash return will be lower than for the good duplex, unless what?"

"You pay a lower price for the bad duplex?" ventured Jane.

"That's exactly right, Jane. To get the same return when you have to put in more cash, you have to pay a lower price. Would the seller accept a lower price? Of course she would. She would know that any buyer would see the problems and realize it's going to take money to make things right. If the seller wanted to do it herself and not lower the price, most likely she would have done so before starting to show the duplex for sale.

"Incidentally, this might well be one of those situations where you'd want to ask the seller to pay all or some of your closing costs. Remember we discussed this technique once before? Tell the seller you need to conserve cash in order to buy her property and make the necessary repairs. The seller quite likely will do so especially if all or part of the closing costs she'll pay are added to the purchase price. So, the seller is not hurt, but you gain by saving cash that you might not even have.

"There's one more thing I need to tell you about fix-up costs before I tell you about a couple of rental property bonuses you'll get beyond the returns we've already talked about.

"As regards fix-up, remember I said to make notes of any suspicious items you saw during your pre-offer physical evaluation? Those apparent problems you didn't feel comfortable evaluating yourself. I used a deteriorating roof as an example. Further, I said to include a contingency clause in your offer that allowed you to get a qualified individual to evaluate the items after the contract was signed. Remember?"

"We do," responded the Andersons.

"Good. Let's suppose a professional says the roof needs replacing and gives you a written estimate of $3,000. At that point, while you're still in the agreed contingency period, do your analysis again factoring in the $3,000 repair. You'll see what, concerning your return?"

"The price will have to be lower!" chimed the Andersons.

"Exactly!" cried a beaming Fred. "Since you're in the contingency period, you can cancel the contract and get your deposit money back. Or, you can try to renegotiate the price. The seller may very well concede, because she knows if she doesn't, she'll have to find a new buyer. Plus, the next buyer may also determine that the roof needs replacing. Of course, even bad looking roofs may have several years of life left before they spring leaks that can't just be patched. Knowing this, the seller may not be willing to cut the price by $3,000. It might work out nicely for both sides if a $1,500 reduction was given. But you get the point, don't you?"

The Andersons acknowledged their understanding and Fred continued: "Now for the bonuses of owning rental property. The first is the tax advantages of owning improved rental property. 'Improved' generally means that the property has a building on it. All of the operating expenses and mortgage interest are tax deductible. In addition, you can divide the value of the improvements by 27.5 and take that amount of money as an expense on your income tax return. For example, suppose you bought a property for $100,000 and the value of the building itself was $82,500. Divide by 27.5 and determine you can claim an extra, tax-deductible expense of $3,000 a year. Every year. It's called depreciation and should be thought of as a paper expense since you don't actually pay out $3,000 every year to get the deduction.

"The value of depreciation is that deducting it from your income along with normal expenses may mean you end up with a loss, on paper. A paper loss means you actually put spendable cash flow money in your pocket, but you don't pay income taxes on it. Your income is said to be sheltered from taxes.

"There are great tax advantages to owning rental properties, but I'm not going to discuss them fully now although I will later. Why? Because tax advantages, while they exist and are very worthwhile, should not be a primary reason why you—especially as beginners—buy a particular property. Stick to the analysis we've talked about. Only buy a rental if it makes good business sense to own it regardless of tax advantages.

"The second bonus you get from rental property ownership is that of a gain in equity from the loan principal paydown. We haven't focused on it, because I want you to concentrate on annual cash flow divided by acquisition cash as a measure of return on investment. Buy or don't buy based on that measure. However, your return, or at least your gain, is actually higher than our standard analysis shows.

"You see, each time you make your monthly mortgage payment you are paying off some of your loan's principal. In the early years of your loan, your payments consist mostly of interest. But with an amortizing loan there's always some principal paid off, and the amount grows month by month. Remember when we were first discussing a loan for our hypothetical duplex? In the first trial we figured the monthly payments would be $692 a month or just over $8,300 a year. Then, we figured about $680 of that was paydown of principal with all the rest being tax deductible interest.

"The $680 principal paydown increases your equity in the duplex. Equity is the part you own, the difference between the duplex's market value and what you owe on it. There's no doubt your wealth went up $680 during the course of the year as you made your mortgage payments. But we haven't paid attention to it until now because it's sort of a hidden gain. You can't spend it like you can cash flow. In fact, you can't release its value to you unless you sell the building. Then you'll benefit. Nevertheless, by owning rental property, your wealth increases year by year through loan principal paydown along with other things. Although you can't easily spend it, you can measure its benefit easily.

"For the third trial of the duplex we took a loan which had payments of $668 a month, or $8,016 a year. My calculator told us $655 of the yearly amount is paydown of loan principal. When we were just considering one lender for this trial, we found we would get $2,424 cash flow on a cash investment of $13,024. That worked out to a return of 18.61% on the cash invested. Here comes my point and another bonus for owning rental property. You see, your true gain for the first twelve months of ownership is $2,424 cash flow *plus* $655 in principal paydown. Your total true gain is $3,079 in 12 months. Since your cash investment is still $13,024, total gain on your investment is 23.64% not just 18.61%. The benefit of principal paydown in this case is 5.03%! Not bad, eh? And every year you pay down an increasing amount of principal through your normal mortgage payments.

"It's worthwhile to do this bonus calculation once you have determined your return from the regular cash flow analysis. It will inspire you, but don't let the bonus return calculation cloud your thinking. You still want to make your purchase based on the cash flow return analysis. Think of the bonus as gravy. Something to enhance the meal. Or should I say, deal?" Fred mused over his rhyming.

The Andersons were astounded. They were already amazed at the high returns that would come from properly purchased rental property. Now this paydown bonus, as Fred called it, just about beat all! Also, there were tax advantages to be had as yet another bonus! They could hardly stand it. Joe looked at Jane. Jane looked at Joe. They both looked at the Madisons. All four of them started to smile. Joe and Jane were ready to buy some property!

As was their custom, once home after a training session with the Madisons, Joe and Jane discussed what they had learned. They now knew how to do a final analysis once a preliminary analysis and a physical evaluation had been done, financing possibilities explored and closing costs estimated. They knew how and why at least three final analysis trials have to be performed using various prices and financing plans. Only then could they determine the maximum price that could be paid for a property in order to get an adequate return.

PART 3:
ACTUAL
ACQISITIONS

11

First Property Put Under Contract

Each Sunday afternoon the Andersons drove by all the rental property offerings newly listed in the newspaper, on the Internet or in real estate advertising booklets they had picked up at the supermarket entrance. They had even contacted two realtors concerning rental properties they were advertising. The Andersons correctly figured the agents who listed the properties for sale would be named in the advertising. They also assumed, incorrectly, that these agents would be very knowledgeable about their listings. Unfortunately, neither could answer most of the questions Joe asked. To be sure, both agents offered to find out and call back, but Joe told them he would drive by the properties and call them back, if he and Jane liked what they saw.

When they drove by, neither he nor Jane was impressed by these particular offerings so they didn't call the listing agents back. To their surprise, however, the agents didn't call them either! They asked Fred about it. Fred was surprised, too. Even though Joe told the agents he would call back if interested, Fred said on-the-ball agents would have gathered the missing information and called to offer it to the Andersons.

Fred admitted there were lots of real estate agents who were duds when it came to rentals. He hastened to point out that there were some excellent, conscientious and competent agents as well. He advised Joe and Jane to keep looking and not to hesitate to call realtors for information they needed. When they found someone they liked and who seemed interested and competent, they could stick with him or her. They had no obligation to continue working with a dud agent, unless the dud turned out to have listed the one property the Andersons liked best.

It had been ten months since the Andersons had started discussing wealth-building with the Madisons. During this time, Joe and Jane had been trying very hard to put 10% of their gross income into their investment account every month. At first, it had been quite a struggle as they adjusted their spending patterns. Then, over the last six months it all seemed to come together. They got used to doing without the top 10% as they called it.

What really helped in keeping them on the thrifty road to investment savings was to remind themselves that they were going to become millionaires. They were starting to accept that as a fact of life; they were internalizing it. Once they were millionaires they could indulge themselves any way they wanted. Joe saw himself driving a brand new, fully loaded BMW or maybe even a Lexus SUV. Jane visualized a nice house of their own with a pool for their future kids to enjoy. Yes, they were starting to think like millionaires. They were being frugal, living well below their means and visualizing a life with plenty of money. Most of all, they were optimistic about the future, were confident about their abilities to master the rental business and willing to plan for and work hard toward specific goals.

Joe had informally redone their net worth statement several times since they did their first formal one under Fred's direction. At first he had groaned when he saw how little net worth upward movement there seemed to be. Nevertheless, there was movement! They decided a new formal net worth statement was in order and came up with the following:

Joe & Jane Anderson Net Worth Statement
April 30, Wealth-Building Year #2

ASSETS:

Household furnishings	$	3,300
Joe's car		5,600
Jane's car		7,900
Regular checking account		700
Cash for rainy days		1,500
Cash reserves for big items		600
Cash for investing		7,000
Total Assets	$	26,600

LIABILITIES:

Installment loan on TV	$	50
Anderson credit card debt		25
Loan on Joe's car		3,200
Loan on Jane's car		5,180
Total Liabilities	$	8,455

NET WORTH (Assets - Liabilities) $ 18,145

Joe and Jane couldn't believe it. Could their net worth have increased over $8,300 in ten months, from $9,800 to $18,145? They re-checked and re-checked again. The figures weren't lying. They had been very diligent in setting aside $4,500 in fresh cash. That was their 10% off the top, plus general cutting back on their spending. Just as important, they had paid down all existing debts by making all scheduled payments. Their TV was about to be fully paid off. No new debts were added and they tried to pay off every credit card statement as soon as it arrived. Maybe they were going to get somewhere, yet when they thought about it, they realized that they had hardly even started!

Within their assets they had separated out $1,500 as their untouchable rainy day fund. Also, they split out their reserves for big items, such as car repairs, car insurance and holiday gifts. Reserves for big items, they decided, would never be allowed to drop below $300 and would be funded at the rate of

$75 a month. Jane declared they had $7,000 they could invest in a rental property. In fact, by the time they found something to buy, then worked through to closing on it, they could very well have $8,000 to dole out!

They also produced a new income statement. Effective the first of January, Joe had gotten a 4% salary increase to $26,000 a year. Jane had received a 5% raise which brought her to $22,050. They still planned to put 10% of their combined gross into their investment fund. In actual fact they had been salting away somewhat better than 10% in recent months. Thanks to their salary increases they had $1,845 a year more—about $150 a month—for general living expenses than they had when they did their first income statement the previous June. It gave their tight budget some welcome relief. The Andersons' new income statement:

Income Projection Statement
April 30, Wealth-Building Year #2

Joe's gross annual salary	$ 26,000
Jane's gross annual salary	22,050
Total Anderson family gross income	$ 48,050
Planned set-aside for investments ($400.42/mo.)	4,805
Gross funds available for all else	$ 43,245/yr.

Just two weeks later, Joe and Jane figured they hit property pay dirt. Of the four new listings they drove by on Sunday afternoon, two seemed like distinct possibilities. Both were in acceptable neighborhoods and both seemed to be in fairly good condition, on the outside.

One offering, on Alton Way, was advertised as a rental house for sale at $50,000 by the owner, a Mr. Cory Whittaker. The other was a realtor-listed duplex on Green Drive with an asking price of $74,500. By Thursday afternoon, thanks to a flurry of phone calls, including to lenders, they had gathered all the data needed to make preliminary analysis charts. The fifth lender they called said she could do a 90% loan-to-value loan on investment property provided they had class A credit reports. She could offer a one-year adjustable-rate mortgage with an 8.5% initial interest rate. One loan discount point would be required but zero origination fees. The loan would be amortized over 30 years. Caps were one per year, five for a lifetime.

One of the lenders Jane talked to invited the Andersons to come in and get pre-approved for a loan. That way, the lender said, they'd know just how much they were qualified to borrow and therefore how much they could buy. Jane said she'd think about it and call the lender back. Then she called Wendy and arranged for her and Joe to drop by to get the Madisons' opinions about pre-qualifying for loans.

Once at the Madisons' home, Fred told them: "Don't bother trying to get pre-approval for loans, although you undoubtedly will be urged to do so by some lenders and some realtors. If you're buying a property for use as your prime residence pre-qualifying is okay, but avoid it when you're after rental property.

"If you pre-qualify prior to pursuing rental acquisitions you may become inhibited by what the loan clerk says. If the clerk and the lender's guidelines are conservative, you'll be told you qualify for a loan amount smaller than you probably can actually borrow. You'll be inclined to adjust your buying sights downward accordingly. This could be unfortunate.

"In addition, the amount you can qualify for is magnified when you're buying rentals. Most lenders will allow 75% of the scheduled annual rental income—sometimes of net income after allowance for vacancies—to be added to your other income in the qualifying formula. Boosting your income obviously boosts the amount you can borrow. If you pre-qualify before finding the rental property you won't know the amount by which your income should be boosted.

"Further, there are common means of borrowing beyond the first mortgage loans that orthodox lenders offer or in combination with them. Think about second mortgages and owner financing, for instance. You don't want to be stifled in your acquisitions by feeling your loan limit is X when it's possibly X plus Y plus Z.

"Finally," Fred concluded, "in my experience lenders respond better to being presented with the signed contract you have on a rental property. Ask the lender if they wish to participate by providing the primary financing. Show your analysis proving it's a good deal for you and safe for the lender. Approached this way, lenders will be flexible to the extent of their hunger for loans and flexibility of their policies."

"But what if you're turned down?" Joe asked.

"Just because one lender turns you down doesn't mean the contract is dead. Try other lenders. If after a diligent effort you can't get financing, you may be able to re-structure the deal so it's more lender friendly. Ultimately, if nothing works, you can gracefully back out of the deal by invoking the financing contingency clause which must be a part of any contract you sign."

"Have you had to back out of deal because you couldn't get financing?" Joe asked.

Wendy stepped in. "No, but we've had to go to more than one primary lender. One time Fred went through six lenders before getting a re-finance loan he wanted. The main thing about financing is to have the deal structured so it's a good, profitable deal for you. The numbers must prove that the deal makes sense and will be profitable for you even after debt service is covered. And, of course, it can help a lot to be creative in financing ideas. Don't saddle yourselves into thinking about only one lender or only one way to finance."

The Andersons thanked their mentors for the advice and went home. The next day, Jane called the lender who had invited her to pre-qualify and politely declined. That evening, she and Joe prepared the following:

Analysis of Price/Financing
Alton Way House & Green Dr. Duplex

	Alton House		Green Duplex	
	Asking Price	Trial 2	Asking Price	Trial 2
Price	50,000		74,500	
Down Payment—10%	5,000		7,450	
To Be Financed—90%	45,000		67,050	
Monthly P&I				
Debt Service	346		516	

Analysis of Income, Expenses and Cash Flow
Alton House

	Trial 1		Trial 2	
	Mo.	Yr.	Mo.	Yr.
Gross Potential Income	590	7,080		
Vacancy Loss 5.0%	30	360		
Net Effective Income	560	6,720		
Operating Expenses				
Taxes	70	840		
Insurance	16	192		
Repairs Done by Others	20	240		
Maintenance Supplies	13	156		
Landlord Paid Utilities	3	36		
Yardwork (Do self)	0	0		
Advertising	3	36		
Miscellaneous	2	24		
Total Operating Expenses	127	1,524		
Net Operating Income	433	5,196		
Debt Service (P&I)	346	4,152		
Spendable Cash Flow	87	1,044		

Analysis of Income, Expenses and Cash Flow
Green Duplex

	Trial 1		Trial 2	
	Mo.	Yr.	Mo.	Yr.
Gross Potential Income				
(2 x440 for duplex)	880	10,560		
Vacancy Loss 5.0%	44	528		
Net Effective Income	836	10,032		
Operating Expenses				
Taxes	76	912		
Insurance	22	264		
Repairs Done by Others	40	480		
Maintenance Supplies	26	312		
Landlord Paid Utilities	5	60		
Yardwork (Do self)	0	0		
Advertising	3	36		
Miscellaneous	3	36		
Total Operating Expenses	175	2,100		
Net Operating Income	661	7,932		
Debt Service (P&I)	516	6,192		
Spendable Cash Flow	145	1,740		

With the help of one of the lenders they had been speaking to on the phone, the Andersons came up with the following estimate of cash required to close:

Analysis Chart for Cash Required to Close

	Alton House		Green Duplex	
	Asking Price	Trial 2	Asking Price	Trial 2
Down Payment	5,000		7,450	
Points 1.0% of Loan Amount	450		671	
Mortgagee Title Insurance	380		440	
Owner's Title Insurance	60		70	
2 Endorsements	50		50	
Settlement Fee, Title Search, etc.	110		110	
State Taxes $.55 per 100 of loan	248		369	
Application/Appraisal	300		300	
Survey	225		225	
Credit Report	55		55	
Recording	25		25	
Tax Service Fee	50		50	
Flood Certification Fee	25		25	
Miscellaneous	20		20	
TOTAL CASH TO ACQUIRE	6,998		9,860	

Cash-on-cash return for Cory Whittaker's Alton Way house was calculated as $1,044 divided by $6,998, multiplied by 100, or 14.92%.

Return for the Green Drive duplex was calculated as $1,740 divided by $9,860, multiplied by 100, or 17.65%.

Since the current rate for one-year certificates of deposit was 6.3%, the minimum return needed from a rental property investment was 18.9%.

Joe and Jane happily went through a couple of trials on each property to determine the maximum price they should pay for each. They were following Fred's advice.

For the house, manipulating their analysis determined about $47,500 was the maximum they should pay. For the duplex, the maximum was calculated as $72,500. The Andersons, of course, would try to pay less than the maximum amounts to get an even better return. They felt much better, armed with the knowledge of what the properties were actually worth based on a logical financial analysis. They understood their valuations were preliminary. After all, they hadn't done physical evaluations yet. Maybe the buildings needed lots of work.

Jane was quite excited about the Alton Way house. She thought it might be perfect. She assured Joe, however, that her sense of what looked right from the outside wouldn't overshadow a cold, hard analysis of the property based on its numbers and true physical condition. But if they had to start somewhere, her vote was to go after the house first. Besides, she reasoned, they could handle the cash requirements of the house out of their own investment funds. To buy the duplex they needed to come up with about $2,700 more than they had or the seller had to pay some closing costs. Not impossible, but not a certainty either.

They discussed everything with the Madisons and got ready approval on what they had done so far. Joe asked Fred if he would consider going with them to view the properties and talk to or deal with Mr. Whittaker about the house and the realtor about the duplex.

Fred declined. He told them, "I'm happy to be your behind-the-scenes advisor but you need to do certain things yourselves. What good does it do you guys for *me* to get more experience? You need the experience of looking through buildings and talking directly to owners and realtors. The more you do it the better you'll get and the more comfortable you'll feel. I want to teach you to be fisherman," he concluded, borrowing from a famous adage, "I don't simply want to give you fish." They understood.

A meeting was set with Mr. Whittaker for Wednesday at 10 A.M. Fred reminded the Andersons to try to visit rental property when the tenant is not there. Mr. Whittaker said he would call his tenant Tuesday to set up the Wednesday showing for when the resident would be at work.

Cory Whittaker turned out to be an unfriendly individual with tight lips and a dour expression. He was barely cordial to the Andersons. He led them through his rental house and answered their questions using as few words as possible. It was almost as if he resented their intrusion, yet he was trying to sell his property!

The rental house was in good shape although the appliances were clearly dated. They were in colors popular years ago. Cory Whittaker made it very clear that everything worked since he maintained everything himself and said that was the only way you could make money from a rental house. He looked at Joe with some disdain as he tried to evaluate Joe's handyman skills. Evidently, he didn't think Joe measured up since he turned away shaking his head.

Jane tried her charming best to engage in pleasant small talk relating to the property and its tenant but got essentially nowhere with Mr. Whittaker. He did reveal, however, that just the month before he had signed a one-year lease renewal with his tenant who had lived there six years. The rent was increased by $20 to $590 at that time. Immediately, Joe realized the rent wouldn't be changing for at least 11 months.

As they were leaving, Joe casually said he and Jane liked the house and complimented Mr. Whittaker on its condition. He added that they would be putting their heads together to see what kind of offer they could make on the property. Joe was being friendly but perhaps too open. In any event, rather than take Joe's remarks as encouraging, Cory Whittaker took offense.

"So it's an offer you're thinking of, is it?" Whittaker said with a snarl. "Well, let me tell you I'm not the horse trading kind. My house is in good shape—you admit it is—and the price is the price. You get what you pay for and I've got a good place."

"Indeed you have, sir!" Joe hastened to say. "But your price does seem a little high to us. Surely you're open to a little negotiation?"

"Look," sighed Whittaker. "I've put a lot of work into this place. You have no idea. I don't need to sell it but I'd like to. I'm not selling unless I get my price." Then he softened a bit adding, "Well, maybe I'd go down $500 but that would be it and only providing there was no other funny business."

The meeting ended.

The next evening Joe and Jane described the Whittaker incident to Fred and Wendy. Fred listened, then sighed heavily.

He told the Andersons not to worry about it but they could forget getting Whittaker's house at their maximum price of $47,500 let alone below it.

"Cory Whittaker is the type of person who should be using a realtor," declared Fred. "Trouble is, he's a good maintenance do-it-your-selfer and figures he can sell as well as anyone. He can't. You've described someone who seems to lack people skills and who ends up working against himself. You two probably aren't the first prospects he's turned off and you won't be the last. But not all for-sale-by-owner types are like Whittaker so don't be too discouraged."

Wendy jumped in. "Actually, Fred used to sell all his own stuff before he ever became a licensed realtor. Were you a nasty fisbo Fred?" She used the realtor's jargon for a for-sale-by-owner type.

"No, I wasn't nasty. But then I enjoy wheeling and dealing, whereas Cory Whittaker obviously doesn't. I've always thought of negotiating as a rather interesting game—sometimes with high stakes. I actually like it and sold maybe eight or nine of my own properties before getting a license. Whittaker sees negotiation as a personal attack against him. Forget him. Why don't you see what you can do with the duplex?"

"We will," said Jane, but she was disappointed her first choice wasn't going to work.

"Yeah, I'll call Danny the realtor tomorrow," added Joe, but without enthusiasm. Joe was somewhat dejected by their experience with Cory Whittaker.

Danny turned out to be the opposite of Cory Whittaker. He was definitely a people person but not overbearing. Jane had heard that realtors were pushy. Danny was not pushy. Instead, he was attentive and quick to respond to any questions thrown at him. Joe had only talked on the phone with him before; this was their first face-to-face encounter.

They met at the duplex Monday afternoon. Danny had left notes for the absent tenants on Sunday telling them of the upcoming showing. Neither resident was home. They looked first inside side B. Jane wondered why they didn't start with A, since that would be the logical starting point, but said nothing.

Side B looked fairly average. It looked "tired" and the walls were yellowed by age and possibly by a smoker. The plastic bathroom sink, in an oval shape, was cracked around its rim. It would need to be replaced. The bathroom floor vinyl was discolored and also needed to be replaced.

Overall, unit B was acceptable to the Andersons. They felt they could whip it into shape whenever it became vacant. They went outside and headed across towards the door for unit A. Danny, who until that point had kept up almost a constant chatter, was strangely quiet.

Finally, as he was turning the key in the lock after knocking loudly several times, he said mildly, "I should tell you something about the resident of unit A before we go in. But what the heck, you might as well see for yourselves. Then I'll tell you about him."

Jane gasped as they stepped inside. The place was a wreck, an absolute mess. Newspapers and pizza boxes were everywhere. Crumpled clothes and magazines were strewn about haphazardly. The sparse amount of furniture was battered and cheap looking. In the bedroom was a mattress on the floor but no box spring and no bed frame. Bed sheets and a blanket were a twisted horror, wrapping around a badly stained pillow. The kitchen sink and counters were heaped with greasy dishes, pots, pans and glasses. Torn fast food bags and plastic utensils littered the small formica table.

It was hard to find a clear path to walk through the apartment. Certainly there was no clear place to sit. Books, newspapers and magazines tottered on every chair. The strong sour odor of garbage led them to a tall, baby blue plastic garbage can near the side door. It was overflowing. The short hallway wall leading to the bedroom had two fist-size holes blasted into the plaster. One bedroom wall had a four-inch hole punched into it also.

The Andersons were appalled. Their mouths remained slightly open as they picked their way around. It didn't take them long to see all they wanted; they were anxious to get back out to fresh air as fast as possible.

Once outside, Danny composed himself as best he could, coughed lightly to clear his throat, then said, "Obviously side A could use a little dust-up." None of the three could restrain themselves at this outrageous understatement. All three burst into laughter.

Danny took them to a coffee shop to discuss the situation.

"I'm sure you noticed we went to side B first. That was on purpose. I felt you might not want to bother looking at B if you saw A first."

"Good thinking, Danny!" said Joe.

"Yeah, right," Danny responded. "Actually, I've already shown this duplex to four other prospective buyers in the seven days it's been on the market. All of them have said no thanks once they saw unit A. Guess you'll be doing the same thing. Right?"

"Not necessarily," offered Joe who was suddenly excited as possibilities occurred to him. "What does the owner think of it all?"

Danny perked up at Joe's question. "Well, he's very upset about it, that's for sure. In fact, unit A is why he wants to sell the building. Are you possibly interested in it?" He raised his eyebrows to emphasize his curiosity.

"We may be," answered Jane, who thought she might be thinking the same thing as Joe. "Would you say the seller is . . . what do they call it . . . motivated? Or is that even a fair question?"

"Yes it is, in this case. The owner has authorized me to tell anyone who shows interest after seeing it that he is anxious to sell. Translation: he's open to offers. But let me be very candid. The seller has authorized me to tell you what I'm about to say. He thinks it's only fair. But you need to know anyway because it's a material fact."

The Andersons leaned forward toward Danny in anticipation of a shocking revelation. Danny continued. He didn't disappoint them.

"Jeremy Foss, esteemed resident of duplex side A, hasn't paid rent in more than three months. My owner, Don Majors, who is really a nice guy, is fit to be tied. He doesn't know what to do. That's why he wants out. You see he inherited the duplex from an uncle about two years ago. The duplex was fully rented when he got it and remained so until five months ago when side A moved out. Don had no real landlord training or experience, but he got side A cleaned up, advertised it and unfortunately attracted Jeremy Foss. Foss is the proverbial tenant from hell.

"Foss gave Don just $300 to get the keys so he could move a few things in that night. Gave Don a pitiful tale of woe so Don agreed to let him pay the deposit and, get this, the rest of the rent the next Friday. Foss also said he was in too much of a hurry to sign a lease then but would take one with him to read. Said he'd bring it back signed when he brought the rest of the rent and the deposit. Well, surprise, surprise! Guess who didn't have any money the next Friday? You got it. No signed lease either. All Jeremy had for Don was another tale of woe. Don's sick about it. It's a real shame. Don's been to see him time after time to get the rent, or at least some of it, but Jeremy just gives him a song and dance. Oh, one time Jeremy gave him $100, but then he told Don to stop bothering him. Don's a nice guy, as I said, but apparently not cut out to be a landlord. Jeremy's into him for almost $1,400, plus the deposit! Don wishes the whole nightmare would go away. He really doesn't know what to do. Hope you guys do. You might be able to get a good buy here. Mr. Majors authorized me to tell anyone truly interested that he is anxious to sell."

After a bit more discussion, the Andersons took their leave, promising to let Danny know their intentions in a day or so. Alone in their car, Joe and Jane compared notes. They both figured a good opportunity might be presenting itself if something could be done about Jeremy Foss. Jane called the Madisons and set up a meeting for the next afternoon.

The next day, Joe and Jane took turns in telling Fred and Wendy about the Green Drive duplex, Jeremy Foss and the predicament of owner Don Majors. Both Wendy and Fred smiled knowingly to each other and to the Andersons as the opportunity conclusion was presented.

Fred waited until the Andersons said all they wished to say, then spoke. "Joe, Jane, I think you're absolutely correct. A great opportunity seems to be presenting itself. I'm real pleased you two concluded that yourselves. Here's an owner who sounds like he'll take any reasonable offer and any reasonable terms. Plus, you say the duplex seems basically sound and is in a good neighborhood. Your only concerns are Jeremy Foss and his messy apartment and a few wall holes. You know what I think? I think you don't have to worry about Foss at all or any of the rest. Let me tell you what I'd do. I smell a great deal just ahead." The Andersons were all ears.

Fred told them to get out the analysis sheets that the Andersons had brought with them. He asked to see them starting with the price chart. Looking at pricing, he reminded himself of the $74,500 asking price and the approximately $72,500 maximum price the Andersons determined they could pay. He stroked his chin thoughtfully. A moment later he declared it was time to be bold.

"Mr. Majors is asking for an offer," said Fred. "And it's a messy situation. Let's jolt him with an offer of $63,000."

The Andersons gasped. Someone had told them a properly priced property usually sold at about 97% of asking price. Even Wendy seemed a bit taken aback; she was frowning a little.

Fred explained himself: "If you think I'm being aggressive, just focus on the mess Mr. Foss has created and Mr. Majors allowed to happen. The duplex may have been properly priced if it was in good order, but it ain't. Jane, you told us the garbage smell of side A about made you gag. Surely the place isn't worth top dollar. But if Mr. Majors thinks you're being too hard on him, what are the three things he can say in response to your low offer?"

"Yes, no, or hell no!" said Joe with a laugh.

"Great, Joe! You're learning. Don't be afraid of rejection. You're not buying someone's treasured homestead or a quaint little nest for your family. We're talking rental property here. No emotion should be in your decisions. In this case, my guess is the seller won't take the 63, but he's so anxious to get out of his sticky situation he'll be very cautious in his counteroffer.

"You don't have to do another analysis at this point since we know you're not going to pay as high as your 72.5 maximum. Course if it goes all the way, we'll want to do an analysis based on the final price and terms. It'll look pretty good, I'm sure . . . something over 20% cash-on-cash.

"By the way, isn't this the property for which you didn't have enough cash to meet the 10% down payment, plus closing costs? If so, better plan to ask the seller to hold a second mortgage for 15% of the price. That will put the primary lender down to 75% LTV so they shouldn't change their minds and suddenly say they need you to pay PMI. Also, once the basic negotiation is done, we'll bump up the purchase price and ask Mr. Majors to pay some closing costs. He'll do it, if he wants to sell. Boy, this is starting to get interesting! Tell you what, why don't you two sleep on all we've talked about. Then, if you want to proceed, I'll tell you tomorrow just how to structure your offer. Fair enough?"

"Deal!" said Joe.

"Deal!" echoed Jane. "But Fred, what will we do about Jeremy Foss? I can't see why we shouldn't be worried about him."

"Well, Jane, we'll just have to throw him out. Legally, of course, but it isn't hard and won't take long. I'll tell you about it tomorrow if you decide to submit an offer."

The Andersons were skeptical but excited at the same time as they left the Madisons. Once in their car, they rehashed everything.

The next day they returned to the Madisons and declared that they were prepared to submit an offer. Since Danny, the realtor, was involved, Fred said Danny should prepare the actual offer using a standard form produced by the local Board of Realtors. Otherwise, the Andersons could do it themselves using a form from an office supply store. If they were going to use an attorney, the attorney could prepare the offer on a form of his or her choosing. However, Fred told them that before getting the actual offer prepared by anyone, they should jot down the main things they want included.

Fred told them: "Start with the legal names of whoever is intending to take title to the property. It must be 'Joseph P. Anderson and Jane M. Anderson, his spouse,' for example, not simply 'Joe and Jane Anderson.' You ought to use the word spouse so the relationship is clear. Otherwise, you can't tell whether Jane is a sister, other relative or just a friend with the same last name. Find out from the courthouse or have the realtor find out who is the legal owner of the property. Be sure to list all owners, as all owners will have to sign to accept your offer. Naturally you want to be very specific as to what you want to purchase. In addition to the street address you need the legal description. The tax assessor's identification number is helpful as well. Be sure to list any moveable items you expect to be included with or have stay with the property, otherwise they may not be there when you take possession. For this particular duplex, Fred suggested they specify two stoves, two refrigerators, installed lighting fixtures and all window treatments.

It was usual to put up a deposit when submitting an offer, Fred said, but he suggested they specify an amount, say $500, to be paid to the realtor's, attorney's or title company's trust account within 24 hours of acceptance of the offer. This type of deposit, which would apply toward the purchase if the deal goes that far, is known as "earnest" money. It's meant to show that they are a serious prospective buyer.

They had to indicate the total amount of the offer—in this case $63,000—and the source of the funds. Fred suggested the following:

Deposit, due within 24 hours of offer acceptance	$ 500
Third party financing—75% of price	47,250
Seller financing—15% of price	9,450
Remainder, cash from buyers, due at closing	5,800
Total Price Offered	$ 63,000

"It's important to specify financing percentages," Fred cautioned, "in case the offered total amount is changed through a counteroffer. With percentages, if the total is changed, clearly the financing amounts are to be changed accordingly."

"Standard offer forms contain most all of the language needed to protect both prospective buyers and the sellers," Fred said, "so I won't go through all that detail. Once the offer is prepared by Danny, but before it's submitted, I will, if you want, go over the standard clauses and explain any which are unclear. But I'm not an attorney. If you're nervous, or feel things don't seem right, are unclear or going too fast, you can consult a real estate attorney.

"As to closing costs, the division of who pays for what is entirely negotiable, but I suggest the following generalities. Buyers should pay for things that are primarily for their benefit or are required to get financing. So, Joe and Jane, you should pay for survey, title insurance, the loan application fee, points, state taxes on mortgages and any inspections. The sellers should pay for whatever is needed to sell the property. This includes preparation of the deed, state taxes on the deed, recording of it and any repairs, perhaps with a dollar limit, or treatments required because of a termite or similar inspection."

Fred said, "Most important are special clauses added to any standard contract and made part of it. Specially added clauses override any preprinted clauses if they create points in conflict."

Fred suggested that certain items be covered by special clauses. "First," he told them, "put in contingency clauses for primary financing, secondary financing and inspections. A contingency gives you the privilege of canceling the contract— if the offer is accepted thus creating a contract—should you not get the financing you need or like the results of inspections.

"In this case, you should put in a contingency clause that you be able to obtain a loan and first mortgage for 75% of the purchase price from a lender of their choice at terms and conditions satisfactory to them. If you don't qualify, or if the interest rate isn't acceptable, you can back out of the deal and get your earnest money deposit back.

"Your second contingency must be for the seller to hold a loan, secured by a second mortgage, for 15% of the purchase price. The loan is to be at 7.5% fixed rate with a 30-year amortization, monthly payments of principal and interest and a balloon payment as the 120th payment.

"Your third contingency should allow you to, within seven working days of the contract date—meaning the date the last signature was added to the contract—inspect, or have inspected at your expense, all aspects of the duplex and any leases. Results of inspections must be satisfactory to you or you can declare the contract null and void."

Fred told them to also add the following as special conditions of their offer:

Buyers have a right to inspect all mechanical equipment and appliances, plus electrical, plumbing, heating and air conditioning systems, approximately ten days before closing. Each device or system is to be operating satisfactorily or it will be fixed by seller, at seller's expense, prior to closing.

Fred explained that there was little point in doing a detailed inspection at the offer stage since something may go wrong in the time between offer and closing. If the Andersons found a stove burner or a water heater inoperative ten days before closing, the seller still could easily get it fixed before closing.

Jane asked: "Do sellers sometimes put into the contract that they agree to repairs only up to a certain dollar limit?"

"Yes, they do," replied Fred, "but if they do it's usually one of several points made in their counteroffer of the prospect's initial offer. Most commonly it would be a limit on wood rot repairs and it would also give the buyers the chance to back out of the deal if repairs were going to go over the limit. Any limit specified should be reasonable or it could scare the buyers away by making them think the sellers know something they're not telling. Plus, if the A/C in a rental unit is inoperative, for example, the seller should know they've got to get it operational before closing regardless of the cost. An aware buyer is not going to accept a low limit."

Fred then suggested that they add a contingency clause regarding rents:

Seller to use his best efforts to keep units rented at not less than $440 a month. If units become vacant prior to closing, they are to be put into clean, rentable condition by the seller, at seller's expense.

Fred explained that this would keep the pressure on Don Majors so he didn't let the units go unrented if they became vacant and would prevent him from quickly filling a vacancy by offering cut-rate rent. Fred also pointed out that it was in Majors's interest to fix up any vacancy and to try to rent it in case the deal with the Andersons fell apart.

Rents are to be prorated as of the day of closing with the day of closing considered as belonging to the buyer. Proration of occupied units is to be based on the assumption that scheduled rents have been collected for the month. Buyers are not responsible for collecting any due rents not paid. Past due rents belong to the seller.

Fred pointed out that it shouldn't be up to the Andersons to go after unpaid rent, although they should cooperate with the seller in trying to collect it. The seller could avoid dealing further with Foss, including not pursuing delinquent rent. However, the seller would end up paying the rent out of his own pocket at closing as if he had collected it. Fred emphasized that if the seller was tolerating, albeit unhappily, a non-paying resident it was his problem. The Andersons shouldn't expect rent if an apartment was vacant, but they shouldn't have to accept a freeloader during the month of closing. The clause would keep pressure on the seller to keep trying to collect outstanding rents.

Another clause that Fred puts in all of his rental property acquisitions is:

Existing leases, tenant records and tenant security deposits are to be transferred to buyers at closing. Deposits are to be transferred via separate check from seller to buyers.

Fred said that this would highlight the importance that must be placed on money belonging to the tenants. He told Joe and Jane that many landlords co-mingled tenant deposits with their own money, but it was illegal to do so in their state unless a bond covering the total amount was acquired and the tenants so advised. The separate check from the seller provided a good trail of where the money came from and where it was going. Otherwise it could be "lost" in the many entries on the closing statements and used, technically illegally, in a netting-out process. Tenant deposits are best put into a non-interest-bearing trust account. The Andersons said they would establish one.

If it's not provided elsewhere as part of standard form language, Fred also suggested that they specify a "time is of the essence" clause. Also specify a deadline time and date for the offer to be accepted after which it automatically becomes null and void.

Fred had found that three days was a reasonable length of time for in-town sellers to mull over any offer and decide how to respond. More time should be allowed if there are multiple owners in different locations since it takes time to communicate, get signatures and transfer paperwork.

"Allowing just one or two days for response may make a seller feel unduly pressured and react unfavorably. On the other hand," Fred stated, "in a highly competitive situation I might very well specify one day to minimize the chances of the seller waiting to see what else came in. Of course the seller might take his time anyway but a short time for response would cause him to do so at the risk of losing me. I may have other things to bid on."

Fred also reminded Joe and Jane they could withdraw their offer any time up to the point they were notified it had been accepted by signature of the seller.

Finally, Fred told them to specify a closing date 40 to 50 days hence, but in any event somewhere between the 15th and 20th of a month. This would mean they took over after all the rents had been collected for the month, and their share would be handed to them at closing. Unless a new problem arose immediately, they would then sail through to the start of the next month before anything had to be done. Plus, if there was a vacancy they would have ten to fifteen days in which to get someone to rent it, with occupancy starting with the first day of the new month or even before. In addition, a closing mid-month or later would cause the lender to specify the first day of the second month after closing as the date on which first mortgage payment is due. They would be required to pay some prepaid interest but putting off the first full mortgage payment was to their advantage.

At last the Andersons were ready to take their notes to Danny to get their offer formally prepared. Fred advised them to convey to Danny—who would convey to the seller—that they were leery about making any offer at all because of the existence of Jeremy Foss, tenant from hell. The Andersons said they would certainly tell Danny this because they were, in fact, very leery. Fred told them not to worry about Foss.

Danny the realtor was, of course, pleased to hear from the Andersons and agreed to meet with them Saturday morning. He hoped something would work out with the Andersons that Don Majors could live with. If it did, Danny would claim the commission for both the listing side and the selling side rather than have to split it with another realtor.

Danny was taken aback, however, when he heard what Joe and Jane proposed as their offer. He hemmed and hawed and went over the merits of the property. He also said he doubted whether Mr. Majors would accept it and might be offended. The Andersons listened sympathetically. Obviously a selling realtor would prefer to take a full price offer, or something close to it to his principal, the seller. Fred had forewarned them about Danny's probable reaction.

Once Danny finished telling them all the reasons why their offer should be increased, Joe said to him firmly: "We understand your disappointment, Danny, but we figured out what the property is worth to us, especially considering Jeremy Foss. It may be worth more to Don Majors. If so, perhaps he should keep it. Besides, we don't have a lot of cash and will have to conserve a bunch of it to fix up side A. This is our offer. We're asking you to submit it as is and do your best to make your seller see its merits. If he wants out, here's the way."

"I'll see what I can do," replied a subdued Danny. "Probably I can present your offer today."

Two days later, at about 7:15 P.M., Danny called the Andersons and asked if he could come to their apartment. He had a response from Don Majors.

When he arrived, Danny first conveyed how hard he had worked to prevent Mr. Majors from rejecting their offer out of hand. He said he went over all the offer's good points and gave Don his advice. Don had called him mid-afternoon with his decisions. At that point, Danny pulled out the offer document. Since the seller had changed some things, Danny told them, it was now his counteroffer to them. He had specified 5:00 P.M., three days hence, as a response deadline.

Majors had changed only three primary items, but this had the effect of causing other items to be changed accordingly. First, Danny said, Mr. Majors wouldn't take any less than $66,000. Second, he would hold a purchase money mortgage as a second mortgage, but it must be amortized over 15 years not 30. Finally, his loan must balloon in 7 years not 10. The use of percentages had caused the size of the primary and secondary financing to change as well.

Joe and Jane asked a few questions then thanked Danny for trying his best. They said they would think over the counteroffer and get back to him by the deadline if they wanted to proceed. Knowing Danny would be reporting their reactions back to his seller they emphasized their unfortunate shortage of cash. Danny left. He worried about their cash situation.

The next afternoon, the Andersons met with the Madisons to discuss the latest developments. Fred was both surprised and pleased.

"This is great!" he declared. "I thought Majors would counter at not less than $67,500 and maybe 69 or 70. The 66 he came back with should make your numbers look great!"

"What about the 15-year amortization instead of 30 years?" asked Jane.

"It should be just fine. The real answer is to run our complete analysis using the counteroffer numbers. Then we can decide whether to accept Majors' proposal or counter his counter. My guess, though, is that your return is going to be fabulous!"

They prepared to completely redo their earlier analysis and Joe headed up a blank Trial column as the Final column. Wendy and Jane objected to the designation since they didn't know yet whether the numbers would change again. Fred, who had something further up his sleeve, said, "They're right," and had Joe change the label to Semi-Final Trial. Using 8.5% for the prime lender's mortgage and 7.5% for the seller's second, here's how the new analysis looked:

Analysis of Price/Financing
Green Dr. Duplex

	Asking Price	Semi-Final Trial	Trial 3
Price	74,500	66,000	
Down Payment 10%	7,450	6,600	
Primary Financing	67,050 (90%)	49,500 (75%)	
Owner/Secondary Financing	0	9,900 (15%)	
Monthly P&I Debt Service	515.56	472.38	

Analysis of Income, Expenses and Cash Flow
Green Drive Duplex

	Asking Price		Semi-Final		Trial 3	
	Mo.	Yr.	Mo.	Yr.	Mo.	Yr.
Gross Potential Income						
(2 x440)	880	10,560	880	10,560		
Vacancy Loss						
Allowance 5.0%	44	528	44	528		
Net Effective Income	836	10,032	836	10,032		
Operating Expenses						
Taxes	76	912	76	912		
Insurance	22	264	22	264		
Repairs by Others	40	480	40	480		
Maintenance Supplies	26	312	26	312		
Landlord Paid Utilities	5	60	5	60		
Yardwork (Do self)	0	0	0	0		
Advertising	3	36	3	36		
Miscellaneous	3	36	3	36		
Total Operating Expenses	175	2,100	175	2,100		
Net Operating Income	661	7,932	661	7,932		
Debt Service (P&I)	516	6,192	472	5,664		
Spendable Cash Flow	145	1,740	189	2,268		

Analysis Chart for Cash Required to Close
Green Drive Duplex

	Asking Price	Semi-Final Trial	Trial 3
Down Payment	7,450	6,600	
Points 1.0% of Loan Amount	671	495	
Mortgagee Title Insurance	440	420	
Owner's Title Insurance	70	60	
2 Endorsements	50	50	
Settlement Fee, Title Search, etc.	110	110	
State Taxes $.55 per 100 of loan	369	327	
Application/Appraisal	300	300	
Survey	225	225	
Credit Report	55	55	
Recording	25	25	
Tax Service Fee	50	50	
Flood Certification Fee	25	25	
Miscellaneous	20	20	
TOTAL CASH TO ACQUIRE	9,860	8,762	

"Well, look at this!" said Fred, with a whistle while he manipulated a small calculator as Joe watched. "Cash flow of $2,268 divided by cash required of $8,762 multiplied by 100 gives you a cash-on-cash return of 25.88% Not bad! Not bad at all!"

Jane joined Joe in staring at the calculator display. They were amazed and very pleased.

"But there's a fly in the soup," intoned Fred somberly. "Don't get too excited yet." The others stared at him.

"As it stands, you guys can't enjoy the almost 26% return because you don't have the $8,762 cash. I think you said you had about $7,000."

"We should have about $8,000 by the closing date," Jane added hopefully.

"Still not enough; you've got to have fix-up money besides. But part of your training is to use your imaginations when problems arise. In this case, a fine prize is within your grasp and the seller wants you to grab it. You would but you're short of funds. How can you get more cash or reduce the amount of cash you need? Think about it."

"Increase the price!" shouted Joe a moment later.

"Bingo! Joe, you've learned your lessons well. You remembered we had discussed raising the price and asking the seller to pay closing costs a while back. Good for you!" Jane looked baffled, but Wendy nodded knowingly.

Fred explained what to do. After some discussion, Joe was told to call realtor Danny. Joe was to tell him they were inclined to initial their acceptance of Majors's counteroffer, but on the other hand didn't have enough cash to do the deal. Could they get with Danny to discuss it? Danny would agree readily. Once together, they were to explain to Danny that they were about $2,000 short of covering closing and fix-up costs. They were to wait a few moments to allow it to sink into Danny that his sale was sailing away. Then, they were to say they would do the deal if the seller would pay $2,000 in closing costs for the Andersons. As soon as they said that, Danny would undoubtedly protest.

At that point, they were to calm Danny by telling him they were willing to pay Majors $2,000 more, if he did pay $2,000 of their closing costs. In other words, they would raise the price to $68,000. Danny probably would then tell them in that case he could sell his seller on the plan. Finally, Joe was to point out to Danny the arrangement was essentially a wash. Majors wouldn't be hurt since the $2,000 outgo was matched by a $2,000 inflow, especially since Danny would accept commission based on a $66,000 price. Danny's eyes would widen but then he would start to smile and nod approvingly. He could do it. He could convince Majors. He could save the deal!

And that's what happened. Danny added a clause to the counteroffer in accordance with Joe's instructions and got their initials beside it and all other revisions. A day later, Danny arrived back at the Andersons' apartment and happily told them they were on their way to becoming landlords. Don Majors had agreed with their plan! He had initialed the counter-counteroffer thus converting it to a contract. Joe, Jane and Danny were all smiles!

Fred and Wendy were excited, too, but Fred insisted they do a final revision of their analysis. He told them they would be pleased by the effect of putting up less of their own cash.

Analysis of Price/Financing
Green Dr. Duplex

	Asking Price	Semi-Final Trial	Final Plan
Price	74,500	66,000	68,000
Down Payment 10%	7,450	6,600	6,800
Primary Financing	67,050	49,500	51,000
	(90%)	(75%)	(75%)
Owner/Secondary Financing	0	9,900 (15%)	10,200 (15%)
Monthly P&I Debt Service	515.56	472.38	486.69

Analysis of Income, Expenses and Cash Flow
Green Drive Duplex

	Asking Price Mo.	Yr.	Semi-Final Mo.	Yr.	Trial 3 Mo.	Yr.
Gross Potential Income						
(2x440)	880	10,560	880	10,560	880	10,560
Vacancy Loss						
Allowance 5.0%	44	528	44	528	44	528
Net Effective Income	836	10,032	836	10,032	836	10,032
Operating Expenses						
Taxes	76	912	76	912	76	912
Insurance	22	264	22	264	22	264
Repairs by Others	40	480	40	480	40	480
Maintenance Supplies	26	312	26	312	26	312
Landlord Paid Utilities	5	60	5	60	5	60
Yardwork (Do self)	0	0	0	0	0	0
Advertising	3	36	3	36	3	36
Miscellaneous	3	36	3	36	3	36
Total Operating Expenses	175	2,100	175	2,100	175	2,100
Net Operating Income	661	7,932	661	7,932	661	7,932
Debt Service (P&I)	516	6,192	472	5,664	487	5,844
Spendable Cash Flow	145	1,740	189	2,268	174	2,088

They made the following revision of cash required to close:

Analysis Chart for Cash Required to Close

	Asking	Semi-Final	Final
Down Payment	7,450	6,600	6,800
Points 1.0% of Loan Amount	671	495	512
Mortgagee Title Insurance	440	420	430
Owner's Title Insurance	70	60	65
2 Endorsements	50	50	50
Settlement Fee, Title Search, etc.	110	110	110
State Taxes $.55 per 100 of loan	369	327	337
Application/Appraisal	300	300	300
Survey	225	225	225
Credit Report	55	55	55
Recording	25	25	25
Tax Service Fee	50	50	50
Flood Certification Fee	25	25	25
Miscellaneous	20	20	20
Seller's Closing Cost Payment			(2000)
TOTAL CASH TO ACQUIRE	9,860	8,762	7,004

Fred handed his little calculator to Joe and Jane for them to determine the revised cash-on-cash return. They divided the $2,082 annual cash flow by the $7,004 in cash they would have to put up and multiplied by 100. They saw the result, looked at each other, then did the calculation over again. Next, Joe handed the calculator to Jane for her to do it by herself. They could hardly believe it. Every time the answer was the same: 29.73%. Not too bad. Not too bad at all for beginners!

"Hold on, guys!" called Fred as Joe and Jane jumped up and down cheering and hugging each other. "You've got a duplex under contract and it'll probably close, but you've then got lots of work ahead."

"We don't mind!" squealed Jane.

"Good! So, let me give you something more to celebrate."

Joe and Jane stood still and stared big-eyed in anticipation.

"You must have forgotten one of the bonuses of real estate investing. Remember loan principal paydown as you make your monthly mortgage payments? You can't spend it like cash flow but nevertheless your equity increases so it's a real gain to you.

"While you were jumping around the room I figured that in the first 12 months of mortgage payments you'll be paying down your loan principal by $768.18. Add that amount to your cash flow of $2,082 and you get $2,850 as your total 12-month gain. Divide by the $7,004 in cash you invest and guess what your return on investment is?"

There was dead silence. Finally Jane asked, "What is it?"

"40.69%."

"40.69%?"

"That's what it is, 40.69%!" exclaimed Fred.

Joe and Jane resumed jumping, hugging and cheering. Wendy cheered, too. The Andersons were on their way!

Once home again, the Andersons reminisced about their experience in getting their first property under contract. They had found a house and duplex they liked and analyzed both. Jane had been most interested in the house, but they were turned off by the rigid seller. Inspection of the duplex revealed a major problem: a non-paying occupant. Fred had helped them prepare an offer and outlined negotiation tactics. A counteroffer was received which they in turn countered. Finally a contract was signed! Then a real estate bonus was calculated and, considering it, they would realize an outstanding return on investment.

12

First Property Closed

The Andersons duly applied for a primary loan on the Green Drive Duplex and were approved in about 30 days. Prior to submitting a loan application, they exercised their contractual privilege of inspections within seven working days but didn't see anything they hadn't seen on their pre-offer walk through. Jeremy Foss was as messy as ever.

A survey was done. No encroachments. An inspection for wood destroying organisms including termites was done as well. It showed wood rot in eight places at the bottoms of exterior door frames and exterior siding. Don Majors cut out the bad wood, rather expertly installed new material, then painted over his patches. The termite inspector was called back to re-inspect. He judged the repairs as satisfactory and accordingly issued the clear report, which the lender specified had to be in hand by closing.

Joe and Jane selected a title company from a list of five the lender said had done good work for them in the past. Closing was set for the 18th of July, which was a Wednesday. Fred had told them to close no later than a Thursday to give at least Friday as a fall back day in case of delays. Wendy told them delays were commonplace. One thing or another would not be ready when it was supposed to be. The key to avoiding delays, according to Fred, was to use a checklist and keep checking on people. Don't assume people will, without being reminded, get around to doing what they're supposed to do on time. Keep after them, in a friendly manner of course.

An appraisal was done and showed the duplex was worth $73,500. A full-price offer would have been too high. The Andersons were getting a good deal with their $66,000 or $68,000 purchase.

It was important to have insurance for their new duplex go into effect on the day of closing. Not only was it a requirement of the primary lender, it was prudent common sense as well. With a binder from the insurer, the premium could be paid at closing.

Fred advised them to get replacement cost insurance rather than the ordinary type since the latter only covered current value. In the case of a loss, the preferred type would pay for what it took to replace the damage. The current value type would only cover the depreciated value of whatever was lost. Fred advised Joe to discuss coverage amounts with their insurance agent. However, to give them a general understanding, he told them that in order to get replacement cost insurance they would have to buy coverage for at least 90% of the cost to totally replace the building. Land wouldn't be insured because it couldn't be destroyed, and the foundation and driveways would likely survive anything.

He also strongly urged them to get loss of rents insurance coverage. If for any covered reason apartments became uninhabitable and not rentable, such as because of fire damage, the insurance company would pay the rent normally generated. This was very important. Whether their apartments were rentable or not, their lender would still expect timely mortgage payments.

The title company found no impediments to conveying the title from Don Majors to the Andersons so it was ready to issue title insurance. Existing mortgage liens recorded against the property were not considered clouds since these would be paid off at closing.

On Monday afternoon Joe picked up a copy of the proposed settlement statement from the title company. Closing was scheduled for 10 A.M. Wednesday. The settlement statement, whose form is mandated by the United States Department of Housing and Urban Development, listed all costs and proceeds attendant to closing the deal. It showed who paid what to whom and who got what and why. Danny the realtor said he would preview the report to see if it was correct from the seller's viewpoint. He said he would go over the buyer's figures as well. Joe asked Danny to let him know if anything appeared incorrect. Danny said he would and advised the title company. Joe's unstated intention was to go over the statement with his mentor Fred.

Fred did go over each settlement statement item with Joe and Jane since this was their first closing. He told them the title company's closing agent would go over everything, too, but it would be useful for them to have a basic understanding before the event. Besides, he said, at the actual closing, documents would be flying fast and furious, and they'd be signing this and that. They could easily lose track of what was going on without an advance briefing. It wasn't hard to understand; there just were a lot of details.

Fred's explanations of prorations and prepaids were particularly useful to the Andersons.

First he explained rent prorations, since they were simplest. The assumption being utilized—because it had been written into the contract—was that the seller had collected $440 rent for July from each of the two tenants. Since closing was to be on the 18th of July and the day of closing was considered as belonging to the buyers, the Andersons were entitled to 14 days worth of July rent—from the 18th through the 31st. What was a day's rent worth? The title company multiplied $880 per month by 12 to get the rent for the year, then divided by 365 days. This was their standard procedure to avoid differences that would occur in the varying lengths of months—28, 29, 30 or 31 days. In this case the Andersons were "given" $405.04 in rent. Accordingly, the same amount was "taken" from the seller's side. The seller's proceeds would be reduced by that much.

Taxes worked a bit differently. Whoever owned the property November 1st would be expected to actually pay the total property taxes for the entire year. Taxes for the year were estimated to be $912, but that could change by the time tax bills were issued. July 18th was the 199th day of the year so the seller would have owned the property and would be responsible for 198 days of taxes. This was 54.247% of the year. Hence, $494.73 would be "taken" from Don Majors as his share of the year's taxes. His proceeds would be reduced by that much. The Andersons would be "given" Don's $494.73 insofar as the settlement statement was concerned, so they could pay the entire year's taxes when the tax bill came out early in November.

It wouldn't be possible for Joe and Jane to enjoy spending the tax money in the meantime, since their prime lender would grab it at closing. Most lenders require borrowers to pay 1/12 of the estimated cost of taxes and insurance along with their monthly payment of loan interest and principal. In fact, mortgage payments are termed as PITI payments since they generally include principal, interest, taxes and insurance. The lender holds the accumulating amounts for insurance and taxes in an escrow account for the benefit of the borrower and for their own convenience. When escrow accounts exist, the insurance company and the tax assessor send their annual bills to the primary lender. The bills are then paid with funds from the borrower's escrow account. The system works well. The lender doesn't have to worry that insurance and taxes won't be paid, and the borrower doesn't have to worry about having enough money when the bills are due.

At closing, the lender collects not less than two months worth of insurance and taxes to establish an escrow account for the borrower. For example, if insurance is $264 a year, its premium could be considered as $22 per month. At closing, the lender would require the full $264 premium for the first year's insurance be paid and $44 to start off the escrow fund for next year's premium. Once regular mortgage payments start coming in, another $22 is added to insurance escrow each period. When the anniversary of the closing rolls around and it's time for the insurance premium to be paid for year two, there's 12 times $22, or $264, in escrow to pay it. A neat system.

The first year's insurance premium plus the $44 to initiate the insurance escrow fund are considered as one of the prepaids that add to the need for closing cash from buyers.

Regardless of the date of closing, it's best to pay taxes in November to take advantage of the maximum amount of discount the law allows for early payment. Funding escrow accounts for taxes takes this timing fact into consideration. Since the Andersons were closing in mid-July, their regular mortgage payments wouldn't start until September. Therefore, only two regular PITI payments—for September and October—would come to the lender before the tax bill arrived very early in November.

At the July closing, the lender would require the Andersons to pay a whopping ten months' worth of taxes. This would result in a full twelve months' worth of taxes being in escrow by November 1st. But wait! Remember, the seller had to fork over about six and a half months' worth of taxes, or $494.76, to the Andersons. The Andersons immediately turned over the $494.76 to the lender. This six and a half months' worth of taxes plus a fresh three and a half months' worth from Joe and Jane would make up the ten months needed. If taxes were $912 a year, a month's worth was $76. Therefore, the fresh money for the prepaid tax to be extracted from the Andersons at closing would be three and a half times $76, or $266.

Taxes Paid	Months of Taxes
By sellers at closing	6.5 into escrow (approx)
By buyers at closing	3.5 into escrow (approx)
Buyers' Sept + Oct PITI payments	2.0 into escrow
Total Accumulated	12.0 in escrow
Paid to Tax Collector in November	12.0 from escrow

Prepaid interest for their mortgages was another item with which the Andersons would have to contend. Since they were closing past mid-month on July 18th, the lenders skipped August and set their first regular mortgage payment to be due September 1st. Besides escrow payments, their mortgage payments due September 1st would include some paydown of loan principal for September. But, in fact, the bulk of their September payments would be for August's interest on the loans. Interest, unlike insurance, is paid in arrears. This means you get to use the borrowed money and *then* pay interest for having it to use.

If September's payments included interest for August, what about interest for July? Did the Andersons get to use the loans from July 18th through July 31st, interest free? Sorry, not in America or probably anywhere else for that matter. Since no mortgage payments were to be made August 1st, the lenders would make sure they got July's interest in advance at closing.

Overall, it was better for Joe and Jane not to have to make an August mortgage payment. The total potential rent, $880 a month, for both August and September would be in hand before the first mortgage payments had to be made in September. That is, the Andersons should take in $1,760 in rent before having to remit $487 in mortgage payments.

Although payments were due on the first of each month, no late penalties would be assessed so long as payments were in the hands of lenders by the 15th of the month. This allowed the current month's mortgage payments to be paid out of the current month's rent collections.

There could be other situations resulting in prorations and prepaids at a closing, but for the Andersons' first experience they had only to contend with rent as a proration and prepaids of taxes, insurance and interest. The net effect was:

Rent proration to Andersons	+ $405.04
Interest prepaid by Andersons	- 178.23
Insurance prepaid (264+44)	- 308.00
Tax prepaid by Andersons	- 266.00
Effect considering + and -	- $347.19

Jane referred to their earlier calculation of cash required for closing and found it to be $7,004, which matched the settlement statement's total for the same items. However, the closing agent, taking prorations and prepaids into consideration, would tell them to bring a cashier's check for $7,351.19 ($7,004.00 plus $347.19) to the closing. The Andersons were slightly dismayed.

"But we get a $300 security deposit from duplex side B don't we, Fred?" asked Joe excitedly.

"Yeah, but it ain't going to be your money. Remember, security deposits belong to the tenants. You hold them in trust for the tenants. Don't plan to use the tenant's money. That's called co-mingling and it's illegal."

"Oh, yeah."

Jane asked, "Should we recalculate our investment return in light of the fact that we're putting up more money than expected?"

"No, because the prorations and prepaids relate to

operating income and operating costs. Your investment is still the same."

Closing turned out to be straightforward and understandable to the Andersons thanks to the advance briefing Fred had given them. At the end, it was smiles all around. Danny the realtor took charge of a commission check for his broker to divvy up. Don Majors looked mighty relieved as he handed over all keys, tenant records and a deposit check to the new owners. Joe and Jane were new landlords and they felt good.

Danny had formulated a letter that he said he would hand deliver to the tenants of the Green Drive duplex or leave posted to their doors. In essence, the letter advised them that property title had been conveyed to the Andersons. It gave the Andersons' phone number in case of apartment problems and their address to which the rent due August 1st was to be sent. The amount of rent due plus the amount of deposit transferred, for tenant B only, was specified. This was to preclude any questions or claim by the residents that different amounts were due. Don Majors planned to send a separate certified letter to Jeremy Foss demanding the three months of past due rent be sent to him. By agreement, Joe and Jane had no obligation to try to collect the past due amount but agreed to cooperate with Majors and turn over any past due funds they received.

Jane also sent a letter to each tenant introducing herself and Joe as the new owners. Like Danny's letter it outlined what amount of rent was due August 1st, where to send it, and what number to call in case of apartment problems.

During the remainder of July the Andersons had no problem calls from their duplex tenants. On the Saturday following closing Joe took a lawnmower over to cut the lawn. Jane came along too, and trimmed bushes. They met the tenant from side B and liked her. There was no sign of Jeremy Foss, although the tenant in B said that she saw him every once in a while.

The next time they were having dinner together—the Madisons were treating as the Andersons were feeling very cash poor—the topic of their difficult tenant came up.

"What are we going to do about Jeremy Foss?" Jane asked Fred.

"It depends upon what he does regarding your August rent. He has received letters from both Danny and you. He knows what rent is supposed to be paid and how to pay it. Personally, I think he's going to test you by not paying it. But you never know. Maybe the two letters will cause him to have a complete change of heart. You've got to give him a chance to pay the rent August 1st."

On August 1st rent from tenant B arrived but nothing from Foss of unit A. Jane was all for giving him a few days to adjust to the new mailing address, but Fred told her she had to act decisively, right away.

On Thursday, August 2nd, Fred had Joe deliver a three-day notice to Foss. He told Joe that if Foss wasn't home when he hand delivered the notice, to tape it to his door across the lock so it couldn't be missed or blown away. Foss wasn't home. Joe put the notice in an envelope and taped it across the lock as instructed.

"Why didn't I just change door locks and leave a note so he would have to contact me to get a key?" Joe asked Fred later.

Fred explained: "That's illegal in this state as is the old landlord practice of completely removing door locks or, in fact, the entire door for non-payers.

"The three-day is the necessary first step in the eviction process in this state. It gives the tenant three days to pay you the rent owed or to give up possession of the premises. In other words, move out. The three days start the day after you deliver the notice and exclude weekends and any court holidays. Since you delivered the notice on a Thursday, Foss has Friday, Monday and Tuesday to pay or move out."

"What do you think he'll do?"

"Neither. I think he'll continue to test you."

Tuesday passed without the rent arriving. On his lunch hour, Joe went by unit A to see Foss who, of course, wasn't there. A glance through the nearest window, however, showed Joe that Foss hadn't moved out.

Fred said, "That's what I figured would happen. So, today I want you guys to be sure to file with the court what's known as a five-day notice. It's the next step in the legal eviction process."

"The five-day notice," Fred explained, "can be thought of as the intermediate step in the eviction process." It gives a tenant five more working days (again, exclusive of weekends or court holidays) to explain in writing to the court why he shouldn't be evicted. The tenant can request a hearing in front of a judge." Joe filed the five-day notice that day.

"Most rent-delinquent tenants pay up within the required time if they are given a three-day notice," Fred told Jane and Joe that evening. "Once in a while one will move out in the middle of the night. Some will negotiate with you for a couple more days, say, until Friday's pay is received. Going to the five-day notice is fairly rare but when a tenant gets one he usually pays right away. Of course you only settle for the rent owed plus the $110 in fees paid. My guess is that Jeremy Foss will ignore the five-day notice."

And he did. It was time for more action.

Jane returned to the clerk of the court. She was required to fill out a couple more forms. The latest forms were a means of asking a judge for a writ of possession. A judge would review the case records. He or she would want to see if the three-day looked correct, if the five-day looked correct and if the papers had been served correctly. Further, the judge would look for any response, any request for hearing or any deposit of money from the defendant. If all was in order, the judge would issue a writ of possession within a day of its request.

The writ was in essence a court order that possession of the subject dwelling be returned to the landlord. However, again a prescribed procedure had to be followed. Fred explained that many landlords get frustrated by the eviction process and think it takes weeks too long. Not so, was Fred's experience, provided you diligently complete the paperwork, file it as soon as possible and stay on top of it.

The writ could only be served by the county sheriff or a sheriff's deputy. Jane could let it be sent to the sheriff through normal inter-agency channels or she could carry it herself to the sheriff's building. Jane felt she could save one or two days by carrying it herself since the sheriff was halfway across town.

In the sheriff's building there was a warrants department. Jane presented her writ and coughed up $70 to have the notice served on Jeremy Foss. She was told a deputy would be in touch with her once notice was served. The notice, which consisted of the writ being posted to the defendant's door by a deputy, would give the occupant 24 hours to get out. Jane was starting to get excited. This was a drastic action, she told herself, but since Foss was beating them out of their rent he was actually stealing from them. She remembered Fred saying that landlords are in the business of selling time and that you can't go back and re-sell the time if it wasn't paid for in advance.

In the late morning of Monday the 21st, Deputy Markin called Jane at her work to tell her the writ had been posted at 11:00 that morning. He could meet at the duplex any time after 11:00 A.M. Tuesday to oversee the clearing of the apartment

On their way home from the mall just before 9:00 P.M. they saw that the notice had been removed. Going by the time the notice said it was posted, Jeremy Foss should realize he had only about 14 hours to get out. Would he, they wondered.

He didn't. The Andersons found out later from tenant B that Foss was around the duplex at 11:00 A.M. Tuesday. Probably he planned to argue his case and beg for more time. When no one showed up at 11:00 Foss probably figured he had survived another idle threat.

But he didn't survive. Joe arrived just before 2:00 P.M. with two teenagers as helpers. Deputy Markin arrived at one minute to 2, Jane a few moments later. Deputy Markin knocked a few times to see if anyone was home. No answer. "She's all yours," he said to Joe, "I'll stand by to keep the peace. You've got an hour."

With that Joe unlocked the door and the Andersons and their teenage helpers went to work. Everything was added helter-skelter to a curbside pile.

Everyone carried out items as fast as possible. Deputy Markin stood by nonchalantly. However, as the pile grew he had to tell several motorists who stopped that it was a private business and they weren't to touch anything while he was there.

In 35 minutes the duplex half was stripped clean. Joe changed the door locks. Then he put hand printed notices, prepared in advance, on each of the two doors. In large letters the notices said:

APARTMENT CLEARED BY COURT ORDER.
LOCKS CHANGED.
NO TRESPASSING!

Deputy Markin walked throughout the apartment once the Andersons said they were finished. "Good enough," he said. "You've got yourselves an apartment again. And I don't think you'll have any trouble with your former tenant. His type knows how this game is played. He knows he's taking on the sheriff's department and the court if he messes around with this apartment or you."

The deputy, the Andersons and their helpers left. Joe had paid $15 to each of the boys.

Neither Joe nor Jane felt bad. After all, Foss was flat out stealing from them and had stolen from Don Majors.

Jeremy Foss returned just before 6:00 P.M. at which time it was drizzling rain. He went into shock as he saw the pile of his belongings lying by the curb. However, the pile was only about one fifth its original size, and he had to drive off three scavengers who were sorting through his clothes. Everything sizeable and valuable looking had already been carried off except his stained, sopping mattress. He went to the front door, unsuccessfully tried to insert his key into the lock, then stared at the simple notice a full minute. He then looked through the front window at his empty, former living room. He shook his head and cursed loudly as he threw his key into the hedge. Finally, he walked to his flattened pile of scattered belongings and selected some items that he tossed into the back of his pickup. Five minutes later he drove off, according to watchful tenant B. More scavengers came around.

Jeremy Foss was not seen or heard from again.

The evening after the eviction, Joe and Jane returned to the empty apartment. Jane was armed with buckets, mops, sponges, cleaning agents, oven cleaner and paper towels. She immediately started in on the neglected bathroom, then moved to the kitchen. Joe brought his tools and a wall patching kit. He started repairing the four fist-size holes Foss had made in the plaster walls of the hall and bedroom.

Joe hadn't patched a wall before but it was very easy and he was proud of his results. Fred had told Joe he could do it and had run through the steps to make sure they were clear. This was the kind of thing a beginning landlord should plan to do, said Fred. Most apartment fix-up work was easy and plenty of simple how-to books were available. A landlord could save a ton of money by doing things himself or herself, Fred emphasized.

Fred had also told Joe to put the door locks he had taken off the duplex into a plastic bag for storage. Next time he needed to change locks he would re-use Foss's old locks. Fred strongly advised the Andersons to plan to change locks whenever anyone moved out even if the departing resident was clearly an honorable person. With that policy rigidly adhered to, no new tenant could successfully blame the Andersons by claiming some previous resident had entered their apartment using a retained key. Joe and Jane worked three evenings cleaning and fixing up the duplex in light of the condition in which Foss had left it. But it was satisfying work. They were working on a place they owned!

On Saturday morning, Joe laid drop cloths and papers then started painting. Fred had told them to pick one neutral, pleasing color which would be used in every room in every apartment they ever acquired. He suggested Dover White for everything. Wendy had to laugh as Fred gave his paint advice.

"When we started out," she said, "we fancied ourselves as decorators. So we insisted, when we got our very first vacancy, on painting each room a different pastel color. Each was to have very white trim, too. Also, I had Fred install curtain rods for frilly curtains I made for each window. It looked terrific to me. We were so pleased. Of course, we easily rented the apartment.

"Well, then came another vacancy. We started with our decorator-look again, although this time it started to seem like more work than necessary. When we got a second duplex and another vacancy, our enthusiasm was definitely waning, but we decorated once more. By this time Fred was starting to complain about all the different colors of paint we were accumulating. We were creating a monster!

"We learned our lessons the hard way. From that point on we've always used Dover White paint and Alabaster mini-blinds. I mean *everywhere!* It's so easy to touch up or partially repaint. And in storage all we have are one can of flat finish Dover White and one can of semi-gloss Dover White. Our lives became simplified again!"

Joe painted all day Saturday and all day Sunday as well. The Madisons dropped by Saturday afternoon with a gallon of Dover White with a ribbon on top, plus a large pizza and an assortment of cold drinks. Jane pitched in Sunday afternoon as did their in-laws the Archers and friends the Repaskys. These four brought paintbrushes of their own. They pitched in and helped for several hours. As a reward, Jane picked up two more large pizzas and some libations. They all had a good time.

Finally it was done. Fred had told them one professional painter, used to painting rentals, would have done the whole job by himself in about six hours. But there was no denying the Andersons saved paying out money. They were putting in sweat equity by doing things themselves. New landlords, without much money, needed to pay their dues through sweat, Fred declared.

Fred had told them not to bother advertising or showing the apartment until it was completely ready. A good prospect might jump at a well-done, completely ready apartment, whereas from a unit in upheaval they might walk away, never to be seen again. He told them that they would waste a lot of showings if they had to tell prospects how great it was going to be rather than showing them a finished product. And if someone was willing to rent it in a trashy condition, it was probably a renter they shouldn't take. They would have a high closing average if they only showed apartments when they were shiny and ready to move in.

On Tuesday Jane placed a three-day newspaper ad offering their apartment at $465 a month. By Thursday night the Andersons had fielded six telephoned inquiries and had shown the apartment three times. On Friday morning, one of the lookers called back and said she wanted to fill out an application. She wanted to move in the next day—September 1st—if possible.

Joe and Jane went over the application carefully once it was left. They then called the young woman's employer and the two landlords she had listed including the present one. The Andersons signed their first ever lease Friday evening August 31st. They were very pleased with their success.

The opportunity for more success came three months later when tenant B gave her 30-day notice. The Andersons took solace in Fred's admonition to think of every vacancy as an opportunity for an even better resident and higher rent.

Once unit B became vacant, Joe and Jane descended upon

it immediately. They did all of the cleaning and fix-up work themselves. Once it was fully ready, they placed a two-day ad in the newspaper and quickly received four inquiries. The second person to actually look at the unit ended up renting it. The new rent matched the rent of unit A, $465.

The Andersons were pleased. Already they had a great deal of confidence in their landlording abilities. It wasn't really all that hard to rent apartments that were clean and orderly.

Since they had increased rents by $25 a month for each side of the duplex, Jane figured they were getting a spendable cash flow of $224 a month or $2,688 a year. Dividing by their original $7,004 cash investment they were now getting a return at the rate of 38.38% per annum. If you threw in their 12-month principal paydown of $768.18 as a gain, albeit unspendable, they were enjoying a 49.35% return. Not bad for beginners!

Their duplex was worth more now since both sides were fixed up, the landscaping had been cleaned up and the rents had been increased. They asked Fred to estimate its worth now.

Fred said, "A quick revaluation of the same property over time can be done simply. However, I strongly emphasize that the method is a totally inadequate means of thoroughly analyzing a new property for a purchase decision.

"Determine the annual gross potential rent at the time you bought the duplex and divide into the purchase price. For your duplex that would be $880 times 12 to get $10,560 annual potential. Divide into the $68,000 price to get a multiple of 6.44 which is sometimes called the gross income multiplier. Stated differently you could say the duplex at time of purchase was worth 6.44 times its annual rent. That is, 6.44 times $10,560 equals about $68,000 which was the purchase price.

"What's the duplex worth now? Well, in my experience good condition duplexes and quadraplexes in good locations sell for around 6.6 times annual rent. Of course, you can find bad duplexes and quads in poor locations all the way down to 4 times annual gross. Let's use 6.6 as our multiple because your property is in at least good condition, maybe even excellent condition now. Your potential annual gross rent is $465 per unit, times two, times 12 or $11,160. Multiply gross rent by 6.6 to get a value of not less than $73,656 for your duplex. If you were trying to sell it you might put it on the market at $78,000 and I'm confident you would readily get 74 or higher.

"Don't forget there was a formal appraisal of $73,500 on the property before it was fixed up. The same appraisal company re-doing their figures and looking it over again might very well bump their valuation by three to five thousand. However, appraisers use evaluations based on income as only one of at least three valuation approaches they employ. General condition, age and comparable sales can keep their appraisals moderate. Personally, I put most weight on income when I'm considering rental property, and, as you know, I really determine what should be paid for a property by working backward from a minimum acceptable return on cash investment."

"We're sold on your approach, Fred. We've done well by it," Jane offered. "Did we ever thank you?"

"No."

"Well then, *thank you!*"

"Don't mention it. Glad to help out."

At the end of the year, the Andersons again calculated their net worth and prepared an income statement.

Joe & Jane Anderson Net Worth Statement
December 31, Wealth-Building Year #2

ASSETS:

Green Drive duplex	$ 74,000
Household furnishings	3,500
Joe's car	4,900
Jane's car	7,100
Regular checking account	800
Cash for rainy day	1,500
Cash reserves for big items	300
Cash for investing	1,900
Total Assets	$ 94,000

LIABILITIES:

Green Drive mortgage #1	$ 50,875
Green Drive mortgage #2	10,075
Anderson credit card debt	25
Loan on Joe's car	2,200
Loan on Jane's car	4,300
Total Liabilities	$ 67,475

NET WORTH (Assets – Liabilities)	$ 26,525

Once again, the Andersons could hardly believe it. Could their net worth have increased $16,725 in the 18 months since they started keeping score? They looked smugly at each other.

They entered their Green Drive duplex spendable cash flow onto their new income statement. Their 10% of gross set aside now amounted to over $5,000 a year, while at the same time their gross available for other things had gone up by over $3,000. It made them feel good to see they were finally getting somewhere. The figures didn't lie. They felt good about their future. They were firmly committed to their wealth-building program. In fact, Jane thought they could do better than their $5,074 goal and squeeze at least another $2,500 into investment funds over the next 12 months. If so, with the $1,900 they already had, they'd have at least $9,500 for another rental property in about a year.

Income Projection Statement
December 31, Wealth-Building Year #2

Joe's gross annual salary	$ 26,000
Jane's gross annual salary	22,050
Cash flow from Green Drive	2,688
Total Anderson family gross income	$ 50,738
Planned set-aside for investments ($422.82/mo.)	5,074
Gross funds available for all else	$ 45,664 /yr.

What would they buy next? The Andersons did not know. Nor did they know that they would be millionaires in less than 14 years.

In looking back over the experience of actually acquiring their first property, Joe and Jane were glad Fred had explained the closing process before they got to the closing table. Of particular value to the Andersons had been his explanations of prorations of rents, taxes, etc. and prepaid interest and escrows for taxes and insurances. Then, as new duplex owners, the Andersons had to contend with a deadbeat tenant. They lived through their first eviction with his apartment contents being put at the curb. It was also quite an experience fixing up the duplex and getting a new resident for their first vacancy.

13

First Owned Residence

For months Joe and Jane relaxed while gradually gaining more experience as landlords. There wasn't much more they could do at this stage since it was necessary to build up their investment money fund—their war chest as Joe preferred to call it. They simply didn't have enough in the chest to make another deal. They stuck to their savings plan, however, and Jane was able to salt away more than their 10% of gross minimum. Being frugal and living below their means was becoming ingrained in them. Fred said this was to be expected since they were now focusing on long-term wealth accumulation rather than immediately satisfying every whim.

Calls from their tenants came sporadically. The problems were not big and between Joe and Jane they were able to handle all of them without hiring professional tradesmen. The home handyman book Joe had was extremely helpful and easy to use. Fred and Wendy were available for advice, too, but the Andersons preferred to figure out problems and to do things on their own if they could.

Wendy told them she had enjoyed doing minor fix-ups in their early days as landlords. Sometimes, when Fred was out of town and she herself had an office job, she would show up at an apartment during her lunch hour with her little toolbox. Lots of times she astounded tenants by showing up in her business suit to repair things they had reported. Men always watched her carefully, she said, to learn how to avoid having to call her again. They seemed embarrassed they couldn't fix things themselves. Probably they simply hadn't tried. Women tenants were invariably impressed as well when Wendy would do something such as clear a clogged disposal while in her high heels.

The only thing that bothered the Andersons was that they were still renters. Their apartment was adequate, but small. However, now that they were landlords it rankled them to still be tenants. Finally, Fred suggested a solution which excited them.

"You know," he said one evening in August while they were visiting, "you guys ought to consider buying a quadraplex and living in one of the units. You could rent three apartments and more than cover your own costs of living. Besides, lenders give the best possible interest rates to owner-occupants. They know the risks of loan default are less if a person's primary residence is on the line."

The Andersons looked at each other. What an awesome notion, they thought, to live practically rent-free in one unit of a multi-family building! Why hadn't it occurred to them before?

"Well, we still don't have enough in our war chest to buy anything," declared Joe, by way of excuse or maybe explanation.

"Maybe you do," countered Fred. "For prime residences, lenders will let you in with as low as 3 or 5% down. Probably you've got that much."

"Are you a veteran, Joe?" asked Wendy. "The reason I ask is that the Department of Veterans' Affairs has a program that allows former military men and women to get a home with nothing down. Can't beat that! They're called VA loans."

"No, neither of us has been in the military Wendy, so that idea's out. I was in R.O.T.C. while in high school, but that doesn't make me a vet."

"I suggest you two start looking for a quadraplex to live in. You might not find anything suitable, but on the other hand, you might. Doesn't cost you anything to do a little lookin' around. And you might call Danny, the realtor, to see if he knows of anything."

"Hold on now," said Joe in an exasperated tone. "Aren't we starting to move a little too fast here? After all, quads run $130,000 to $170,000. I don't think we'll be able to qualify for any of them. Don't the lenders calculate what you can buy based on your income?"

"That they do, Joe, but let me tell you another benefit of buying income property. For loan qualification purposes, lenders will consider as part of your income 75% of the income of whatever rental property you're thinking about buying. For example, let's suppose you find a quad you like that has rents of $520 for each of its four apartments. You're planning to occupy one unit as your primary residence, so you expect three times $520, or $1,560 a month, rental income. Lenders would consider 75% of $1,560, or $1,170 a month, as part of your family's income. It can really help in qualifying for a loan. Let's see what your annual income is using this special fact."

Joe jotted down the following with help from the Andersons:

Annual Income if Quad Bought
as Primary Residence

Joe's annual salary	$ 26,000
Jane's annual salary	22,050
Net cash flow from Green Drive duplex	2,688
Allowed income from quad, $1,170/mo.	14,040
Total Anderson annual income	$ 64,778

"Gee, our income is really getting up there! Look at that, Joe!" exclaimed Jane.

"As a very rough rule of thumb, lenders consider tht you should be able to buy a home equaling up to three times your annual income. In this scenario you qualify for about $194,000. You should be able to get a pretty good quad for that kind of money. Fact is, it's the income *from* a quad which will enable you to buy it. Another version of the old saying about the rich getting richer, wouldn't you say?"

"I like it!" said Joe.

"Me, too!" agreed Jane.

So the Andersons began their quest for a quadraplex to live in. To their dismay, there weren't any on the market when they first started looking.

Mentor Fred told them to be patient; good quads did come on the market from time to time. However, he said, since they were buying for themselves there was no reason they couldn't be activists in their search. He explained it was necessary for a person to be licensed as a realtor to be buying, selling or leasing real estate for others for commission money. However, a person could sell, buy or lease their own property without being licensed. Therefore, they could tour around the city for quadraplexes they thought they might like, go to the courthouse to find out who owned them, then contact the owners to see if they were interested in selling. They should be sure to tell the owners they weren't realtors, didn't want a listing and weren't thinking about commissions; they simply wanted a quad to live in themselves.

This approach was yet another revelation to the Andersons. However, with a few basic instructions from Fred and the kind, patient help of two courthouse employees, they soon were finding out who owned some quads that interested them. Still, none of the owners wanted to sell. That is, not until they encountered Mr. Chen on their eleventh call.

Mr. Chen had long owned a fairly nice looking quad at 5191 Shalimar Drive. He and his wife Lucy seemed to be just a few years older than the Madisons. Their current thought as they approached retirement was to buy a powerful diesel pickup truck and a fifth-wheel type camper. The Chens were planning to live in one as they toured the 49 continental United States plus part of Canada. Jane's call had come just at the right time; they had been thinking about calling a realtor to list their quad for sale.

Mr. Chen revealed they had owned the quad for 14 years and it had been very good for them. He had been watching what came on the market for the last 6 to 8 months and had seen what prices were being asked. In addition, he had found out what several of them had actually sold for.

Ming Chen was candid with the Andersons. He told them he and his wife figured they would be putting their quad on the market at $165,000 and would hold out for at least $160,000. But they had been figuring on having to pay a realtor 6% commission so that would have meant not much more than $150,000 net for them. Of course, they had paid much less for it—$90,000—and over the years had paid their mortgage down to about $55,000. They figured they would take about $92,000 away from the closing table after paying the other expenses typical for sellers. He said if the Andersons could fit in with his numbers, they could make a deal.

Joe said they were certainly interested but would have to think about it. In the meantime they'd like a tour of the quadraplex. Mr. Chen gave them a tour of each apartment during an early lunch hour just two days later. Two units were in quite good condition, one was average and one was "tired." Overall the quad was quite acceptable to Joe and Jane. As with the Green Drive duplex there was some wood rot on the siding and at the bottoms of door jambs. Chen declared straight out he would get it all fixed.

"No problem," he told them. "I've got an excellent carpenter who I've been using for years."

Joe told Ming Chen he'd get back to him no later than Monday. That evening, the Andersons met with the Madisons and discussed everything.

Wendy pointed out that a realtor with gumption could easily have gotten the Chens' quad as a listing and made about $10,000 in commission. All it would have taken was a phone call just as the Andersons had made. Many realtors were lazy, Fred said, and most didn't like making cold calls to get listings. The field is wide open for any realtor who is a little aggressive and has gotten over fears of initial rejection. But the loss for a realtor was a gain for the Andersons. Joe and Jane beamed over their good fortune.

Jane contacted three likely lenders on Friday to see what kind of financing they would offer them as owner-occupants of a rental property. The best plan she found was a 7.25% fixed mortgage with 1.25 discount points and no origination fee. They would require at least five percent down and pay for private mortgage insurance (PMI), since the loan to value (LTV) ratio would be greater than 80%. Again, one of the lenders invited Jane in to pre-qualify for a loan. Again, Jane followed Fred's advice against pre-qualifying and declined the invitation.

The Anderson-Madison foursome got together Saturday and Fred went over the numbers Chen had given. Rents were two apartments at $510, one at $505 and one at $500 for a total of $2,025 a month. They seemed reasonable as did the cost figures Chen had given. Wendy and Fred guided the Andersons through the same analysis routines as had been done for the Green Drive duplex purchase.

Annual cash flow was calculated to be $6,917 using a 7.25% interest rate, assuming the Andersons did the management chores and took care of the yard. It turned out that a price of $161,000 would give the Andersons 18.90% return on cash investment. Since three times current annual CD rate was 18.75%, a $161,000 price would be acceptable. However, their analysis was also based on the Andersons' paying 20% as a down payment and paying $4,400 in closing costs for a grand total of $36,600. It was late in September. Jane projected that in early November they probably would have $9,700 in their war chest. Even if a closing could be achieved around mid-November, the Andersons would still be $26,900 short! Fred told them not to worry because he was mulling over a strategy for them and he was pretty sure it would work. He told them to come by at 1:30 P.M. Sunday and he would detail his plan. If they liked it they could then contact the Chens.

The next afternoon Fred told them to offer the Chens $152,000 for their quadraplex. This was about $1,500 more than Ming Chen expected net of realtor commission so he should be pleased. After they had agreement on price, the Andersons were to say that they could only make a five percent down payment, but Ming needn't worry since a lender would give them a 95% loan, because they were going to occupy one apartment as their prime residence. Once Ming Chen had accepted that, they were to ask him if he would consider holding a second mortgage for 15% of the purchase price so only an 80% primary loan was necessary. They were to point out to Ming Chen that he and his wife Lucy would save taxes if the proceeds of their sale were partly in installments rather than entirely in one lump sum of cash. Also, Fred figured Ming Chen was probably a nice enough person to help them avoid PMI, providing he could do so without harm to himself.

If they reached agreement on the second mortgage, Fred said to offer the same fixed interest rate the bank thought was fair, with a 30-year amortization but with a ten year balloon.

They were then to bring up one more thing. They were to ask the Chens if they would pay $3,200 of the Andersons' closing costs if the purchase price was raised by $3,200 to $155,200. Fred thought the Chens would almost certainly go along with this idea, especially if Mrs. Chen thought she was helping a cash-starved young couple get started. And they were cash-starved . . . without a doubt.

Fred told them they wouldn't, for the second mortgage, have to pay the one and one-quarter discount points the primary lender required. If so, the total cash the Andersons would need would be $7,760 as a 5% down payment on the $155,200 quad and about $1,050 in closing costs, with the sellers paying another $3,200. Total cash from the Andersons: $8,810 leaving about $890 in their war chest for prepaids.

Regarding a closing date, they were to request November 19th, a Monday. This would give the Andersons about $800 in prorated November rent at closing and put off their first mortgage payments until January 1st. Thus, they would be able to collect full rents for December and January before they had to make mortgage payments.

The Andersons liked Fred's strategy. They called Ming Chen and made an appointment to meet with him and his wife.

Discussions with the Chens went well. Lucy Chen said she was most impressed with what Joe and Jane were trying to do at their young ages.

"Why, we were in our late forties when we finally got up enough nerve and had saved enough money to buy our quadraplex. It's been a good thing for us. We only wish we had started in the rental business much sooner and had figured out how to buy more property. It's quite a proposal you've outlined to us and I'm impressed. As far as I'm concerned it sounds like it will work out well for us as well as for you. And we hated the thought of having to pay a realtor. We would have, of course, because we were getting ready to sell. But no realtor called us before you did. Good for you two! Mr. Anderson, I'm really very impressed that you figured all this out!"

"I try," responded Joe. Then he sheepishly turned away from Jane's quick glance.

The deal was agreed to verbally. Ming Chen said he preferred to have his personal attorney draw up the contract and handle the closing. This was fine by the Andersons. Then Ming brought out the leases and showed them that one ran until next April and one until the end of June. The initial terms of the other two leases had expired one and two years ago. Therefore two tenants, one upstairs and one down, were on a month-by-month rental basis.

"Good," commented Jane, "that means as soon as we close, we can easily give one of them a notice to vacate. We'll want to live in a downstairs unit. I hope the one we'll get is one of the nicely fixed-up apartments. One of the downstairs units looked kind of weary." She looked hopefully at Ming.

Ming Chen shuffled his leases and peered intently at one. "Sorry, Jane. You lose. The downstairs month-to-monther is Taylor in unit 2. Downstairs on the right as you face the building. His apartment was a little weary, as you say, when he moved in almost three years ago. But he was in a hurry so he said he'd take it as is."

"Figures," said Jane, shaking her head resignedly.

The Chens gave the Andersons coffee then excused themselves to talk over the proposal privately. In six minutes they reappeared and declared: "It's a deal." Everyone shook hands while smiling broadly. All felt like winners.

Ming told the Andersons to write up their offer on plain paper and bring it over to him. He would take their offer to his attorney to be put on a proper form with all the necessary legalese. Then, they would all sign it to formalize it as a contract.

And so it was done. Besides the usual special stipulations that were added to the Green Drive offer, Fred had the Andersons add the following:

It is the Buyers' intention to occupy 'Unit 2' in the building as their sole residence. Assuming Unit 2, which is presently occupied by a month-to-month tenant, is occupied at time of closing, Buyers, within five days after closing, will give occupant notice to vacate by the end of the first full month after closing.

Such a clause was necessary, Fred explained, to convince the primary lender they were sincere in their intentions to move in as owner occupants. It would assure the Andersons of getting the low interest rate available only to owner occupants.

Once the contract was signed, the Andersons had the Madisons over for a simple celebration dinner. Wendy pointed out that if the closing was November 19th, the tenant in unit 2 would be asked to leave by the end of December. Once the apartment was vacant, it would have to be fixed up for the Andersons to move in. Wendy suggested as soon as the closing occurred, Jane try to negotiate a mid-January move out from their present apartment with payment of only one-half a month's rent for January. A small landlord might very well agree providing they like you, Wendy said, and you give them plenty of notice.

Fred told them they should allow $1,200 to put in new carpet, new carpet pad and new kitchen, bathroom and laundry area vinyl. He assumed they would take care of repainting, minor repairs and cleaning. The $1,200 should be included as part of their cash investment for calculations of investment return. This was because it was an expenditure immediately necessary for the unit to be properly rented or inhabited by themselves.

Luckily, Fred continued, they would have the full December rent and rent from three of four units for January before a mortgage payment had to be made. There should be enough to cover the mortgages and the $1,200 carpet/vinyl cost. Major item expenses come up from time to time with rental properties, he reminded them, and it was important to start building a major items reserve fund. They had to be able to readily fix up any vacant apartment regardless of its condition or to replace a worn out air conditioning compressor. An apartment reserve fund was just as important as a rainy day fund for a household.

Joe and Jane agreed to get a major items reserve fund started once they were in their new apartment. Then, they opened a bottle of champagne.

Three hours later, after dinner, dessert and coffee, Fred suggested they calculate the cash-on-cash return they would enjoy, based on the deal as finalized and including the $1,200 fix-up cost. They should continue to figure on getting rent from four units even though they were occupying one. After all, most everyone has to make a mortgage or rental payment to someone for their dwelling place. The Andersons might as well consider they were paying themselves. But since they were going to be fixing up the old $500 apartment, they might as well consider that with new carpet it should rent at $525. This meant they would get $25 a month more for unit 2. Therefore, they should add 12 times $25, or $300, to the annual cash flow of $6,917 previously calculated. On the other hand, they were now going to be paying on a second mortgage amounting to 15% or $23,280 of the purchase price. Cost of servicing the second mortgage would be $158.81 a month, or $1,905.72 a year, which had to be deducted from annual cash flow. New cash flow equaled $6,917 *plus* $300 *minus* $1,906, or $5,311.

The cash investment was going to be:

Down Payment, 5% of $155,200	$ 7,760
Closing Costs Paid by Self	1,050
Immediate Fix-up Costs	1,200
Total Cash Investment	$ 10,010

Cash-on-cash return would therefore be $5,311 divided by $10,010 times 100 or 53.06%!

The Andersons, and truthfully the Madisons as well, were astounded. That was a fabulous return! It was all thanks to leverage, Fred said. They were going to be owning and moving into a property worth at least $160,000 for just $10,000. "Very, very, good," he said contentedly.

The closing took place as expected and notice to vacate by the end of December was duly given to Taylor in apartment 2.

Fred pointed out a few more things to Joe and Jane. Since they would be occupying one of the four apartments, only 75% of the rental building's operating expenses would be tax deductible. They couldn't, for example, take depreciation or the cost of repairing a broken window as deductions on their own residence. However, since even for a prime residence real estate taxes and mortgage interest are deductible, the Andersons could get tax and interest deductions for the quarter of the building they would occupy. But they would have to be itemized as deductions on income tax schedule A rather than with rental property expenses on schedule E. Between schedules A and E the total amount of taxes and mortgage interest for the Shalimar Drive quadraplex would be tax deductible.

At the end of December, the Andersons went through their ritual of calculating their net worth and preparing an income statement. Here's how they looked:

Joe & Jane Anderson Net Worth Statement
December 31, Wealth-Building Year #3

ASSETS:	
Shalimar quad (by appraisal)	$ 162,000
Green Drive duplex	75,850
Household furnishings	3,800
Joe's car	4,000
Jane's car	6,400
Regular checking account	1,100
Cash for rainy day	1,800
Household cash reserves for big items	500
Major apartment item reserves	200
Cash for investing	600
Total Assets	$ 256,250
LIABILITIES:	
Shalimar mortgage #1	$ 124,160
Shalimar mortgage #2	23,280
Green Drive mortgage #1	50,480
Green Drive mortgage #2	9,680
Anderson credit card debt	0
Loan on Joe's car	1,500
Loan on Jane's car	3,500
Total Liabilities	$ 212,600
NET WORTH (Assets – Liabilities)	$ 43,650

The net worth of the Andersons had increased over $17,000 in one year! They were delighted. They remembered they had less than $10,000 total net worth on statement #1 when they calculated it in June of wealth-building year 1 just 30 months ago.

Fred pointed out they were starting to have a number of things working for them. First, their properties would naturally increase in value as long as they were maintained and even more so if they made improvements. Second, their mortgage loans would steadily be paid off, albeit slowly. Third, with more income they would be able to save more and buy more property. Fourth, because their income was growing, they could spend more on other things to enjoy life.

Both Joe and Jane had been told by their bosses that they would be getting 5.5% salary increases effective January 1st. For the coming year their income statement looked like this:

Income Projection Statement
December 31, Wealth-Building Year #3

Joe's gross annual salary	$ 27,430
Jane's gross annual salary	23,262
Cash flow from Green Drive	2,688
Cash flow from Shalimar	5,317
Total Anderson family gross income	$ 58,697
Planned set-aside for investments ($489.14/mo.)	5,870
Gross funds available for all else	$ 52,827 /yr.

Jane figured they could live as well as they wished, at this stage, on about $46,000 a year. If so, they could add another $6,800 to their investment war chest beyond their planned $5,870. That would mean $12,670 available for another property. They were starting to roll!

What would they buy next?

They still didn't know, of course, that they would be millionaires in less than 13 years.

The Andersons reflected upon their recent experiences. As they had gained experience as duplex landlords, they had gotten the urge to buy a home for themselves. They wanted to get out of their rental apartment but really didn't want to use their investment savings. Then Fred had guided them into buying a quadraplex using a 5% down payment with the plan of moving themselves into one apartment while they rented the other three. They were pleased that their latest net worth and income statements showed increasing wealth.

14

A Different
Way to Buy

In mid-January, with the help of their old friends the Repaskys and in-laws the Archers, the Andersons moved out of their old small apartment and into the refurbished apartment #2 of their Shalimar quadraplex.

Jane felt that both couples were somewhat envious of the fact that she and Joe now had a duplex and a quadraplex. Mitzi Repasky felt they were pretty darn lucky. Brianne Archer asked if Joe had gotten a fancy new promotion to be able to afford yet another new property. Mitzi and Marty Repasky, who had their own house, started making remarks about how they wouldn't really want to live in the same building with people who might call on them to fix their toilet. Brianne then kidded Mitzi that she'd feel differently if her neighbors all started bringing her rent checks every month.

Joe and Jane took all the ribbing in good spirits. They were happy with what they were doing and appreciated the help of their old friends. Joe told them they hadn't seen anything yet and to just wait until they saw what they bought this year. That got their attention and the ribbing stopped. They started looking at Joe with a new degree of respect. Joe, however, really didn't have any idea of what they'd buy this year, if anything at all.

Months passed. There really was no problem living in the same building with their own tenants. Of course all the tenants were pleasant and Joe promptly handled any problems that came up. Wendy advised them to be as cordial as possible with their tenants but to avoid real socializing. If they got to be too buddy-buddy someone might start asking for things that would be hard to refuse. Or, they would find it hard to clamp down if anyone started doing things not permitted under their leases.

Even though all was going well, in early April Jane mentioned she wouldn't mind looking for a separate house of their own.

"But what about our rental property buying plan?" asked Joe.

"I'm not saying we should buy anything right now but Brenda Piccardi, at work, is a part-time realtor and she said she'd keep an eye open for something we might like. What about looking at a few places if Brenda comes up with anything?"

During their next social encounter with the Madisons, Jane mentioned she and Joe were starting to look around with a realtor named Brenda Piccardi.

"If that's what you both want to do, then fine," declared Fred. "My only advice is to not mislead Brenda into thinking you're more serious or anxious than you actually are. People seem to abuse realtors a whole bunch. Remember, Brenda will only be spending a lot of time with you in the hopes you'll buy something through her so she can get a commission. Nothing wrong with that but be careful about using a lot of her time and then buying a house from another realtor."

"Wouldn't Brenda get at least half the commission if we had been working with her? She uses MLS, the local realtor's Multiple Listing Service."

"Most residential realtors use their local MLS, but Brenda will still only get a commission if you buy a house she herself has listed for sale or if she is the procuring cause for you to buy anyone else's listing. More simply put, she has got to be either the selling agent or listing agent or both. She can't get commission simply by saying she knows you or that she showed you a few other properties.

"Be fair to your friend Brenda if she has been working hard for you guys. Remember, if you happen to drive by something you like that has some other realtor's sign in front, contact Brenda to get you info on it or a viewing. However, if she hasn't been doing much for you, tell her you'll be happy to look at anything she brings to your attention and work with her if you like it. But, also tell her if you find something completely on your own you won't feel obligated to tell her. That includes for-sale-by-owner sellers, which I think I told you, realtors call fisbos. If Brenda sees one you might like, leave it to her to talk to the seller and make her own arrangement about commission. Most fisbos will agree to pay any realtor who brings a buyer half the regular commission, just as if the seller was the listing agent and Brenda the selling agent. On the other hand, unless Brenda has been working really hard for you, I don't think you have any obligation to bring a fisbo you find to her attention."

"Sounds fair."

Brenda did show Jane five houses one Saturday afternoon a couple of weeks later and one more on a Sunday afternoon. None of them appealed to Jane so she didn't bother to even drive by them with Joe. Brenda didn't call again.

About a month later, the Andersons were strolling around a picturesque small lake near the heart of town. Suddenly Jane put her hand on Joe's arm to stop him. With her other hand she pointed across the street to a house almost hidden by vegetation. Nailed to a tree was a sign about 6 inches by 8 inches. It read: For Sale By Owner.

No phone number was given. Joe and Jane crossed the road and pushed through the overgrown bushes which had almost closed off travel along the curved front walk. They pressed on a small button beside the front door and could hear a light buzzer trilling away somewhere inside. In a few moments Mrs. Agnes Saunier opened the front door with a big smile.

Mrs. Saunier soon revealed she was 78 years old and loved company. Oh yes, she had decided to sell. She had gotten an appraisal because her dearly departed Neville had told her years ago that was what she should do. The appraisal, just two weeks old, said her house was worth $110,000. It was almost 1,700 square feet and was built in 1933 when they weren't building many houses. She wasn't the first occupant but had lived there for the last 41 years. With that she gave them a tour of her home which they found to be most interesting.

Jane was enthralled by the house, but Joe less so. Once they left he pointed out all the kitchen appliances would need to be replaced and the deep red carpet over most floors was threadbare in places. He also said the air conditioning was having a hard time keeping up with the late May heat. Mrs. Saunier had said the heating and air system had worked like clockwork since it was installed 22 years earlier. All I need, thought Joe, is to take over an inefficient HVAC system on its last legs. He figured it would take a fortune to fix the place up.

Jane, however, continued to be intrigued with 1461 Lakeview Drive and insisted they return three more times. Naturally, Jane told the Madisons all about the adorable house she had found. Wendy was very impressed and went over with Jane to see it. Then both of them were extolling its features and the charming Mrs. Saunier.

Jane had calculated that they should have just under $9,000 in their war chest by early September. She felt it would cost them all of that to acquire the place even using any creative financing ideas of Fred's. Then they would have an empty, worn out, overgrown house needing thousands and thousands of dollars to fix it up. Joe felt depressed. Not only that, he moaned to himself, if they put every last cent into this old place for the next year their wealth accumulating plans would come to a total halt. It would take them years to get back into the financial condition to buy another good rental.

When they got together with the Madisons, Joe was not at all pleased when Fred seemed to pick up the enthusiasm of Jane and Wendy.

"Maybe you've made a major find, Jane," he said. "A nugget. A diamond in the rough." Joe wanted to hide.

"Can you guys afford to buy it and fix it up?" Fred asked Jane. She outlined their investment money situation, plus her ideas about the house. Fred stroked his chin thoughtfully. "Let me think about this. Tomorrow, if you want, I'll give you my opinion as to what I think you should do."

The next afternoon, after church, the Andersons dropped by the Madisons. Jane especially, wanted to hear Fred's views.

Fred explained that there were many routes to achieving wealth. Also, he reminded them that he had told them before not to devote themselves to saving money and investing constantly to the exclusion of all else. A happy life was one of balance. They shouldn't deprive themselves of all pleasures as they chased after a rising net worth. But buying and fixing up this house for their own use could be both a pleasure and a wealth builder. That is, providing Joe could become as enthusiastic about it as Jane. Everyone looked at Joe.

Feeling their questioning stares, Joe felt compelled to comment. "Jane and I discussed the old place at length last night. I admit it has some great possibilities. And its location would be super for us. I'm not afraid of the work of fixing it up, but I am worried about the cost. I just don't see how we can afford to both buy it *and* fix it up. Even if we could, there's the matter of then not having any money for buying rental property for the next two or three years. Other than those concerns, I'm all for it." The others couldn't help but laugh at the way he put it.

"Joe, Joe, Joe," Fred said as he shook his head. "I'm mindful of all the things you're worried about but, providing you and Jane are both willing, I think you should do it. I think you can, financially, and come out on top wealth-wise to boot. Let me tell you how."

Wendy interrupted. "Before either of you think what Fred is going to say is simply too improbable to work, let me tell you we've done it. I know what he's going to tell you. It'll be along the lines we used to buy one of our houses many years ago. Fred's plan can work. It has for us."

"Thank you, my dear. May I proceed now?"

"By all means."

Fred described a different approach to buying. It could fit many rental property situations but was especially suited to buying a fixer-upper house to live in from a person who didn't need all the sale proceeds immediately.

The Andersons were to tell Agnes Saunier they would love to buy her house because it was so charming and had such an ideal location. They were to tell her they thought they could be as happy in it as Agnes evidently had been. Then, they were to point out the obvious need to fix-up the house, update the appliances and so forth. Agnes would have to agree. Once she did they were to reveal they didn't have enough cash money to both buy the house and fix it up. So, they wanted to propose something that could work for everyone.

First, they were to say they accepted the 110 value as per the appraisal Mrs. Saunier had obtained. Next, they were to point out that if she ended up listing it with a realtor, she would end up with only 103-something after paying typical commission. Mrs. Saunier would have to agree.

To save Mrs. Saunier the trouble of listing it, especially since they wanted to buy it, they were prepared to pay her $105,000 with no commission involved. She wouldn't have the hassle of showing it to more people and wouldn't have to worry about just getting 103-something.

Then they were to suggest that Mrs. Saunier have her own attorney draw up an agreement as follows. This would increase Mrs. Saunier's comfort level. It would eliminate any thoughts she might have that she was losing control or something was going to be pulled over her eyes. The agreement: Total price $105,000. Down payment at closing $6,000. Seller to hold a mortgage loan for the $99,000 difference. Monthly payments to seller to be based on current average fixed interest rate and 30-year amortization. However, and this was to be emphasized, the loan was to balloon on or before the 24th monthly payment.

They were to take the Sunday newspaper showing the average interest rate was currently 7.25 percent and tell Mrs. Saunier her monthly payment at this interest rate would be $675.35 and the balloon payment at the 24th month would be $97,011.82. They were to emphasize to Mrs. Saunier that she'd get $6,000 up front, $15,533 in payments over 23 months and a balloon payment of over $97,000. Stated this way—and it was all true—Mrs. Saunier would be thinking of taking in over $118,000 within a short two-year period. She should be pleased.

Fred said, "The real key to a seller's acceptance of this kind of proposal is whether or not the seller must have all of the sales proceeds at closing. My guess is that Agnes Saunier isn't going to be buying anything big and her normal living expenses are already being taken care of. The $6,000 up-front money will allow her to take a nice trip. She'll probably just salt away the monthly payments you send.

"Tell her she should have her own attorney draw up all the papers and handle the closing. You won't need another appraisal and she won't need title insurance. So closing costs will be low.

"Now," Fred continued, "as soon as you close, you get busy on the fix-up. Based on what you've told me, you'll have $2,000 or so to put into fix-up immediately and you'll be saving for investment at the true rate of over $900 a month. Put it all into fix-up. That's about another $11,000 cash in 12 months. Move into the house as soon as you've got the basics done. Live at one end while you fix up the other end.

"Buy all the new appliances you need right off the bat. If you buy them all at one store you can probably get them to finance them at a good rate; maybe even interest free for a while. Just be sure they're 100% paid off within two years. Go to city hall about your heating and air conditioning system. This city, and I think many others as well, has a rebate and financing plan if you put in new gas appliances.

"Wendy and I took advantage of the program for this house about three years ago. It's a terrific program. It can be used for rental properties as well. You guys should go for it. It'll take care of the problem of Mrs. Saunier's worn out A/C system and it's an affordable solution."

"You should plan to be outside doing the yard work. And you can do all the painting yourselves inside and out. You can make the house look like a jewel! You'll be very proud of it and you'll like living in it."

"Ah, Fred," Joe murmured feebly, "sounds pretty good but you're forgetting one thing."

"What's that?"

"When the balloon bursts in 24 months we'll be blasted apart. We won't have $97,000. Seems like we'll be broke." He looked to Jane for support.

"No, Joe, I haven't forgotten the balloon payment, and you won't end up broke. I just haven't told you, yet, about the main feature of this purchase strategy. Want me to reveal all?"

"By all means! Go ahead. I need to hear some good news."

"Good news it will be then! Here's the deal. Once your new house is all renovated it should look gorgeous inside and out. Right?"

"It definitely will, Fred," responded Jane. "It will be a jewel just like you said. We'll make sure of it."

"Okay, then. Once you've got it looking like a jewel, you call an appraiser. A different one than the one who did the appraisal Mrs. Saunier has now. The new appraiser will see a jewel in a unique, attractive, desirable setting . . . facing one of the prettiest little lakes in this city. The lawn, flowers and bushes will be in great shape. The building already has good lines but by then it'll be freshly painted. Inside everything will be immaculate. Everything will be freshly and attractively painted. All the appliances will be new. The A/C or heating will be modern, quiet and efficient. The appraiser will ask and you'll report it's all new. Guess what will happen?"

"What?"

"The appraiser will put her emphasis on condition and uniqueness of setting plus all the obviously new items. Of course, you'll tell her something like $18,000 has been poured into it ,exclusive of labor. That will be the $13,000 or so you guys put in plus the perhaps $5,000 the city finances for your heating/cooling system. Not included will be the value of your personal labor."

"Yeah, I can see the appraiser will be impressed," commented Joe, "but how does that help us?"

"Joe, I foresee an appraisal of something like $138,000. Maybe more."

"Wow!"

"So, armed with the new appraisal you go to a lender and apply for an 80% loan. You should get it easily since you'll already be living there. Eighty percent of $138,000 is $110,400. The lender will pay Agnes Saunier her $97,000 and give about $13,000 to you. Presto, Joe! You'll have a big part of your investment war chest back! How about that?"

"That's fantastic! War chest back and a fine house to live in, all fixed up. Do you really think it'll work?"

"You betcha. It worked for us as Wendy told you. You can do it!"

And they did. At first Agnes Saunier said she wasn't interested in financing anything. Joe and Jane kept talking, however, and gradually she could see some merit to what they said. Two things clinched it. One was she liked the Andersons and wanted them to have her home. She thought they would be suitable for it because they seemed to appreciate its charm.

The second clincher was her attorney. When Agnes consulted him, he saw nothing wrong with the plan. He would make sure the loan and mortgage would completely protect Agnes if the Andersons even thought of defaulting. Also, the two-year balloon was most attractive. If all remaining principal wasn't paid within 24 months she'd get her house back. And that was after she had taken in the $6,000 down payment and $15,000 or so in mortgage payments. He endorsed the plan.

Just three weeks later the closing was held. The Andersons immediately got to work on the fix-up. They did what Fred said to do concerning appliances and the heating/AC system. They did most fix-up work, including painting, themselves but did hire experts as needed. The project was finished in 15 months. They had their jewel.

It was finally time to call an appraiser and apply for a loan. The appraiser came, inspected everything, asked questions, took measurements and photos. Jane presented a list of all the items they had purchased to fix-up the house including replacement of the heating/cooling system. Total: $20,643. She emphasized to the appraiser that most labor cost was not included in the total cost since they had done most of the work themselves.

"You've been busy," he said.

About a week later the appraisal was ready for Jane to pick up during her lunch hour. It was in an envelope. She decided to wait until she and Joe were together that evening to open the envelope. The afternoon dragged on and on.

She couldn't wait until after dinner. As soon as Joe stepped in the front door, she exclaimed, "It's here! It's here! Come on, let's open it!"

Joe took the envelope and dramatically turned it this way then that. Finally he opened it, pulled out the document and skimmed over the first five pages. Then he found the sought-after number. He turned to Jane with a smile.

"$140,000."

Jane squealed with delight. Joe gave a mighty hooray! Their efforts were paying off.

Within a few days, they were in front of the lender who seemed to offer the best rates. He examined their appraisal. He had them fill out the usual application. He told them it would take a few days to get them tentative approval but he foresaw no problems providing their credit was good. "By the way," he asked, "do you want an 80 or 90% loan? The 90% loan will require PMI, of course."

"Ninety percent," said Joe.

"Right you are," nodded the loan officer. "I'll call you when I've got something to tell you. I expect it'll be good news."

It was good news. They were approved and a loan closing date was set for two weeks hence. They would have to pay for mortgagee title insurance and the loan would be subject to PMI. They could pay for the closing costs out of loan proceeds. Their loan was considered as first time financing on their home rather than a refinancing. This was because the loan from Agnes Saunier was a private, purchase-money loan. The distinction was important since at the time refinancing was limited to 80% of appraisal.

At closing, they accepted a loan for $126,000. From this amount, $97,300 was used to pay off Agnes Saunier's loan and $3,400 to pay all closing costs. At the end, the Andersons were handed a check for $25,300.

Now their investment war chest was fuller than it had ever been. In addition, they were in their own house, a house of which they were very proud.

What would they buy next?

Close to December 31st, at the end of the fifth year for which they had been keeping score, they again calculated their net worth. They used a different format for their report this time, as it was more efficient for the increasing number of entries they had to make.

They had learned from the newspaper that the value of properties in their city had gone up an average of 2.5% for each of the last two years so they increased the values of their rental properties accordingly. The principal balances of their loans continued to go down. As usual, they didn't list their trust account containing tenant security deposits since the money didn't belong to them.

Of course, they also made an income statement reflecting their anticipations for the upcoming year. During the past two years they had raised rents about 3% each year but 1% of that was lost annually to higher costs. Result: Rental income rose a net of 2% each year. They were now getting rent from others on all four quadraplex apartments since they had moved into their own house. Jane had gotten 4% salary increases in each of the last two years. Joe got a 3% salary increase one year; in the past year had been promoted to supervisor with an 11% raise.

Here's what their scorekeeping reports looked like:

Joe & Jane Anderson Net Worth Statement
December 31, Wealth-Building Year #5

ITEM	ASSET VALUE	LIABILITY		EQUITY
BANK ACCOUNTS (CASH)				
Regular checking account	1,500			1,500
Rainy day fund	2,000			2,000
Big routine items fund	700			700
Major apt. items reserve	900			900
Investment war chest	27,000			27,000
Cash Subtotal	32,100			32,100
REAL ESTATE				
Lakeview home	140,000		126,000	14,000
Shalimar quadraplex	170,000	Mrt 1	121,765	
		Mrt 2	22,800	25,435
Green Drive duplex	79,600	Mrt 1	49,575	
		Mrt 2	8,800	21,225
Real Estate Subtotal	389,600		328,940	60,660
MISCELLANEOUS				
Household furnishings	4,500			4,500
Joe's car	2,400			2,400
Jane's car	4,400		1,200	3,200
Heating/air system loan			4,700	(4,700)
Misc. Subtotal	11,300		5,900	5,400
TOTAL ASSETS	$433,000			
TOTAL LIABILITIES		$334,840		
NET WORTH (Assets - Liabilities)				$98,160

Income Statement
December 31, Wealth-Building Year #5

Joe's gross annual salary	$ 31,360
Jane's gross annual salary	25,160
Cash flow from Green Drive	2,800
Cash flow from Shalimar	5,530
Total Anderson family gross income	$ 64,850
Planned set-aside for investments ($540.42/mo.)	6,485
Gross funds available for all else	$ 58,365 /yr.

Jane declared they could easily make do with $50,000 a year, which was more than they had ever used before. If so, over the next 12 months they would have their planned 10% set aside or $6,485, plus $8,365 for a total of $14,850 fresh money for their war chest. Once again, they were amazed at how well they were doing. If Jane's frugal thinking actually worked out, they would have the present $27,000 war chest plus $14,850, or $41,850, for purchasing rental property. In their eyes, especially considering where they had come from financially, it was an absolute fortune!

Jane reflected on the fact that they didn't have any IRAs listed as assets on their net worth statement. After all, many of their friends had IRAs. On the other hand, she considered, their friends didn't have any investment properties. Jane nodded her head to herself. She'd rather have real properties, she thought, instead of IRAs. Having rental properties was a much more promising retirement program.

A very good question was: What would they buy next?

The Andersons, in thinking about their recent buying adventure, shook their heads in amazement. Owning a single-family home of their own was one of their dreams. They had found a charming old house in need of extensive fix-up but the total cost of buying and renovating seemed beyond them. Fred showed them how to buy and renovate and still end up with more cash in their investment war chest than ever before. And, they could now rent all four apartments of their quadraplex.

15

Buy Right, Buy Boldly

With their six rental apartments, their new house and regularly adding to their war chest, Joe and Jane Anderson were quite content . . . for about three months. They found managing rental property, at least their few units, wasn't hard provided you took care of problems as they arose. They followed Fred Madison's advice to attend to reported problems quickly and thoroughly.

"Things don't fix themselves," Fred said repeatedly, "so if you're going to have to fix something anyway, you might as well do it as fast as possible. Then you get brownie points for being an extra good landlord. Tenants are impressed with fast action and become content. Contented tenants stay longer so there's less turnover cost. Contented tenants will also treat you right in terms of paying the rent on time, taking care of their place and cleaning up thoroughly when they eventually move."

Fred had also drilled into them that they had to buy right. You've got to keep your eyes open, he emphasized, to find the good properties just as soon as they hit the market. Then, you must carefully analyze any properties that interest you. You must establish the maximum price you can afford to pay in order to get the minimum cash-on-cash return you consider acceptable, then try to buy at a price lower than the maximum. You've also got to use as much leverage as possible while you're in the acquisition mode of life. Finally, you've got to be as creative as possible to see special situations and to deal with them.

"If you buy right," Fred had stressed, "you'll enjoy good cash flow from the day of closing. If you aren't enjoying good cash flow from day one, you've made a buying mistake."

Fred said buying used residential rental properties was less spectacular but a much more certain road to wealth than speculating on raw land or buying commercial properties. In Fred's opinion, residential rentals were by far the best investment for a beginner starting with little capital.

"To move ahead while you're looking for a good buy," Fred said one evening, "you two ought to consider getting state real estate licenses."

Jane asked why.

"Well, having a real estate license is by no means essential to the wealth-building process, but it can be helpful. Although retired, I still maintain an active real estate broker's license. Wendy has never had one.

"In fact, for the first eight years after I bought my first duplex, I didn't have a license either. Didn't need one. As you know, you can buy, sell, trade or lease your own property or for your own account without a license. Before you start doing that stuff for others with gain to yourself, you must get a state license.

"I decided to get my license partly to sell real estate for profit to others and partly to get more in tune with what real estate was coming on the market. I was a general commercial realtor for several years before specializing in small residential rental properties, which is where my heart lies. I liked analyzing and helping others sell or buy rentals. Naturally, the fact that I owned and operated rental properties myself helped a lot since it gave me credibility with clients.

"Being a realtor allowed me to more easily remain aware of what was available, at what price and so forth. Also, I could consider whether any new listing I heard about would fit Wendy and me for our own account. Obviously 99.9% of them didn't fit. Occasionally we ran across something we thought was a winner."

"Fred, isn't there an ethical problem about the salesman or broker buying for his own account?" asked Jane.

"No, providing full disclosure is given up front to everyone involved. If I submitted an offer, the first special clause would

be something like: *It is hereby disclosed that the undersigned,*
Fred L. Madison, is an active real estate broker licensed by the State
of . . . who wishes to purchase the subject property for his own
account. The presumption is that someone active in the real
estate business has a knowledge or expertise advantage over a
layman. The disclosure put everyone—seller, other realtors
involved, attorneys and lenders—on notice. Never had any
problem with it.

"The biggest advantage to me, first as a salesman and
even more so as a broker, was it enabled special deals involving
the commission. Nothing secret mind you, all on the up and
up and in the open, but special deals nevertheless. It's for the
special deal possibilities as much as anything that I recommend
that you, or anyone building wealth through owning rental
real estate, get real estate licenses. But let me reiterate: having
a real estate license is by no means essential for becoming
wealthy through ownership of rentals."

Fred gave examples of the flexibilities and opportunities
licensed realtors enjoy. For one thing, to complete more deals,
a broker, or even a salesman with his broker's agreement and
involvement, could sell properties to cash-short buyers by
agreeing to take the commission in the form of a promissory
note.

"Suppose a $150,000 sale was about to fall apart because
the buyer is short $9,000 in cash and the seller won't hold a
second mortgage. Suppose the commission would be 6%, or
$9,000, payable at closing. In this case it may be wise for the
broker to finance the commission by accepting a promissory
note for $9,000 with maybe 7% interest from the buyer in lieu
of commission from the seller. The buyer agrees to pay the
broker, say, $180 a month for about 60 months. Or, the broker
could accept assignment from the seller of a second mortgage
and note payable by buyer. Is this risky for the broker? Somewhat. But if it's not done the deal might never be completed
and no commission is payable if there's no closing. What is the
risk in light of no deal at all? I've arranged for commission to
be paid via promissory note three times. And I've never had a
problem being paid in full."

Fred continued: "A shaky deal might be salvaged by the
listing broker agreeing to a reduction of the planned commission

with the further agreement of any other broker involved. If such a reduction was proposed by the seller who was responsible for paying the commission, the broker might get angry. A broker doesn't have to agree to reduction of the commission specified in a listing agreement. But an experienced realtor can tell when a deal is truly stalemated. When it is, it may be wise for a broker to suggest that the buyer, seller and realtors all give a little. I've been a party to such arrangements five times. I never liked it but I'm a realist. In each case, I felt, the deals would not have closed if all parties had not given up something."

But Fred was adamant that if it seemed the seller was suggesting a commission reduction just to increase the seller's net proceeds, the broker shouldn't agree to it. When the broker refuses under such circumstances, the seller quickly realizes he is about to lose the sale due to his own greed and changes his tune.

"Given a negotiated 6% commission payable by the seller, 3% usually, but it's negotiable, ends up as the listing side with the listing broker and 3% as the selling side with the selling broker. A transactional broker may end up with both sides. Usually a salesperson rather than the broker actually gets the listing and/or makes the sale. However, salesmen must work for brokers and are prohibited from getting commissions except from the brokers with whom they have placed their licenses.

"Typically a salesperson gets between 40 and 100% of the side of the transaction he or she can claim. That is, the listing side, the selling side or both sides. Whether it is 40% or closer to 100% relates to the salesperson's experience, business he or she has brought into the brokerage firm that year and previous years and the distribution plan of the particular brokerage company. Agencies that allow salespeople to retain 100% of the commissions they earn require the salespeople to pay an office services fee every month. That is, an agent may have to pay $800 to $1,500 a month for being part of the agency, to have an office and full clerical facilities and to keep all commissions he or she earns. Not the kind of place a beginning realtor should start a career! Many times it takes months for new realtors to make their first sale and commission checks aren't issued until closing, which is 30 to 90 days after a sales contract is signed."

Jane interrupted. "I'm confused. Is a realtor a broker? And is a broker on a higher level than a salesperson?"

Fred explained: "Anyone who, for money, performs almost any activity on real estate owned by someone else, must be licensed by their state to do so. The basic license is a real estate salesperson's license.

"A higher level license is a broker's license. Licensed salespersons, with enough practical experience working under the direction of a broker, can do further study and pass state exams to become real estate brokers themselves. All licensed real estate salespeople must affiliate themselves with a broker and work under the broker's general guidance.

"All real estate commissions are received by brokers who then distribute a certain percentage to other brokers or salespeople involved. By the way, the terms salesperson and realtor seem to be used interchangeably these days. The term Realtor, with a capital R, is copyrighted by the National Association of Realtors or NAR. It indicates a realtor who is a member of NAR and who adheres to their Code of Ethics and so forth."

"Okay, I get it," said Jane. "Fred, what are you?"

"I'm retired as a practical matter but I still hold an active broker's license. And I'm a member of the National Association of Realtors so I'm a Realtor with a capital R. I'm also a member of the state association of realtors."

Buying for their own account, brokers or salespeople can think of whatever commission is at stake for them as their down payment or at least part of it. In a sense, it's almost like getting the down payment, or part of it, free. Or, as Fred put it, some rental properties seemed to call to him saying: "Buy me, down payment free!"

"Here's how it works," Fred explained. "Suppose a realtor lists a rental property for sale and does all the usual things to market it. The realtor handles quite a number of inquiries and shows the property to likely prospects, but no offer is forthcoming. Suppose the list price is $165,000 and the seller has agreed to pay a 6% sales commission. At some point, the acquisition-minded salesperson might begin to see himself as the buyer. To make sure no one thinks there is a conflict of interest, if it is his listing, the agent should, in consultation with his broker, make sure that a wide variety of prospects learn about the property and have an opportunity to acquire it. Given no immediate success on the open market, the agent could talk to the seller about the agent buying the property for himself.

"Probably the seller doesn't care who buys the property providing an acceptable price is obtained. The seller is also probably well aware of the marketing efforts that have been made and roughly the price her property will ultimately fetch. The agent could then offer a price thought to be fair and likely to be acceptable to the seller, say, $160,000, providing analysis shows that price is acceptable from a buyer's standpoint, with a special stipulation in the offer. The stipulation would be that the agent's share of commission be applied as a portion of his purchase down payment. If the agent's cut was to be 65% of the total $9,600 commission to the broker, the free down payment portion would be $6,250. The salesperson's broker, of course, must be in agreement."

"Why is the $6,250 free?" Joe asked.

Fred responded: "Because if the salesperson doesn't make the deal he doesn't get any commission, whereas by agreeing to be the buyer they get $6,250. It's as if $6,250 was sitting on a table waiting to be picked up.

"In the scenario I just outlined, unless the salesperson arranges for the broker to be at the closing prepared to issue a commission check, the closing would have to go into escrow until the salesperson can deliver the commission check. This is because a salesperson cannot accept a commission check directly from the seller or closing agent; commissions are payable only to brokers. If the closing goes into escrow it still should be able to be finalized no later than the next business day."

Fred continued: "In the example I just gave, it should be clear how much better the salesperson would fare if he were a broker. If he were a broker/salesman, in business by himself for himself, he could 'find' the entire $9,600 commission on the table ready to be used toward a down payment. In addition, the broker would have the power to accept the total commission check from the closing agent then simply endorse it back to the closing agent as down payment.

"In this type of transaction, the question usually arises as to whether it is better to accept the commission and use it toward down payment or just negotiate a lower price, meaning agreeing on the price, determining the commission and lowering the price and not pay commission at all. If this is done, income tax on the commission is saved by the realtor. There are no capital gains savings to the seller, however, since if a commission is paid it is deducted from sales price as a selling expense. Since the seller's gain is based on net selling price, gain would be the same whether commission is paid or selling price is reduced."

Despite the income tax potentially payable on his earned commissions, Fred almost always chose to take the commission rather than have the price reduced by the amount of commission. He always felt it was better, overall, to have the record show the true price paid for the property. A price artificially reduced to avoid income taxes would result in a distorted price on the official records. Appraisers, other realtors and potential buyers refer to official sale records to determine comparable sales figures when evaluating properties. It's in the overall interests, with the exception of tax assessments, of property owners with selling on their minds to have their holdings evaluated high. Anyone in the real estate acquisition mode accumulating wealth should also consider himself or herself a potential seller. One never knows when an opportunity to advantageously sell or trade a property might present itself.

Following Fred's suggestion, both Andersons enrolled in real estate training courses which were a prerequisite to taking the state real estate salesperson's test for licensing. Both enjoyed the training and both passed the course finals. However, when they sat for the state exams about a month later Jane passed but Joe didn't. This brought a torrent of kidding to Joe and he suffered mightily. He also crammed and, with help from Jane, passed a re-test a month later.

Both Andersons planned to keep their day jobs but managed to place their new licenses with one of the few brokers who would take part-timers. Their commission split was to be 50% to start and could rise in stages to 80% if they brought $60,000 in gross commissions to the agency. It was their intention to each put in ten hours a week with the agency through evening and weekend work.

Two months passed. Neither Joe nor Jane had gotten a listing or sold anything. Joe was averaging about 6 hours of real estate work a week and Jane usually did 8. They could see several full-time agents in the firm doing very well. But besides being full-timers, they were seasoned agents who seemed to know everybody and everything. Finally, in her third month Jane listed two houses and in the fourth month was selling agent of a $120,000 house. Her commission share: $1,800. She hated to think about how many hours she had put in to earn the $1,800. Nevertheless, she was pleased and encouraged.

Jane felt she got some listings in part because she had mastered her fear of cold calling. She had done plenty of cold calling when searching for properties to buy for herself before becoming a licensed realtor. She also remembered how some realtors she and Joe had dealt with had let business slip through their fingers through not being aggressive enough.

Both Joe and Jane were learning a lot although Joe didn't make a sale until his fifth month. His commission was $2,300. But Joe did meet Carla Pearson and it turned out to be a most rewarding association. Carla was petite, forty-something, vivacious and energetic. She was a part-timer, too. She had six listings of her own and always seemed to have some closing pending. Her husband Ricardo, to whom Carla was devoted, was an ophthalmologist.

One Saturday, Carla off-handedly revealed to Joe that she was about to list two quadraplexes that she and her husband owned. Joe was immediately intrigued and got all the income and expense information he could from her. He then drove by both properties, one on Bigelow Street and one on Lauren Court. The quadraplexes were similar in appearance although on separate but close-by streets. Both seemed to be in good shape. Carla was listing them at $159,000 each.

Joe did an analysis the way Fred had taught him and determined a price of $156,000 would be the maximum they should pay for one of the quads to achieve a cash-on-cash return of 18.3%—three times the current CD annual rate. The Andersons' investment war chest would be about $38,000 in another month. Buying one of Carla's quads seemed a perfect use for it. They'd put up to $31,200 as 20% down, pay closing costs and have several thousand left over. After he and Jane had thoroughly discussed it and concurred, they went to the Madisons to outline their latest plan to Fred and Wendy.

The Madisons listened carefully. Fred was pleased when they showed him their analysis work. Certain expense figures needed to be double-checked and the properties needed to be inspected, but the Andersons seemed to be approaching things in a correct manner. Fred asked questions about Carla, her husband and their reasons for selling. He appeared satisfied with what Joe told him. Stroking his chin, Fred said he needed to mull things over, but if they wanted, he would give them his opinion as to what they should do the next evening. The Andersons agreed to come back.

The next evening, Fred outlined the approach he suggested they use. The Andersons were all ears.

"First," Fred said, "you should go after purchasing *both* quadraplexes, not just one." The Andersons gasped. Joe turned pale.

"I can tell you're shocked but sometimes you've got to be bold. Just hear me out. To begin with, it's probably a safe bet that the Pearsons would probably prefer to dispose of both buildings in one transaction. That being so, they'll probably give you a better deal for two quads than for one. Let's suppose they would accept $150,000 each . . . providing you buy both."

The Andersons gasped again.

Unperturbed, Fred went on. "As selling agent as well as the buyer, Joe, you could claim half the commission on each of the two sales. What would your piece of the pie be?"

Joe tapped on his pocket calculator. "Looks like $9,000 to our broker and she would pass on $4,500 to me. I'm still at the 50% commission level."

"But that boosts your war chest from $38,000 to $42,500. Therefore, think of $21,250 as available for each building. Why, I believe you bought your Shalimar quad for less than $10,000, didn't you?"

"Yes, but..."

"No yes buts about it. If you could do it then, you probably can do something like it now. Let's see. Twenty percent down on $150,000 is $30,000. Plus maybe $4,500 for closing and some for prepaids. Totals up to perhaps $36,000 per building. If you guys have available only $21,250 for each building, what has to happen?"

Silence. Then, "Someone has to give us about 15 big ones for each building!" exclaimed Jane.

"Who might do that?"

"The sellers!" yelled Joe. "Carla and Ricardo Pearson!"

"Bingo!"

Joe first approached his broker to outline the plan to roll Joe's commission into a down payment if he could pull off the deal to purchase the two properties. She was receptive to the idea and promised to attend the closing to facilitate the use of the commission toward down payment. Joe then approached Carla on the basis suggested by Fred.

Fred had correctly sized up the Pearsons' situation; while they wanted to get rid of their quads, they really weren't pressed for money. Therefore, he guessed correctly that they would be amenable to holding second mortgages, especially if they could deal with just one set of buyers.

After some verbal back and forth, the plan was committed to two formal offers since they involved distinctly different properties at different locations. Fred had the Andersons add two special clauses to the offers that otherwise mimicked offers used by the Andersons for their previous acquisitions. The first special clause was:

It is hereby disclosed that one of the buyers and one of the sellers are active real estate salespersons licensed by the state.

The above disclosed to all that neither transaction side should have a specialized knowledge advantage over the other side. The second special clause was:

This offer/contract shall not become effective unless a similar offer, bearing the same offer date, on the property known as 28 Lauren Court is also accepted and becomes a contract.

Effect of the above was to ensure neither buyer nor seller would end up with a sale/purchase contract on just one property since sale/purchase of both quadraplexes was the intent.

All went pretty much as anticipated with the Pearsons, except they countered at $153,000 per building and wanted seven-year balloons on the second mortgages instead of the ten-year balloons offered. The Andersons accepted the counteroffers.

In the end, the acquisition plan for each quad was:

Price	$ 153,000
Mortgage # 1, 8.0%	122,400
Mortgage # 2, 8.0%	15,000
Cash Down Payment	15,600
	$ 153,000

With $4,700 in closing costs for each building, the cash investment totaled $20,300 per building. After projected rent prorations were taken into account, prepaids of $500 to $600 were anticipated for each property. Prepaids were prepaid operating costs and were not considered as acquisition costs even though payable at closing.

Based on the final price and financing plan, the cash flows from the two buildings were projected at $4,980 each per year. Their original analysis had shown that 20% down on one building at a price of $156,000 would result in an 18.3% cash-on-cash return. However, the final prices were lower and obtaining second mortgages increased leverage by requiring less cash. Therefore, cash-on-cash return turned out to be $4,980 divided by $20,300 multiplied by 100, or 24.5%!

At this discovery, cheers erupted from the Andersons and Wendy until Fred shushed them with downward waves of his forearms. "Your real return is not 24.5%," he said, pausing for effect. Then he rapidly clicked new figures into his hand calculator. A moment later he turned to them and spoke.

"This is one of those cases where the property seemed to call out to you and say 'buy me, down payment free.' Well, the down payment wasn't entirely free, but in a sense a portion of it was. Joe, you'll be getting $2,250 commission for each of these buildings if you buy them and no commission if you don't. That being the case, you could think of your cash investment as being the money you had accumulated already, meaning $20,300 *less* $2,250, or $18,050 per building. You get the same $4,980 cash flow for less money removed from your investment war chest. Therefore, your cash-on-cash return can be fairly thought of as 27.59%!"

Again, cheering erupted. This time Fred himself smiled broadly and made no attempt to stifle the others.

Formal appraisals on the quads came in at $156,000 and $155,000 so the $153,000 purchase prices were good. Closing was uneventful. The Andersons knew all the routines by now so had few questions for the closing agent. It was getting to be easy.

Over the next three months two of their quad tenants moved out, one without giving notice. However, the Andersons had absorbed Fred's philosophy of thinking of vacancies as opportunities. With this frame of mind they were able to get two quite satisfactory new tenants who paid $15 and $20 a month more rent than their predecessors.

As the year ended, Joe and Jane felt really good about their progress up the wealth ladder. Their net worth statement was starting to be impressive. They couldn't help but compare their present financial condition to what it would have been, had they not acquired the discipline to live within their means and implement a program of real estate acquisitions. They counted their blessings and gave sincere thanks to their guiding forces.

They had used a 2% appreciation rate on their rental properties and 2.5% for their house. Both factors were obtained from the newspaper and were accurate enough for this purpose. They referred to loan amortization schedules provided by their closing companies to determine outstanding balances for their loans. Of course, anytime an adjustable-rate mortgage interest rate and payment changed, a new amortization schedule had to be constructed for the remaining number of years. Jane found she could easily develop one from any of the many loan programs accessible through the Internet. In addition, amortization schedules also were available through the realtor computer programs the Andersons could now use.

The fact that they were the legal owners of over $700,000 in real estate simply amazed them. Their good friends, the Repaskys and Archers, both had their own houses now, worth about $150,000 each. However, it was probable they had got into them using low down payments such as 5%. Even now it was likely that each family had less than $15,000 equity in their house. The Andersons might have been in about the same position without their wealth-building plan.

Joe & Jane Anderson Net Worth Statement
December 31, Wealth-Building Year #6

ITEM	ASSET VALUE	LIABILITY		EQUITY
BANK ACCOUNTS (CASH)				
Regular checking account	1,800			1,800
Rainy day fund	2,400			2,400
Big routine items fund	900			900
Major apt. items reserve	1,300			1,300
Investment war chest	1,600			1,600
Cash Subtotal	8,000			8,000
REAL ESTATE				
Lakeview home	143,500		124,780	18,720
Bigelow St. quadraplex	156,000	Mrt 1	122,400	
		Mrt 2	15,000	18,600
Lauren Court quadraplex	155,000	Mrt 1	122,400	
		Mrt 2	15,000	17,600
Shalimar quadraplex	173,000	Mrt 1	120,300	
		Mrt 2	22,550	30,150
Green Drive duplex	81,200	Mrt 1	49,050	
		Mrt 2	8,300	23,850
Real Estate Subtotal	708,700		599,780	108,920
MISCELLANEOUS				
Household furnishings	5,000			5,000
Joe's car	1,500			1,500
Jane's car	3,400		200	3,200
Heating/air system loan			3,500	(3,500)
Misc. Subtotal	9,900		3,700	6,200
TOTAL ASSETS	$726,600			
TOTAL LIABILITIES			$603,480	
NET WORTH (Assets - Liabilities)				$123,120

Fred emphasized how important it was to own as much real estate as you can even though you may have little equity in any one property. "Rental real estate may have appreciated just 2% in the last year but some years it goes up 5, 7 or 10%. If you own $700,000 worth of property and there's a general rise of real estate values of 7%, your net worth goes up $49,000 from appreciation alone. Regular monthly mortgage payments currently decrease your loan balances 2 to 2.5% a year and will decrease them at a much higher percentage as the loans mature. But even a 2% paydown adds $12,000 more equity to your net worth for a total of $61,000. Just think of that! And if you didn't own any real estate, your net worth may not have increased at all."

Income Projection Statement
December 31, Wealth-Building Year #6

Joe's gross annual salary	$ 32,300
Forecast of Joe's commissions	5,000
Jane's gross annual salary	26,160
Forecast of Jane's commisions	5,000
Cash flow from Green Dr.	2,900
Cash flow from Shalimar	5,700
Cash flow from Bigelow St.	4,980
Cash flow from Lauren Ct.	4,980
Total Anderson family gross income	$ 87,020
Budgeted for normal living expense	56,000
Fresh funds available for investments	$ 31,020/yr

Through becoming part-time realtors, acquiring two more quads, raising rents and receiving small salary increases, the Andersons expected to increase their income by over $22,000 above the previous year! They were amazed. This amount of increase was like adding another wage earner to their family! For the previous year they had exceeded their income projections by $8,600 thanks to Jane's single $1,800 commission and Joe's $2,300 and $4,500 commissions.

These chunks, unexpected at the start of the year, had enabled them to add more funds to their reserve accounts as well as helped them buy the new quads. It also was causing them to pay more income taxes.

Both Andersons were quite busy managing and maintaining their home and 14 rental units and working part-time jobs in addition to their regular full-time jobs. Busy or not, they were very happy with how everything was going for them. Neither of them had ever been lazy, so having lots to do didn't faze them. Indeed, they were pleased with the fact that they could see a direct payoff for their efforts. Their lifestyles were evolving. They were eating out more, of course, and spending more on clothes and dry-cleaning. They felt more need to keep up appearances, considering potential new clients they were regularly meeting as realtors.

While being frugal and living well below their means was totally ingrained within their psyches, Jane concluded they needed $56,000 for living expenses for the upcoming year. The big jump was primarily caused by their decision to get new cars. Their present vehicles were seven and nine years old. They looked fine and ran smoothly but were getting dated. As part-time realtors, they felt they needed to carry clients around in something fresher.

Providing their forecasts proved correct, they would have $31,000 for real estate investments by the end of the coming year. Since they were easily putting aside so much of their gross income, they decided to discontinue their practice of formally taking 10% off the top for investments.

It was a good thing all was going well; soon after the new year started, Jane discovered she was expecting their first child. They still didn't know they would be millionaires within nine years. However, they were now realtors and had learned to be bold buyers.

16

Cars, Depreciation and More Income

Jane was excited as she told Wendy about the new SUV they had almost decided to buy. "It's perfect," she said. "It has a high rating in *Consumer Reports*, but it's not one of those big things that makes you hitch up your skirt in order to climb in. This little sweetie is easy to get in, like a car, but it's still higher than a car and it's got great visibility all around. Why, I don't think a lot of people see me in my little car anymore."

"So, are you going to get it or not?"

"Yes! I mean no! I mean probably! We aren't sure whether to lease it or buy it and if we buy it, what's the best way to finance it. Finally, we decided to hold off and ask Fred if he has any opinions one way or another."

"You mean *my* Fred? Of course, he'll have an opinion! That man has an opinion on everything under the sun. Have you ever known him to be neutral or indifferent? He'll be home any minute and you and Joe can ask him then."

After Fred got home he heard Joe and Jane's questions and then said, "It's a no-brainer really. You two are in the process of becoming wealthy. You're doing it by buying rental property and getting high cash-on-cash returns. Doesn't that tell you a few things?"

"It should occur to you that if you can make money renting something, it must be a good thing to own. You own apartments because you get a good return leasing them. So always plan to buy to own . . . if you can . . . it's part of the wealth-building process."

"You guys should buy, not lease, and if you can, keep your cars well beyond the time they're paid-off. It's a nice feeling not to have car payments of any sort."

"Ah hah!" exclaimed Joe. "You said paid off so you must think we should finance the car and make payments rather than paying cash for it. Oh, what am I saying? We don't have the money to pay cash anyway! Plus, I need a new vehicle, too."

"Even if you had the money, Joe, you shouldn't pay cash for it. That should be a no-brainer, too, considering your success in buying real estate."

"Whaddayamean?"

"Well, undoubtedly you can finance Jane's new car for anything from a dealer's promotional 2% interest through maybe 11% from the typical bank. But just think about the kind of return you've been getting from your real estate buys. Seems to me you've never closed on anything producing less than 24% cash-on-cash return. Why would you waste cash, on which you can get a 24% or more return, just to avoid paying maybe 8% interest on a car loan? A no-brainer. Save as much cash as possible to devote to buying more real estate."

Fred went on: "One last comment. It's about the kind of vehicles you should buy. I realize you both want to get nice looking cars, but don't get flashy luxury cars to drive to your apartments. It's entirely the wrong image. You can't properly rent moderately priced apartments and convince tenants of the absolute need for rent increases when you drive around looking like Mr. or Mrs. Fat Cat. How can you convince tardy tenants it's essential for your business that they pay on time if they see you all the time in a prestige car? They'll conclude that 'there's something wrong with this picture.' And there would be. Whatever you drive to your apartments should be a non-luxury, bread-and-butter vehicle. It can be clean, it can be shiny, it can be new, but it can't obviously be top-of-the-line expensive."

Subsequently, the Andersons traded Jane's car in on the brand new SUV she wanted. The SUV's value when picked up was $21,500. Financed after trade-in was $16,000 at 9% for 5 years.

Joe bought himself a two-year-old mini-van that seemed to be in excellent shape and a good vehicle for carrying his tools, supplies and lawnmower. Drive away value was $17,000. Financed after trade-in was $15,000 at 9% for four years.

In March, as the Andersons were amassing their records preparatory to doing their income taxes, Joe quietly telephoned Fred and asked him to go over the matter of depreciation with him. "Jane seems to understand it pretty well," Joe told Fred, "and she does our tax returns. But how about you going over depreciation sometime with me . . . without telling Jane."

Fred agreed.

One evening, while Jane was showing houses to a prospect, Fred and Joe met at a coffee shop to discuss depreciation. Not surprisingly, Fred had a notepad and his calculator. Joe had been asked to bring the closing statements and appraisals of their rental properties.

Over coffee, Fred explained that the availability of depreciation was a fantastic advantage that improved real estate had over many other investments. There was nothing like it for stocks, coins, commodities or even unimproved land, meaning raw land without anything built on it. The only thing close was the depletion allowance available to owners of such things as oil fields and mines.

Fred hastened to point out that while he wasn't an accountant or a lawyer, he knew enough about the subject to give Joe a general overview. The general theory, he explained, was that the functional life of some things was limited and, as time passed, the item became less valuable. An oil field originally containing 20 million barrels is clearly less valuable six years later, after two million barrels a year has been pumped out of it. Similarly, if it is decided a new building will last thirty years, it is functionally less valuable after it has endured 18 years of use.

The powers that be decreed that the Internal Revenue Service (IRS) should give depreciation allowances on real estate improvements and any equipment used in the production of income. There are charts, tables, rules and conventions to follow but in essence, residential real estate improvements are depreciated over a 27.5-year period. This means a depreciation allowance of 1/27.5 of the original acquisition cost of the improvements can be taken each year. Forgetting the partial year of acquisition to simplify understanding, it works out to 3.636% of the cost of the improvements for each of 27.5 full calendar years. The allowance is taken on your income tax return as an expense deductible from rental income. You pay tax on net rental income, which means total rents you collect less any expenses the IRS considers deductible, including depreciation.

While about any expense you incur to operate a rental property is deductible, all of them except depreciation involve outlay of money that tax year. For example, if you spend $22 to buy a new lock for one of your apartments, you can take $22 as a tax deductible hard expense on your tax return. It's considered a hard expense since it's a dollar out for a dollar deduction. On the other hand, if you are able to claim a $5,000 depreciation allowance on a rental, you didn't put out one dime that year. Some call it a paper expense because you do not pay out dollars each year to get it. And you can claim the $5,000 paper expense each year for 27.5 years!

Fred explained: "As a dramatic example, suppose you have a quadraplex generating $500 a month rent per apartment, or $2,000 a month for the building. That's $24,000 a year. If you had $19,000 in hard, deductible expenses you would have a cash flow of $5,000 left over on which the IRS would figure you should pay income tax. Then, just before you send in your tax return you remember to claim your allowed $5,000 depreciation expense. The depreciation deduction offsets your cash flow. The IRS is foiled! By their own rules you now have zero taxable income for that property. Fact is, you actually had $5,000 cash flow to spend on a nice vacation, but it was tax sheltered by the depreciation. Hooray!

"Taking my example a step further, if you had $21,000 in hard expenses your cash flow would have been $3,000. In this case your $5,000 depreciation would first totally shelter the $3,000 cash flow from this building and also shelter $2,000 cash flow from another building.

"Only depreciation provides true tax sheltering, although some people loosely consider any tax deductible expense as providing shelter. A hard expense reduces net taxable income, but only depreciation shelters you or protects you from having to pay tax on otherwise taxable cash flow."

Fred then philosophized on depreciation as being an accounting technique and a nice tax-reducing procedure but usually having no real relationship to the physical life of the real estate improvements to which it's applied. Supposedly, it means a residential rental building will last 27.5 years, but that's nonsense. A building will last as long as it's properly maintained, which could be for hundreds of years as is common in Europe. Not only that, the depreciation write-off period is arbitrarily changed from time to time. Fred said he had to use a 40-year period for his earliest rentals. That meant 2.5% of cost per year on a straight-line or equal amount per year basis. Then, he recalled, the depreciation period dropped to 15 years, was raised to 18 years and then to 19 years. No rhyme or reason to it that he could ascertain except it related to how much of a tax break federal Congresses over the years wanted to give to rental property owners. He wasn't complaining since it was such a nice benefit, but it was a most peculiar one.

Joe wanted to know how much deprecation could be claimed for each of their properties. He opened up his records on the Green Drive duplex. Fred examined the appraisal and closing statements.

"Price of the Green Drive duplex," Fred said while jotting figures on a notepad, "was $68,000 and $7,004 was paid as closing costs for a total acquisition cost of $75,004. The appraisal indicated that of the $73,500 total appraised property value, the land was considered to be worth $11,000. This meant the improvements were worth $62,500 or 85% of the total appraised value. Applying this percentage to the actual total acquisition cost of $75,004 meant $63,753 was spent to acquire the improvements. Applying the 85% to the total including closing costs recognizes that a portion of closing costs were for land and a portion were for improvements. Multiplying $63,753 by 3.636 indicated $2,318 could be claimed as a depreciation expense for each of the next 27.5 full years."

Fred's jotted notes were:

Property cost	$68,000
Closing costs, etc.	7,004
Total acquisition costs	$75,004

Appraisal indicates land value	15%
Appraisal indicates improvements	85%

Therefore total depreciable value of
   improvements is 85% of $75,004=$63,753

Depreciate residential rentals over 27.5 years
   which equals 3.636% per full year

Depreciation/year = 3.636% of $63,773=$2,318

Fred again stressed to Joe that he wasn't an accountant and had simplified the calculations to make them easily understood. He suggested that Joe or Jane consult a CPA or study a tax manual to learn the fine points. Then, they should establish a depreciation record for each property and keep it for all time. The record would show how the amount to be depreciated was determined, how much depreciation was taken each year and the value of improvements remaining to be depreciated. Fred told Joe he had set up and maintained his own depreciation records manually and that it was easy to do so. Once set up they only needed to be referred to and updated at tax time or whenever they were going to sell or trade a property.

Fred and Joe then looked at the records for the other rental properties the Andersons owned and calculated the approximate full-year depreciation for each. They made a list:

DEPRECIATION ALLOWANCES
(FULL YEAR)

Green Dr. Duplex	$ 2,318
Shalimar Quad	4,772
Bigelow Quad	4,931
Lauren Quad	4,931
Total	$16,952

Fred pointed out that the Shalimar depreciation amount applied to when all four units were rentals. During the time the Andersons lived in one unit they could not claim depreciation for the entire building; only of the three-quarters rented to others.

Joe asked about their Lakeview house. No depreciation can be taken on your personal residence was the answer, only on rental properties.

Joe admitted that when Jane had talked about depreciation each year as she worked on their tax returns he hadn't paid much attention. Now that he understood the basics he could see what a great thing it was for them.

"Absolutely," said Fred. "For this tax year you'll have almost $17,000 in tax-free cash flow! How much that's worth really depends upon what your marginal tax rate is, assuming you didn't have the depreciation. For example, if you exclude depreciation, you might find the income tax on your taxable income amounts to 22%. If so, you could consider depreciation was saving you 22% of $17,000, or $3,740, in income taxes. Using the highest tax rate that applies to your last dollar earned—sometimes called your marginal tax rate—is a simple approach that gives you a quick approximate answer. However, putting in depreciation as an expense may cause the resultant lower income to drop to a lower tax rate so the savings calculation is a little more complicated. The most accurate way of figuring the true tax savings, if your income tax is done on a computer, is to calculate what taxes will be considering depreciation, then temporarily take depreciation out. The computer will spin its wheels and come up with a new, higher tax due figure that will amaze you. You'll really understand the benefit of depreciation then.

"You know, Joe, I've always advocated buying rental property on the basis of its merits as a business proposition without regard to its tax savings aspects. Sure, I'm well aware of the tax savings aspects but prefer to think of them as gravy or icing on the cake. Rental properties used to be bought by some wealthy people with tax sheltering as a primary rationale for buying. That's not done so much anymore because of changes in IRS regulations. I've preferred to evaluate properties by determining if the deal made good business sense, putting tax aspects aside. That's what I recommend for you and anyone else. Buy with your decision based solely on the business sense of the deal ignoring tax aspects. If you do decide to buy, only then should you calculate the bonus you'll get through tax savings."

Joe spoke up. "Well, that's what we've been doing so far anyway 'cause I didn't fully understand the benefits of depreciation. Guess we'll continue buying the same way even with my newfound knowledge."

About two weeks later over iced tea around the Andersons' patio table, Jane thanked Fred for giving Joe a course on depreciation. "I thought I'd answered all of Joe's depreciation questions as they came up in the past, but I guess I didn't get through. He seems to understand it pretty well now, so thanks."

Fred tipped his head in acknowledgement.

"But," she continued. "I've got a couple of questions of my own that perhaps you can answer. Would you mind?"

"Not at all. I'll try."

"I think these are related but a couple of things confuse me. First, when I compare the rental income and expense I enter on income tax schedule E to what we had figured would be the cash flow for a building, we always seem to have more profit than predicted. That's after taking into consideration the understandable differences between actual and estimated costs. Second, when I look at the total income line on our 1040 tax return, it's always noticeably lower than the money I know we've actually had during the year. Any ideas?" She looked at Fred hopefully.

"Yeah, I do. Fact is you've got more income than you think you do or at least more than your reports directly indicate. Why don't you grab the notes and figures I did when we were analyzing the Green Drive duplex you bought years ago?"

Jane went to the study where she and Joe kept all of their real estate records. She returned a minute later victoriously holding aloft a folder labeled "Green Dr. Duplex."

Fred riffled through the pages for a second before pulling out a sheet with numbers scratched on it. "Here's what I was looking for. The third trial in your analysis of income and expenses. Let me jot down key elements from this chart and then I think I can tell you where your confusion lies." He listed:

Net Effective Income	$10,032
Total Operating Expenses	2,100
Net Operating Income	7,932
Debt Service	5,844
Cash Flow	$ 2,088

"As I understand it, you're puzzled why your income on your tax form usually beats the predicted cash flow. Is that it?"

"Basically."

"Well, Jane, I think it's probably very simple and it's something we discussed at the time you were thinking about buying the duplex. What I just wrote down as debt service includes both interest and principal. On the other hand you only enter the interest portion as a deductible expense on your tax return. You know, the figure on the little slip your lender sends you each January. The notes here say $768 of your first full year of debt service was loan principal paydown. Principal paydown is a benefit in addition to cash flow. Add the two together and you'll see your true gain was almost $2,860. Cash flow always understates true gain since principal paydown forms a portion of the debt service that is subtracted from operating profit to calculate cash flow.

"Not only that, the amount of interest you pay on an amortizing loan goes down each year whereas principal paydown goes up. I would guess you paid off at least $1,000 in principal on your duplex this past year. So, you would seem to have made about $1,000 more than your old cash flow calculation shows.

"You're still in your first year on the latest quads you bought, but I'll bet on your other rentals you're paying the principal down $2,500 to $3,000 a year. It's more income than you thought you were making! Course you don't have it in your pocket to spend since you already paid it to your lenders, but it was real income. That is, unless your lenders allow you to pay them imaginary dollars!" They all laughed.

"Remember way back when I was telling you how to analyze a property? I told you to determine the cash return to you considering the cash you had to spend to acquire the property. You were to base your buy or not buy decision on that return. At the same time, I said you actually got a bonus return when you considered that in addition to getting cash flow that could be spent, you were also gaining from paying down mortgage principal which couldn't be spent. Paying down principal decreases your debt and increases your equity in the property, but equity is not released until you sell or trade the property. Get it?"

"We do."

"Good. The total income figure on your 1040 tax return includes money you actually used to pay down mortgages. Understand?"

"Yes, sir."

"Jane, regarding your other question, I believe all you have to do to get the total amount of money you think you had use of is to add the total depreciation you took for the year to your 1040 tax return total income figure. Anyone who claims depreciation has to do that if they want to know the true total money amount they've had in their hands for the year. Total depreciation you took for the year shows on the first page of your income tax schedule E.

"As an example, at the end of last year before the effect of your two latest quads kicked in, I think you told us you figured you would have a combined total income of about $65,000."

"Pretty close. Our total income was a shade under $67,000."

"Okay. To get your true income you have to add on the depreciation you took for the year. Joe and I worked on this just a couple of weeks ago. Seems to me that for Green Drive and Shalimar you would have taken about $7,000 in depreciation. Add $7,000 to your $67,000 and your true income had to be something like $74,000. Does that jibe with the figure you had in mind?"

"Actually, I think it does," replied Jane hesitantly. "I didn't have a specific figure in mind but it seemed to me my total income was at least $5,000 too low. Fred, I think you're right. I didn't consider depreciation."

"Again, you guys had more income than you thought you had. Don't forget the nature of depreciation. You can deduct it as an expense and thereby lower taxable income, but it's a paper expense. That means an expense for which you didn't have to pay out dollars during the tax year. You actually kept the $7,000 in your pocket even though you wrote it down as a tax deductible expense. Got it?"

"We do."

"Yup."

The year progressed. Jane did better at her part-time real estate than she expected and earned $9,400 in commissions. Joe did better than expected, too, but only slightly at $6,100.

The Andersons' first child, Jennifer, arrived in late August. Life would never be the same for them! Although Joe and Jane had decided to start a family after they got their first home in order, baby Jennifer had a different idea; she decided to wait a while before she entered the world. They were totally happy with their new addition, although both were busier than they thought they could be. Babies, of course, demand a lot of attention. Jane was away from her salaried job for a total of seven weeks to have her baby and care for her.

Jane then started using a day care center in order to return to her regular full-time job, but, as often happens, she felt uneasy about her baby being away at so young an age. She quit her job effective November 15th. She would become somewhat of a stay-at-home mother. She felt somehow she could become more active in her real estate selling activities to partially make up for the salary she would no longer have. Wendy reminded her of the need for balance in their lives. You had to be happy overall, she told them, and developing a family was one of life's primary satisfactions. Building wealth could go on the back burner for a time.

The Andersons acquired no new properties during calendar year 7 but they had purchased upgraded vehicles and had a new baby. Plus, a new year was coming and their war chest was growing. And, as Fred reminded them, their net worth was growing even without new acquisitions due to property appreciation and loan principal paydown through monthly mortgage payments. They felt good, too, having learned about depreciation in more detail and how it shelters income from taxes.

17

Trade, Don't Sell, to Move Ahead

Since she was no longer engaged in an out-of-the-house, full-time job, Jane had more time to check on what was for sale. She watched the newspaper and checked offerings through the local Board of Realtors' Multiple Listing Service (MLS). As a part-time realtor she had access to the MLS through their home computer. After driving by a few properties that she rejected because of location or immediate surroundings, she found a quadraplex she liked.

It was on Hall Street within half a mile of their quadraplexes on Bigelow Street and Lauren Court. It was listed by a realtor from another agency at $167,000. Joe and Jane worked their usual analysis and determined it was worth up to $163,000. At that price, with 20% cash down, $5,000 in closing costs and financing at 8.25%, they would get a return of 18.9% cash-on-cash return. This was the minimum return acceptable to them; three times the current annual CD rate. Of course they would try to buy the property for a lower price and on better terms to boost their return above 18.9 percent.

A more immediate problem was cash. Twenty percent of $163,000 was $32,600 and the estimated $5,000 closing costs increased total cash needed to $37,600. Their investment war chest had grown to $30,000 during the last year, which was a little less than they had anticipated. This year, since Jane did not have a salaried job, they had budgeted a lot less fresh money to go into the chest each month, just $600. If they closed in early March the Andersons might have as much as $31,200. Still not enough, but close, if they got commission as realtor/buyers.

They couldn't delay long if they wanted this quad. It was a pretty active market. Anything in decent shape, in a decent location and priced reasonably was under contract within three weeks of going on the market. No one was going to wait for Joe and Jane to save the funds they were short.

Joe immediately thought about the usual seller-held second mortgage but Jane said it wasn't in the cards. She had discussed the idea briefly with the other realtor, Juan Cortez, but he said it was a divorce situation. The couple's assets had to be divided; each wanted half of the quad proceeds in cash.

It seemed so unfortunate. Here was a nice property they'd like to buy. They had more money in their investment war chest than they ever thought they'd have. Yet, it wasn't enough and time was running out. Perhaps Fred would have some idea of what to do. They set up a Friday evening get-together with the Madisons.

Wendy and Fred were happy to hear about their hopes of buying another rental property. A whole year without buying something new and the arrival of the delightful baby Jennifer had worried Fred a little. He was concerned that the Andersons, once off the wealth-building track, might never get back on. This talk about another quad pleased him for their sake.

Joe and Jane showed the Madisons the analysis they had made and explained their thinking. Both Wendy and Fred thought the approach was sound. Too bad they didn't have enough cash to proceed, thought Wendy. Fred went silent then started asking questions about the Andersons' existing rental properties, the three quadraplexes and one duplex.

Finally, after another bout of silence and some stroking of his chin, Fred said: "I have an idea as to what you should do, but want to mull it over. If you want my advice, perhaps we can get together tomorrow."

This sounded hopeful to the Andersons so a gathering at 10 A.M. Saturday was arranged. Fred asked them to bring the records of their rental properties.

As soon as the Andersons arrived Saturday, Wendy asked them to take Fred and her on a drive to see the Hall Street quad from the outside. "It'll give us a better idea of what has got you excited," she declared. "It's always good to know first-hand what someone is talking about."

"I'm surprised," said a startled Joe. "Fred hasn't wanted to take pre-closing looks at our prospective properties before."

Wendy responded. "We've always been interested in your prospects, Joe, you know that. But Fred never wanted you to rely on our opinions for your final decisions, other than guiding you through the paperwork analysis. We wanted you to physically size up properties yourselves. Now that you've acquired several properties we don't mind having an early look and giving you an opinion, if you want one."

The foursome drove slowly by the Hall Street quad a couple of times and around the neighboring blocks. Then, they stopped in front of the building, got out, and slowly walked all around the outside.

Back in the car Fred announced the property looked pretty good, at least from the outside. "Now, once I have a cup of coffee in front of me I'll tell you what I think you should do."

Soon they all had coffee in front of them. Fred didn't hesitate any longer. "You need to get rid of your duplex. You know, the one on Green Drive."

The Andersons recoiled. Once again, Fred had shocked them. They hadn't expected to get rid of anything for a long, long time. Why, wasn't the whole idea to buy and hold? To accumulate?

"Well, yes it is," agreed Fred. "At least the whole idea is to accumulate wealth. There's nothing to say you have to own particular properties forever. Wealth-building is a process. You've got to regularly examine and assess your situation and make changes if it's to your advantage."

"How can it be to our advantage to sell our duplex at this stage?" questioned Jane. "Wouldn't we have to pay a bunch of capital gains taxes? That's all we need—more expense!"

"Wait, wait, wait," responded Fred as he waved his arms back and forth in front of him like an umpire. "I don't want you to pay taxes, and I don't want you to *sell* your duplex. I want you to *trade* it!"

He asked Joe and Jane how much they thought they could get if they did sell the duplex and how much they owed. Joe made some calculations while Jane looked up the amortization schedules on their two Green Drive loans. They concluded they could sell the duplex for about $84,000 and they would owe about $56,100 once they had made February's payments. Their equity, meaning the difference between market value and amount owed, was thus $84,000 minus $56,100, or $27,900.

Fred pointed out that selling would cost them up to 20% tax on their capital gain.

Jane punched her calculator for a few moments then said: "We paid $68,000 for it, so if we sell for $84,000 we've got a $16,000 gain. Twenty percent tax on that would mean $3,200 out the window. Sound right?"

"Not exactly!" exclaimed Fred.

Fred then explained that gain on a sale in the eyes of the IRS was basically the difference between adjusted sales amount and the property's depreciated value, not purchase price. Further, it had nothing to do with what they owed on the property. He had them consult their depreciation records for the duplex. It turned out they had taken five full years of depreciation at $2,318 a year plus a half year's worth for the partial first year. Improvements not yet depreciated, therefore, stood at about $51,000. Fred told them to add to that the value of land which never was depreciated. Land value was originally set at $12,250, the records showed. This meant the depreciated tax basis for the duplex, at present, was $51,000 plus $12,250, or $63,250.

Total gain in the eyes of the IRS would be $84,000 minus $63,250, or $20,750. In the case of a sale, up to 20%, or $4,150 ,would have to be paid in taxes. It would be due along with income taxes for the year of the sale.

"However, it's not as simple as I've just described and don't take the number I just came up with as accurate. You really must consider the particular year you bought the property and specifically how much of the apparent gain is due to the depreciation taken. That portion is subject to what the IRS calls recapture. It's not that hard to figure out, but it can be a bit tricky. I would recommend that if you have any questions, you ask your CPA about it. Just understand that the amount of tax to be paid if you do an outright sale is plenty, so you ought to avoid becoming immediately liable for it."

Then Fred explained that all capital gains tax could be

deferred if a trade, rather than an outright sale, was arranged. That being so, they could apply their entire equity in the duplex toward the acquisition of the quad. And the trade—also called an exchange—would be tax-free. Their equity had already been calculated as $27,900 and this could all be applied as down payment towards the quad.

"Sounds terrific," said Joe glumly, "but it'll never work. Jane already found out the quad's being sold because of a divorce. We'll never talk them into taking our duplex as a trade."

"Joe, Joe, Joe," said Fred softly and with a smile, "I don't expect the quad owners to want a duplex. What we need to arrange for here is a three-way trade. You find a buyer for your duplex, and we can arrange a three-way trade easily. I'll tell you how."

And he did. The Andersons subsequently implemented his recommendations.

First they negotiated a deal for the quadraplex. No sense trying to dispose of the duplex until the quad was tied up. A price of $162,000 was agreed to, slightly under the $163,000 maximum the analysis said they should pay. Two additional special stipulations had been put into the offer that had evolved as the Andersons' standard. Their standard offer contained all the applicable stipulations Fred had suggested for their previous deals.

The first of the new special stipulations was:

Closing of this contract is contingent upon it being part of a simultaneous exchange of properties involving another property presently owned by the buyers. The buyers shall have 30 days from date of this contract in which to get their other property under suitable contract to a third party.

This clause was to disclose to the quad sellers the intention to link the two transactions—disposal of the duplex and acquisition of the quad. This was important because the proceeds of the duplex were essential to acquiring the quad. If the duplex wasn't disposed of, and, in fact, disposed of first, the Andersons wouldn't have the wherewithal to close on the quad.

The 30-day stipulation was to put a reasonable limit on how long the sellers might have to wait. Without a short limit, the sellers probably wouldn't accept the offer.

Second of the new special stipulations was:

IRC SECTION 1031 EXCHANGE. Seller acknowledges that buyer wishes to complete the acquisition of the property hereunder as part of a tax-deferred exchange of real property pursuant to Section 1031 of the Internal Revenue Code (IRC). Seller shall cooperate with buyer by ....

...and seller shall not be obligated to incur any costs ...

The primary purpose of this stipulation was to inform the IRS, should it ever audit the Andersons' returns and this transaction, that an exchange was always contemplated. You cannot close, or be ready to close, a transaction and then decide to make it a trade. The IRS would likely frown at such a last minute decision. They would likely determine your motive was to simply avoid paying taxes right away rather than the higher motive of trading like-kind real properties to further your rental property career. The end result: the IRS could declare the transaction wasn't a true exchange. Disastrous finale: You end up having to pay full capital gains tax after you've spent all your money. And as you know, the IRS seems to have methods of making you pay even when you say you have no money. It's best to keep straight with the IRS. It has clout.

The secondary purpose was to inform the quad sellers that while they were expected to cooperate with certain aspects of the exchange, such as signing certain required documents, it wouldn't cost them anything. The exchange is for the buyers' benefit so it's fitting for the buyers to pay whatever extra costs are associated with the exchange. Are there extra costs? Yes. However, the extra costs are small compared to the benefits of exchanging.

A key element of three-way exchanging is that when you dispose of your property, you must not effectively receive money proceeds. Unlike an outright sale, where you expect to walk away from the closing table with a big check, you take away nothing as the first third of the exchange is completed. Your proceeds must be held in trust by a disinterested third party. Frequently a person known as a facilitator or qualified intermediary is used when an exchange is done. Funds and ownership are temporarily held by the facilitator or intermediary until the various phases of the exchange are completed. Naturally, the facilitator charges you a fee, usually based upon a sliding scale relating to the total value of the properties involved.

Under the Andersons' plan, they would turn-in their duplex and the buyers of it would turn in their money (cash plus financing) for it. However, initially the facilitator would hold the Andersons' proceeds and, in essence, the title to the duplex. When the quad sellers came to the closing table, the facilitator would turn over the duplex cash and the Andersons would provide additional cash plus financing for the quad. Once the quad sellers got their proceeds, the Andersons would get title to the quad and the duplex buyers would get title to the duplex.

Fred said he preferred to arrange for all closings involved with an exchange to occur the same day or on consecutive days. However, IRS rules allow for delayed or deferred exchanges. Someone who has closed on his property as one portion of a trade and whose proceeds are being held by a facilitator has 180 days to close on the object of the exchange, meaning all other portions. Moreover, 45 days after the first closing are allowed to identify and declare several properties as candidates for the exchange. At least one of these properties must be closed on to complete the exchange within the allotted time. Then, the IRS is happy. If the exchange is not completed within the allowed time frames, the original portion is considered an outright sale and capital gains tax is due.

Once the quad was under contract and inspections were being conducted, the Andersons started marketing their duplex. They didn't anticipate much trouble getting the price they wanted or very close to it. They had learned a key to an easy sale was good curb appeal. If a prospective buyer drove by and liked what she saw, the deal was more than half done. Of course, examination of the interior and the income/expense figures had to support the good impression created by the exterior. Here, the Andersons had no fear. Every unit in all their rentals was rented in clean, completely fixed-up condition to carefully screened tenants. Also, the building was quite profitable as a rental.

Joe and Jane had inspected the interiors of many rental properties for sale over the last seven years. Some were good, some fair and some were horrible. It was hard to muster much buying interest in apartments that were in horrible condition unless the asking price was clearly low. Prospective buyers of any of the Anderson holdings would be pleased with what they saw and the Andersons would make sure the asking price was reasonable. Buyers didn't mind paying a good price if they were getting a good product.

Asking price for the duplex was set at $88,000. Jane considered it her listing through her real estate agency. It was a fairly hot market for rental property at the time. Eight calls had come in by Wednesday after a newspaper ad appeared in the Sunday newspaper's classified ad section. In the following week, six more calls were received. Jane showed the interior of the duplex to three parties by Wednesday of week two, and they received a verbal offer on Friday. After a bit of back and forth verbal negotiating, Jane drew up an agreement and final signatures were added on Sunday afternoon. Contract price was $85,000.

Jane was the listing agent and the selling agent. For salespeople who were selling their own properties, usually their own residences, her real estate agency had a special deal. Regardless of the prevailing commission split with the agent (Jane was at the 60% level), the agency allowed 90% to go to the agent selling his or her own property. In this case the agency would keep just 10% of the 6% commission offered with the listing. Since Jane was both lister and seller, the $5,100 commission (6% of $85,000) was split $510 to her agency and $4,590 to Jane.

To protect the exchange plan and to get the cooperation of the duplex buyers, Jane added a special stipulation to the agreement. It was virtually identical to the one put into the quad contract headed "IRC SECTION 1031 EXCHANGE." The point was to make it clear to the IRS that this property was part of a trade, the buyers were to cooperate in certain ways, and the buyers were to incur no additional costs due to the exchange.

Closing day finally arrived. Jane had arranged for a real estate attorney, whom they had used before, to handle proceedings, including some aspects required for the exchange. She also arranged for the exchange facilitator to attend the closing, and he had several documents to be signed as well.

The duplex buyers came at 11:00 A.M. with their cashier's check, insurance binder, and so forth. Their closing took only about 25 minutes. The attorney said the duplex would be theirs by the end of the day. At 2:00 P.M. the quad sellers appeared for closing number two. It took about 40 minutes. The attorney then called the duplex buyers back for a few more signings, to get the duplex keys, original leases, and a check from the Andersons covering tenant security deposits. The three-way trade was completed.

From the $85,000 duplex selling price, the Andersons paid $595 for deed documentary stamps, $135 in miscellaneous charges, and $5,100 in commission. Since Jane would get $4,590 commission back from her broker, their gross proceeds were $83,760. Of course the closing agent paid off their two duplex mortgages that amounted to $56,100. Net proceeds to the Andersons were $27,660 and this amount formed the bulk of their down payment on the quad.

The Hall Street quadraplex cost $162,000 as expected but closing costs were only $4,800. However, the facilitator's fees were $750. Grand total acquisition cost—excluding prepaids that were really operating costs—was $167,550. Cash required was $32,400 as a down payment and $5,550 for closing and exchange costs. Total: $37,950. Since Jane was to get $2,916 as her commission for selling the quad to herself and Joe, the fresh cash needed was $35,034.

Duplex proceeds of $27,660 reduced the need for quad cash from their investment war chest to $7,374. Joe and Jane looked at each other and couldn't help but grin. Could this be true? It was. It was primarily a matter of doing what they wanted to do by exchanging a property they owned. They had put all their duplex equity into the quad while deferring payment of the capital gains tax, at least for the moment. In addition, they had paid off their second mortgage to Don Majors about 30 months before its seven year balloon was due to pop.

They took a large pizza and a bottle of wine, along with baby Jennifer, to Fred and Wendy to thank them for their advice and to celebrate the latest rental addition. The Madisons were delighted.

Their good fortune was toasted. Then, Fred speculated that the Andersons' investment war chest must still be in good shape.

"It is," agreed Joe. "We had it up to almost $32,000 but even with prepaids we paid out less than $8,000, after we consider Jane's commissions. Really, it's remarkable. We could buy something else!"

Jane chimed in. "I was telling Mitzi Repasky what we had done and she was pleased for us, of course. Then she threw in that we had always been lucky and we were really lucky I was a realtor."

"Oh, Jane," sympathized Wendy. "Luck doesn't have very much to do with it and being a realtor doesn't either. You guys did the research to find the quad, but Mitzi Repasky could have done that herself. After all, the quad was listed on the open market by another realtor, wasn't it?"

"It was."

"Okay then. As to being a realtor, Fred has told you several times it wasn't necessary to be a realtor to make your fortune in rentals. Oh yes, you tell us you got some commission out of the transactions, but they weren't essential to the deal, were they?"

"No, it was nice to get it, but we had the money to close even without it."

Jane continued: "Sounds like Mitzi is just looking for any kind of explanation to explain why she and husband Marty haven't gotten anywhere with whatever they've tried to do. Lots of people do that. When they are envious, they attribute it to the luck of others. Never would they admit their lack of success has to do with their own lack of gumption, discipline or hard work.

"Plus, they don't seem to have a clue as to how to live within their means. They still seem to be spending more than they take in. Oh, they have lots of things, but Mitzi complains about bills, bills, bills. She says she's always robbing Peter to pay Paul just to get through the month."

"Well, Jane and I do consider we have a secret weapon," Joe said quietly.

"What's that?" asked Wendy.

"Fred. Fred as our mentor."

"Oh, man," Fred squirmed. "I'd give the Repaskys or anyone any advice they wanted. All they need to do is ask. I'm no secret weapon. I only preach common sense and living below your means. Lots of other folks preach the same thing and the Repaskys would know that if they ever put their noses into a bookstore. Say, Wendy, maybe I should write a book! Whaddyathink?"

"Maybe you should."

Fred changed the subject. "While you're all here I might as well go over a couple more aspects of the transaction you've just completed."

With that, Fred asked the Andersons how much more cash flow they expected out of the quad than they had been getting out of the duplex. Jane knew. They had been getting about $3,000 in annual cash flow from the duplex and would get $5,400 out of the quad so it would be $2,400 more. Fred divided the $2,400 by the $7,374 in out-of-pocket cash the Andersons had put up. He determined that they could think of the upgrade from a two-unit to four-unit building was giving them a return of 32.5% on their additional money. Keep making deals like that, he lectured, and you're bound to get wealthy. He then asked what return they were getting on the $24,000 they still had in their war chest. Jane said it was in a money market account paying just under 6%. He advised them to look for more rental real estate deals as fast as possible since they were losing money every day.

The second matter Fred brought up was the tax basis for the Hall Street quad. He said they deferred paying capital gains tax on their duplex by exchanging it but the gain they enjoyed wasn't forgotten or forgiven by the IRS. Recognition of the duplex gain was carried forward to the tax basis of the quad. In essence, the gain from their duplex was subtracted from the tax basis of the quad. Thus, years in the future when they ultimately calculated their gain on the sale of the quad, the calculation would include gain from both the duplex and the quad. They would have a bigger gain to report than just from the quad itself. Then the IRS would get its capital gains tax.

Jane quickly said, "No they won't. We won't sell the quad, we'll exchange it! We'll defer paying capital gains tax by exchanging rather than selling. Oh, I know we'll ultimately have to pay the tax like all good citizens but we'd like to defer for now. If the tax code says it's okay, we'd be dumb not to take advantage of the deferment."

Fred agreed. "Tax deferment through exchanging for like properties is perfectly legal and even encouraged by the IRS. It's a good strategy so long as you can keep it up," he said. "Ultimately, you won't want to acquire any more property so possibly no more exchanges. That's where Wendy and I are headed. We'll have to think about our estate, estate taxes, charities, trusts, and our many grandchildren. But that's end-game strategy and there are lots of possibilities. But you guys are still in acquisition mode. Let's not think about your end-game now."

"Let me explain the tax basis of the property you end up with after an exchange. Remember, I'm not an accountant but I can give you a general idea. First, you determine the gain on the duplex. A short time ago you figured your gain on the duplex was $21,750. Next, figure the depreciable basis of the quad in the normal manner but consider exchange costs as part of closing costs. Earlier you told us that the total acquisition cost of the quad was $167,550. What did the appraisal say the land was worth?"

"$24,000, which was 14.8% of the property's value."

"All right, improvements must amount to 85.2% of the quad property's value. Multiply by $167,550 and you get $142,753 as the depreciable tax basis you'd normally use. But, because this was an exchange, you have to subtract the tax deferred gain of the duplex *from* the quad's tax basis. That means $142,753 minus $21,750 or $121,003 is the adjusted depreciable basis of the quad. Take 3.636% of that and you get $4,400 as the amount of depreciation you can take on the quad for each full year. Got it?"

"We do."

For months all went well with the new quadraplex. The Andersons were very happy with their rental business. Fred, at one point, had to remind them that the residential rental business is not trouble-free. Landlords must remain calm and deal as quickly as possible with whatever problems presented themselves. They must remember that all businesses have problems so landlords shouldn't think they have been singled out for special torment. Landlords must keep their perspective too and a good attitude. Occasional troubles or not, the rental business was profitable—provided the tenants were treated fairly and the landlord knew enough about what they were doing to avoid major mistakes.

Joe and Jane's net worth statement, reflecting the duplex/ quad exchange completed in wealth-building year 8 but with no new acquisitions except new vehicles in year 7, was as follows:

Joe & Jane Anderson Net Worth Statement
December 31, Wealth-Building Year #8

ITEM	ASSET VALUE	LIABILITY		EQUITY
BANK ACCOUNTS (CASH)				
Regular checking account	2,200			2,200
Rainy day fund	2,800			2,800
Big routine items fund	1,200			1,200
Major apt. items reserve	1,800			1,800
Investment war chest	28,000			28,000
Cash Subtotal	36,000			36,000
REAL ESTATE				
Lakeview home	156,700		122,050	34,650
Bigelow St. quadraplex	165,500	Mrt 1	120,275	
		Mrt 2	14,725	30,500
Lauren Court quadraplex	164,400	Mrt 1	120,275	
		Mrt 2	14,725	29,400
Shalimar quadraplex	183,500	Mrt 1	117,200	
		Mrt 2	21,950	44,350
Hall St. quadraplex	166,500	Mrt 1	128,900	37,600
Real Estate Subtotal	836,600		660,100	176,500
MISCELLANEOUS				
Household furnishings	5,500			5,500
Joe's minivan	15,500		9,100	6,400
Jane's SUV	19,500		11,200	8,300
Heating/air system loan			1,100	(1,100)
Misc. Subtotal	40,500		21,400	19,100
TOTAL ASSETS	$913,100			
TOTAL LIABILITIES			$681,500	
NET WORTH (Assets - Liabilities)				$231,600

Guided by newspaper articles appearing toward the end of the year, for each of the last two years they had used a 3% appreciation rate on their rental properties and 4.5% for their house. They referred to loan amortization schedules to determine outstanding balances for their loans.

Their net worth was climbing amazingly fast in their opinions. They checked and re-checked their figures, but all seemed to be in order. One cross check they applied was to consider whether they could sell any of their properties or their vehicles at the prices used as asset values. They agreed they could, so they concluded that their asset values were realistic. The liability figures had to be accurate since they came from amortization schedules. It was true: their net worth had gone up $108,000 over the last two years!

Their bank accounts were getting fatter which meant they were getting more secure financially. Financially, they could absorb harder unexpected blows without being knocked down.

The only assets that weren't appreciating were their vehicles. Luckily they were paying down the principals on their car loans faster than the vehicles were losing value. But driving good vehicles was essential, so the Andersons just accepted the fact of diminishing rolling assets.

Fred pointed out to Joe and Jane that if they had invested in mobile homes, they would see their assets dwindling. "Mobile homes go down in value over time just like cars and trucks," he said. "Only the land they sit on goes up in value. The main attraction of owning mobile homes is low entry fees relative to orthodox buildings and high cash flows. Considering the values of mobile homes, rents are relatively high."

Gross annual income for the Andersons had risen only a couple of thousand dollars over the last two years. However, Jane was no longer tied to a salaried job. She was essentially independent. Setting her own hours and being able to have the freedom to handle baby Jennifer's needs was immensely valuable to her. She was working hard but had time flexibility. Plus, she was getting better and better as a realtor. Joe, on the other hand, wasn't putting in much time as a part-time realtor and his commission expectations showed it.

Both Joe and Jane considered they were living as well as they wanted. Being frugal was now ingrained in them. With their current outlook, $58,000 a year was plenty to spend on themselves.

They didn't feel deprived or disadvantaged. They were content.

Income Projection Statement
December 31, Wealth-Building Year #8

Joe's gross annual salary	$ 35,000
Forecast of Joe's commissions	6,000
Forecast of Jane's commisions	22,000
Cash flow from Hall St.	5,600
Cash flow from Shalimar	6,000
Cash flow from Bigelow St.	5,300
Cash flow from Lauren Ct.	5,300
Total Anderson family gross income	$ 85,200
Budgeted for normal living expense	58,000
Fresh funds available for investments	$ 27,200/yr

Joe liked his regular job well enough but he was glad that he and Jane were developing income sources not dependent upon a particular employer. He got along well with his boss, but he never knew when some even bigger boss would decide to restructure the organization and toss Joe's job, and Joe, aside. Joe had heard some horror stories; it could happen.

In the coming year, if they could actually put aside another $27,000 for investments on top of the $28,000 already in their war chest, they could easily buy another quadraplex, or maybe a six-unit building, if they could find one.

Since sheltering money from income taxes was increasingly important to them, Jane decided to again make a depreciation list for quick reference. They did, of course, maintain detailed depreciation records for their income tax returns. Here's what their latest list looked like:

Tax Sheltering Depreciation
For Upcoming Wealth-Building Year #9

Shalimar Quad	4,772
Bigelow Quad	4,931
Lauren Quad	4,931
Hall Quad	4,400
Total	$19,034

The amount of sheltering depreciation they could claim meant over 20% of their gross income was tax-free! The Andersons felt pretty good about their wealth-building efforts. Now they could see it was just a matter of time before they would be millionaires.

A nice prospect since Jane discovered she was expecting their second child.

Joe and Jane reviewed what they had learned about wealth-building over the last year. They remembered that they had considered selling their duplex to raise the down payment money to buy another quadraplex. Then mentor Fred had explained that outright sales invoke virtually immediate payment of capital gains taxes which reduces the cash available for a new acquisition. Fred explained the merits of tax-deferred exchanges and three-way exchanges which are actually fairly simple to arrange. With exchanges, no cash is lost through immediate payment of taxes but there are some fees associated with it. The Andersons did a three-way trade to get their fourth quadraplex and were pleased with the growth of their net worth.

18

Zero Down Deal

Throughout the first two months of the new year, which was wealth-building year number 9, Jane kept searching for rental properties to buy. No appealing quadraplexes were on the market. She searched for six- or eight-unit buildings, too, but none of those were available either.

Idly looking in the newspaper one Sunday, Joe saw an ad for a 24-unit apartment building. It was in the classified section under "Investment Property." At the bottom of the ad it said "By Owner/Broker" and showed the name of the realty company where both he and Jane had their real estate licenses.

"Hey, Jane, look at this!" he called out.

Jane came over and examined the ad. "Oh yeah," said Jane, "that's one of Kathleen Chennault's buildings. You know, Kathy, our broker. She told us all about it the other day; you weren't there. It's the Beacon Arms apartments on Normandy Boulevard. Kathleen's owned them for years. Not sure why she wants to sell them, but she's into a lot of properties and deals, so who knows. It's an open listing, meaning the listing can't be claimed by any one of us agents. That makes sense since there are 18 salespeople in the agency including you, Joe."

"You mean no commission?"

"Oh, Kathy will pay commission to the selling broker. If she sells it herself, of course, she won't have to pay any commission to anyone. If anyone else sells it, including anyone from another agency, she'll pay their broker five percent. The size of the property puts it into the commercial real estate category and commercial listings are often at 10% commission. But like residential listings, the commission is understood to include a selling side and a listing side. The commission split between the two sides doesn't have to be 50/50 but usually is. That's how she came up with five percent to the selling broker—half the usual commercial commission; she's technically the listing broker but it's an open or non-exclusive listing. Kathy's pretty shrewd.

"Of course, if an individual without a real estate license buys it, she won't pay any commission. Naturally she's hoping an individual will see this ad and call her. Probably most rental real estate is bought by non-licensed people."

"How much is she asking?"

"$576,000. The building is about 20 years old. Block construction, so it's plain. All the apartments are one bedroom, one bath."

"Let's go drive by it."

"Joe, the biggest thing we've got is a quadraplex. What makes you think we could handle a 24 unit? Besides we don't even have the money for a 10% down payment! I don't think we're ready, dear . . . not for a few years yet."

"Let's go drive by the Beacon Arms."

And they did. It was a bread and butter type rental. Nothing fancy but it sure looked solid with its concrete block walls. It was a light yellow color due to dye put into the blocks as they were made. Several of the cars in front looked trashy—not a good sign. On the other hand, the location was excellent. Normandy Boulevard was a bus route and within a few blocks of the Beacon Arms were a strip shopping center with a supermarket, several fast food restaurants, a post office and a small park.

Joe asked Jane to get all the details from Kathleen Chennault on Monday; he was going to be too tied up at his job to get to the agency himself. Jane came home with a sales package containing most of the facts and figures a prospective buyer would want.

Rents averaged $360 a month for the apartments, and income for the previous year was given as just under $95,000. Joe quickly multiplied 360 by 24 to get monthly income and then by 12 to determine that annual rents should have been $103,680. $95,000 was 91.6% of potential so evidently there was over 8% vacancy. Joe felt they could do much better than that. They experienced less than 3% vacancy on their own rentals. Two coin-operated washers and dryers at the Beacon Arms provided about $1,000 more income per year.

The Beacon Arms was managed by a management company controlled by their broker, Kathleen Chennault. In total, the company managed about 1,400 units. They had a resident manager in each of eight apartment complexes which averaged about 160 units each. A smattering of smaller places—like the Beacon Arms—were handled by managers living in the closest, large complexes. Joe guessed the smaller places didn't get the attention they deserved, hence the high vacancy loss.

Head office overhead and computer center overhead showed up on the list of Beacon Arms expenses. While these were typical expenses for a large organization to allocate to its operating units, Joe realized that he and Jane would not have such expenses. Naturally enough, 5% was on the list as management expense. Joe and Jane would manage the units themselves. Maintenance charges seemed high and then Joe found out every property managed by the company had maintenance overheads allocated to it. The true, direct cost of maintenance, therefore, wasn't reflected in the total expense given. Joe figured the direct maintenance cost could be much lower, partly because he would do minor repairs himself.

By the end of three evenings of calculations, Joe concluded that he and Jane could operate the Beacon Arms very profitably, even though the sales package indicated low profits. He saw it as an opportunity. But how could they buy it?

Although the Andersons still considered themselves good friends with the Madisons, they seldom consulted with them anymore on apartment rental matters. Joe and Jane had plenty of experience and had no need to ask about routine matters. Occasionally, something peculiar did come up, and when it did, they asked either Fred or Wendy how to handle it.

Thinking about buying a 24-unit building was something they wanted Fred's input on, however. Once they got together, Fred went over Joe's calculations. Fred also wanted to see the

Beacon Arms so a showing was arranged. There were two vacancies at the time, so Fred could easily look at typical units. He also got to see the coin-op laundry area. Fred thought the laundry room was dismal.

Fred asked Jane to ask her broker about reasons for selling. He realized that straight answers might not be forthcoming but they might get some useful insight. In fact, Jane felt she got a fairly honest explanation from broker Kathleen. The story was that while Beacon Arms had always been pretty profitable, it had become less so in recent years. Plus, Kathleen's interests were now in complexes of 150-200 units, so Beacon didn't fit in her overall plan anymore. Finally, and the candidness of this revelation surprised Jane, Kathleen told her she was trying to convince her banker to finance a new big deal, but the banker told her she needed to get rid of some older debt first. Jane reported all of this to Fred.

Fred listened and stroked his chin. He said he had been doing a few calculations of his own and had some ideas. However, he wanted to mull his thoughts over for another night. If they wanted to hear his advice they could come back Sunday.

On Sunday, Fred asked what the Andersons had determined was the maximum price they should pay for the 24 units. Joe and Jane said they were kind of stuck on that question because they hadn't figured out how they could finance the deal. If they were going to put 20% down they figured about $540,000 was maximum but they didn't have anywhere near the cash required. They asked Fred what he figured. He told them in the low 530s. The bigger question was how to finance the buy. Jane told Fred they would have about $36,000 in their war chest by mid-April.

"You guys clearly don't have enough for an orthodox purchase," Fred declared, "so it's time to be bold. Why don't we try for a zero down deal?"

The Andersons gasped, which was their usual initial reaction to Fred's buying ideas. They had heard and read about zero down real estate purchases and even discussed them with Fred, but hadn't come close to seeing the possibility themselves. Fred had said zero down deals usually work only with a desperate seller, or a highly distressed property, or something in the boondocks. Beacon Arms was a bit tired but by no means distressed, and it was in a good location. And the broker was a wealthy woman, not desperate at all. They looked quizzically at Fred.

Fred savored their mystification for a moment then went on. "It's a property with good potential for energetic new owners like yourselves. I accept that the broker/owner/seller is wealthy and doesn't need the money. What should that fact tell you?"

After a moment, Jane called out, "She'll likely hold a second mortgage!"

"Absolutely! I would think so. She didn't say anything about having to sell Beacon in order to get the money to buy the bigger place, did she?"

"No, she didn't. Kathleen just said the bank wanted her to reduce her loan portfolio before they granted her a new larger loan."

"Right. Now, what should that tell you about the existing loan on Beacon?"

This time Joe had the answer. "Well, maybe it means the bank isn't unhappy about Beacon or the loan, but they think the broker is in danger of becoming overextended if they give her an additional loan."

"Bingo! And what should that tell you?"

Joe again. "Well, maybe we could ask the bank to let us take over the existing loan. You know, assume it."

"Bingo again, Joe!" cried Fred. "You're right on! Any time you're thinking about a purchase, you need to try to determine the owner's real reasons for selling. And, if there's good existing financing, see if it's worthwhile assuming. In this case, I think the bank likes the Beacon loan all right and how it's being serviced. Many times a lender won't let you assume a loan because they'd rather you pay the fees and current rates associated with a new loan. Or they'll let you assume it but you can get a better rate on a new loan or need a bigger loan, so you don't want to assume it. In this case, the existing loan carries an adjustable rate so the rate is okay. Jane, do you know how big the existing loan is?"

Jane looked through the sales package then announced, "$399,160 at the time this was written."

"Okay, let me make a few calculations." Fred worked at his calculator and jotted down a few figures. Finally, he spoke again. "Here's what I recommend you do." The Andersons were all ears and leaned forward.

"First, let's base everything on an offer of $505,000. Mrs. Chennault probably won't take it but we've got to start somewhere. Second, write in your offer that it's contingent upon you first getting an exclusive listing on the property at 8% commission. If your broker objects, you can tell her you only need the listing for three days, because you hope to have it under contract within that time. Jane, what's your share of commissions you earn for your broker?"

"I'm at the 65% level so we're talking—wow—a $40,000 commission here! That would put me up into the 80% bracket. Say 75% as an average. Wow! That would still be about $30,000!"

"Which you would roll into the purchase as down payment. It's one of those deals where the property seems to say: 'Buy me, free down payment!' You know, even if you weren't licensed realtors you could still try this deal in much the same way I'm suggesting. You wouldn't get commission, of course, but you might get some price reduction." He turned to Jane. "You say you've about got $36,000 cash. If you weren't a realtor, you would use the cash you've already got rather than commission. So it's not necessary to have a real estate license to make good real estate deals, but there can be big advantages. Chennault probably wouldn't negotiate a price reduction of another 8% but she's mentally prepared to pay commission to somebody. Might as well be you."

"Ah, Fred, Kathy has only said she'll pay a 5% commission. You invented the 8% idea. I doubt if she'll go for it."

"Time to be bold, Jane. Besides, there are only three things Chennault can say if you ask for 8%."

"Yes, no, or hell no!" the Andersons chimed happily. Everyone laughed.

"Let me go on. If you assume the 398 existing loan and get 30 commission, you're still short 77 if she goes for the 505 offer. That being the case, ask the seller to hold a 77 second mortgage. Same interest rate as existing first and a ten-year balloon. No, wait a minute." Fred thought for a moment, looking upward, then resumed. Let's ask her to hold a second mortgage for the remaining difference plus $5,000. That way, if the price changes, the amount of the second mortgage will still fill the gap."

"What's the $5,000 for?"

"Closing costs. And specify in the offer that seller is to pay $5,000 of your closing costs. I figure $5,000 ought to cover closing costs, because you save a lot of things on an assumption."

"What kind of savings?"

"You won't need an appraisal for the lender since they already like the loan. And the lender won't need title insurance because they've probably already got it courtesy of Mrs. Chennault. Likewise, the lender won't insist on a new survey. And they may want you to pay for a credit report on yourselves but they shouldn't want points on the loan. Probably they'll want a transfer fee, but it'll be a flat fee such as $1,000 rather than a percentage of the loan."

"You'll still have to pay state taxes on the two mortgages and that will run about $2,700. Say $1,000 as a transfer fee and up to $1,000 in miscellaneous fees, recording, and so forth. $5,000 maximum I figure."

Jane spoke softly. "Do you really think this could work Fred? It would be fabulous if it did."

"Actually, I think Kathleen Chennault will change some of the numbers and maybe some terms, but yes, I certainly think it could work.

"The key is how anxious Kathleen Chennault is to move on to her big new project. If she doesn't have other offers she's already considering, I think she might work with you on your offer. She wants to get rid of Beacon because it's holding her back. She won't give Beacon away, but if the numbers look halfway decent to her, I think she'll be flexible. You've got nothing to lose. Time to be bold! I'd go for it, if you're convinced you want it."

"Joe, let's give it a try!" exclaimed Jane excitedly.

And they did. Kathleen Chennault was surprised that Jane would submit an offer at all and a rather imaginative one at that. At the same time, she seemed impressed with aspects of it. Of course, she took it very seriously and had a couple of verbal negotiating sessions with Jane and Joe. Two days later, she returned their offer with a number of changes marked on it and initialed. It was a counteroffer.

Broker Chennault retained the basic acquisition plan but bumped the price from 505 to 535, tossed out the stipulation that she pay $5,000 in closing costs, reduced the balloon period on the second mortgage from ten to five years and knocked the commission from 8 to 7%.

When the Andersons went over the counteroffer with Fred, he said he was encouraged. "She's left your basic buying plan intact and that's the main thing. I'd also say it indicates she thinks the bank will probably go along with your contingency to assume the existing first mortgage. She knows the bankers and what they're likely to do. Probably, she figures they'll be pleased that she'll be getting out from under the Beacon Arms loan. If she does, the bank will likely be pleased to go ahead and finance her big new project. In fact, I'm so encouraged I think you should continue to be bold and counter her counter. That is, submit a counter-counteroffer.

"Accept a couple of the things she changed. You can live with the 7% commission and her not paying closing costs. On the other hand let's split the difference between your offered price and hers. Let's try 518. And let's get at least another year before the second mortgage balloon bursts. Nudge it up from five to six years."

"OK, but Fred, if we pay closing costs we won't have a zero down deal!"

"Sure you will. Zero down generally means zero down payment or actually anything close to a zero down payment such as just 1 or 2%. To get out of paying closing costs as well is pretty rare. It was worth a try, but your broker, in effect, has said hell no. Accept it because by about most anyone's standards you'll still have a zero down deal."

Jane presented the counter-counteroffer to Kathleen Chennault and the revisions were initialed on the spot. The Andersons had a contract!

It turned out that the seller, the buyers and the bank wanted this deal to proceed and close as fast as possible. Fortunately the Andersons' credit rating was top notch and they already had a history of successfully operating residential rental apartments. The bank approved them for assuming the existing first mortgage that had 18 years, 4 months left to run. Balance owing would be $398,000 when the Andersons took it over. The bank required a $1,250 transfer fee, slightly higher than Fred had estimated.

Seven percent commission on the $518,000 final price was $36,260, by far the highest commission Jane had brought in to date and it did push her to a higher commission split level with the agency. Jane's portion was to be 75% or $27,195 which was to be entirely applied as down payment. This meant Kathy Chennault, as seller, would hold a second mortgage, also known as a purchase money mortgage, for $92,805.

No funds were coming out of the Andersons war chest for a down payment so it was a zero down deal. However, $4,649 had to be taken from the war chest to cover closing costs. Not bad for a $518,000 property!

Using the Beacon Arms sales package figures for income and adjusted figures for operating expenses, plus new debt service figures, the expected cash flow was as follows:

Beacon Arms
Expected Cash Flow

Rents	$ 7,900 per month
Laundry Income	90
Total Income	7,990
Operating Expenses	$ 2,186
Debt Service 2 mortgages.	3,339
Total Exp & Debt Service	5,525
Cash Flow	$ 2,465 per month
	Equals 29,580 per year

Fred pointed out they were going to be getting $29,580 a year by putting up just $4,649 in cash to cover closing costs. He worked his calculator, shook his head in disbelief, then worked his calculator again. Finally, he declared, "You'll get a 636% cash return on cash investment. Not too shabby!"

Once the closing was complete and the deed to Beacon Arms officially recorded in their names, Joe resigned from his regular job, effective in three weeks. His bosses tried to talk him into staying and offered an immediate 10% salary increase, but Joe was not persuaded. Becoming his own boss had been one of Joe's dreams since he started working full time. Finally he was not going to be working for anyone other than himself and his family. He felt very, very good.

Comparing the projected Beacon cash flow to the salary he was giving up made it look like Joe would be reducing family income by at least $6,000, even more if he had taken the 10% raise. But Joe and Jane were no longer looking at things in the same way. First, working only for your account rather than for someone else was a quality of life issue. He could no longer be fired! He no longer had to make special arrangements and ask permission if he needed time off. He had flexibility of work hours although he knew full well he might be working even more than before. The best thing, Joe thought, was that he now would have almost total control over what he did and when. Working hard was not an issue; he was prepared for hard work and didn't even mind it. *Control* was the thing!

As far as money was concerned, Joe and Jane weren't worried. They felt the Beacon Arms would pull them through. To begin with, there was income sheltering from taxes through depreciation. Deducting the county tax assessor's figure of $65,000 for land from acquisition cost including closing expense revealed $457,649 of their new property was depreciable. For every full year that meant $16,640 in income-sheltering depreciation could be claimed. That would save them at least $3,300 in federal income taxes.

If they managed Beacon as tightly as they did their other rentals, the Andersons felt they could reduce vacancy loss from the present 8% to 3% or lower. That would mean at least $5,000 more in cash flow. With vacancy loss reduction and tax savings on top of expected cash flow, they already had Joe's salary more than replaced.

But the biggest cash flow improvement would come, they felt, from improvements to the building, the apartments and the quality of tenants.

Of course, immediately after the purchase contract was signed they had inspected all 24 apartments, making notes as they went. A few were in excellent shape, some were average, but at least half were shabby. By examining lease and rental records they also found that in addition to two vacancies, Beacon was housing three occupants who had not paid rent for the last one to three months! Clearly, they would have to clean house.

Joe talked with a painter they had used before and whom

they trusted. Other landlords told Joe that painter Lincoln, his last name and what he preferred to be called, was reliable and a good worker. Plus, he was so good at trim work he was said to have an angel's touch. Lincoln agreed to paint the entire exterior of Beacon for $8,000 as labor. Materials, estimated at $3,000, would be extra. Joe drew up a painting contract and asked Lincoln to get started as soon as his schedule permitted.

Using their inspection notes, Joe and Jane wrote down, apartment by apartment, what had to be done inside to bring each to a good or excellent condition. A few needed new refrigerators, some needed new stoves. Eight units needed new carpet and vinyl. Most needed painting. About half needed new window treatments. Fifteen needed very heavy cleaning. They estimated the cost would be $14,200 spread over the time it would take to renovate.

Both Joe and Jane felt one of the best improvements they could make in the apartments would be to cut a forty-two inch-wide opening in the wall separating kitchen from living room and installing a pass-through counter. Joe found a cabinet shop that would make sturdy formica-coated counters ready for screw-on mounting for $70 each. They would do a minimum of six at a time. Then, Joe found a carpenter who would cut the required hole in the wall, frame it, install the ready-made counters, and trim the openings for $150 each. However, he wouldn't paint the trim.

Installing pass-through counters in all 24 apartments would cost:

Countertop	$ 70
Carpentry	150
Trim wood	20
Total	$ 240 per apartment
Total	$ 5,760 for 24 apartments

Estimated total cost to make over the Beacon Arms apartments would therefore be:

Paint exterior	$ 11,000
Improve interiors	14,200
Pass-through counters	5,760
New sign and flower bed	600
Total	$ 31,560

The new sign was a last minute idea of Joe's. He reasoned that if they were going to get rid of all the bad tenants and make over the building inside and out, it ought to have a new sign. A flowerbed would be developed on a grassy corner and the sign placed within it. Moreover, lest any notoriety exist for the aging Beacon Arms, the Andersons felt they ought to change its name. Besides, renaming was the prerogative of new owners. But what was a good name? This aspect was a puzzler. For days Joe and Jane tossed around dozens of names. It was as hard as naming a new child. Finally they settled on Mayfair Apartments.

It was a clean sounding, fresh name in keeping with the new image they were going to try to project.

Should they sink $31,560 into the Mayfair Apartments? They discussed the question with the Madisons and decided they should. Exterior painting and the new name on a new sign in a flowerbed would, within two months, give a whole new look and good curb appeal to their property. All work would start immediately. The money would come from their war chest.

Once all renovations were finished the Mayfair rent would be $400 per apartment per month. The income increase due to renovations would be $11,520 a year. Return on the investment would be $11,520 divided by $31,560 and multiplied by 100 or 36.5%. Since their war chest was only earning 5.7% in their money market account, putting money into renovations over a year or two made a great deal of sense. It was part of the wealth-building process to be always evaluating alternative uses for your money and to select the one offering the greatest cash-on-cash return for the longest time.

Since he didn't have a salaried job to tie him down, Joe was virtually always available for the next several months to get renovation work started and moving along rapidly. He did many of the easy improvements himself and most of the cleaning as well. To Joe, it was satisfying work. Pregnant Jane was staying close to home. Finally, right on schedule, she had their second child, another girl, whom they named Rachel. Both Andersons appreciated the fact that being free of employment by others gave them wonderful flexibility to tend to their new baby and Jennifer. They now considered their family complete.

They had purchased Mayfair in April and by the end of the year 15 of its 24 apartments had been upgraded. Undesirable tenants had departed and a better tone prevailed. Except for the renovations ongoing at Mayfair they handled turnovers efficiently. Fix-up and make-ready for re-rent was typically done within three working days, and a new tenant was usually installed within a week. This efficiency kept the Andersons' vacancy loss low, despite turnovers.

It was time again to prepare their net worth scoreboard. As to values for their rental properties, Fred suggested they start using a new valuation process.

Fred explained that assuming rental properties are of average quality, condition and location, the main value-raising ingredient is income. Rental property buyers, including the Andersons and the Madisons, were income oriented. Any analysis they made used income as a key factor. Therefore, Fred said, for your own balance sheet, quick reasonable evaluations can be made by using a technique involving multiples of gross annual income. Thus, when rents are raised and annual income increased, the property's value increases proportionally.

Fred emphasized that the technique is not to be used in place of a thorough analysis to evaluate a property you don't own. After all, he pointed out, the gross multiple technique focuses only on income, whereas a proper analysis considers expenses, financing, condition and so forth. Fred went over this caution twice since he felt it was so important.

To use the technique, the starting point is the price paid for a property or a recent appraisal, whichever is higher. This is divided by the gross annual income received at the time of acquisition to determine the multiplier. For example, suppose $150,000 is paid for a quadraplex and the price is supported by a timely appraisal. At the time of closing, each apartment rents for $475 a month, meaning an annual gross of $22,800 for the year. Dividing $150,000 by $22,800 results in a multiple of 6.58 or 6.6. As a check, multiply the annual $22,800 rent by 6.6 and the result is $150,480, which is acceptably close to the proven value or purchase price.

Thereafter, whenever a balance sheet or net worth statement is being prepared, to estimate the value of the quadraplex its then current annual rent is simply multiplied by the multiplier of 6.6. If, for example, rents are raised to $495 a month, gross annual income becomes $23,760. Multiplying by 6.6 gives a property valuation of about $156,800. The valuation increase of $6,800 is reasonable since income has been increased by $960 or 14.1% per year. Just think about how much you would have to invest, and in what, to earn $960 interest per year.

Another cross check on the valuation is to consider whether the property could be sold using the new valuation as the price. Fred said, and the Andersons as realtors agreed, that an income of $23,760 would probably enable a sale at close to $157,000.

For their new Mayfair Apartments, the Andersons divided their $518,000 purchase price by the $96,000 actual income (including laundry income), to get a multiplier of 5.4.

"A multiplier in the 5's is common for medium-age single buildings having more than twelve units," explained Fred. "Quadraplexes are seen as more desirable by many renters than buildings having a dozen or dozens of apartments. Thus apartments in quadraplexes often command more rent than comparable size apartments in larger buildings. Thus, the multipliers for quads turn out to be higher."

Multipliers for their quadraplexes ranged from 6.5 to 6.7 so they decided to use 6.6 for every one of them. Fred assured them this was within the normal range for a good quad.

At the end of the Andersons' ninth wealth-building year, annual rental incomes, multipliers and rental property estimated valuations were as follows:

Rental Property	Gross Annual Income Rate	Gross Rent Multiplier	Developed Valuation
Bigelow Quad	25,680	6.6	169,500
Lauren Quad	25,440	6.6	167,900
Shalimar Quad	28,080	6.6	185,300
Hall Quad	25,920	6.6	171,000
Mayfair 24 Units	108,720	5.4	587,000
TOTALS	213,840		1,280,700

Jane transferred the valuations developed for their rental properties onto their usual net worth statement:

Joe & Jane Anderson Net Worth Statement
December 31, Wealth-Building Year #9

ITEM	ASSET VALUE	LIABILITY		EQUITY
BANK ACCOUNTS (CASH)				
Regular checking account	2,600			2,600
Rainy day fund	3,100			3,100
Big routine items fund	1,900			1,900
Major apt. items reserve	2,600			2,600
Investment war chest	31,000			31,000
Cash Subtotal	41,200			41,200
REAL ESTATE				
Lakeview home	163,000		120,850	42,150
Bigelow St. quadraplex	169,500	Mrt 1	119,075	
		Mrt 2	14,600	35,825
Lauren Court quadraplex	167,900	Mrt 1	119,075	
		Mrt 2	14,600	34,225
Shalimar quadraplex	185,300	Mrt 1	115,450	
		Mrt 2	21,650	48,200
Hall St. quadraplex	171,000	Mrt 1	127,750	43,250
Mayfair Apartments	587,000	Mrt 1	391,450	103,250
		Mrt 2	92,300	
Real Estate Subtotal	1,443,700		1,136,800	306,900
MISCELLANEOUS				
Household furnishings	6,000			6,000
Joe's minivan	13,800		5,300	8,500
Jane's SUV	17,700		8,100	9,600
Misc. Subtotal	37,500		13,400	24,100
TOTAL ASSETS	$1,522,400			
TOTAL LIABILITIES			$1,150,200	
NET WORTH (Assets - Liabilities)				$372,200

As usual, when they calculated their net worth at the end of each year, the Andersons were in a state of shock when they finally saw the bottom line—their net worth. It seemed incredible to them that their worth had increased almost 63% in one year! They knew they had worked hard but didn't realize they had worked that hard!

Fred had assured them that their method for constructing a balance sheet to determine net worth was absolutely legitimate. He could not imagine it not being accepted by any lender. "After all," he stated, "the values used for property assets are fairly readily verifiable by getting opinions from knowledgeable brokers checking the selling prices of comparables. The values won't be exact as if determined by formal appraisal, but they'll be close enough. You might be a little high or a little low on individual properties but lumped together the total value should be pretty close.

"Amounts used for property liabilities should be accurate too since they're taken from amortization schedules." Fred's remarks made them feel more comfortable.

Nevertheless they decided they must dissect their figures to see if they had made some huge mistake in constructing their scoreboard. They re-checked and concluded all figures looked reasonable except one . . . Mayfair. One year ago, there was no Mayfair Apartments. Oh, there were the Beacon Arms Apartments, but Joe and Jane didn't even know where! Now, Mayfair was a line item on their net worth statement showing they had an equity in it of $103,250. Mayfair, alone, accounted for 44.6% of their net worth increase. How did they go from zero to $103,250?

The biggest factor was the increase in Mayfair's value from $518,000 to $587,000—a $69,000 jump. The explanation was that they had put $11,400 into painting and a new sign, plus $12,475 into renovating 15 of the 24 apartments. The improvements, plus tight management, allowed them to reduce the vacancy rate to about 3.5%, and get 15 tenants—10 of them new—to pay an average of $37 a month more than the Beacon Arms' average rent of $360. The gross multiplier technique had amplified the effect of the rent increases. The real test was whether or not Mayfair could be sold at $587,000. Joe and Jane enthusiastically agreed it could. The Madisons agreed as well. Curb appeal was now excellent, 15 apartments looked great inside, and the income figures were getting healthier.

The second biggest factor was that Jane had earned a $27,195 commission that she rolled into the Mayfair purchase as down payment. At the closing, broker Chennault had handed the commission check to Jane. Jane happily waved it around for about ten seconds, while husband Joe and broker Chennault clapped. Jane then endorsed it and turned it over to the closing agent. She almost felt the commission was unreal, merely a bit of paper shuffling. But it was now reflected in their property equity. If it hadn't been for her commission, their mortgages would be that much higher and their war chest that much emptier.

The third ingredient was the paydown of principal on their two mortgage loans. In just eight monthly payments toward each loan, the principal paydown was over $7,000.

They added it up: $69,000 increase in market value, $27,000 in commission and $7,000 as loan paydown. It added to $103,000, which matched their Mayfair equity. Their net worth figure was correct. It had increased almost 63% in one year!

Their bank account balances were gradually getting larger as well. The problem was the Andersons had to keep drawing funds out of one account or another. For example, every once in a while they would have to buy a new dishwasher, stove or refrigerator. Whatever was needed was purchased immediately, by credit card or store account, and paid for within a month from their major-items reserve account. They were pleased with the reserve account concept; it was nice to know funds were always readily available.

While they were putting more in than taking out in order to fatten their reserves, headway was slow. They knew if they suddenly had a really major need, such as $2,700 for a quadraplex roof, they could cover it with funds from their investment war chest. It was their intention, however, to gradually build major item reserves to $10,000.

Primary residence values had risen four percent in their city over the last year, so they increased their home value by that much. Prices for rental properties had risen a smaller percentage, but since the Andersons had decided to use the gross multiplier technique for preparing their scoreboard, they ignored the newspaper's information.

They were pleased to have finally paid off the loan given by the city for their new heating and air conditioning system. Also, as the value of their home rose, their equity grew to more than 20% of its value. Since that meant their mortgage was now less than 80% of the property's value they asked their lender to allow them to stop paying private mortgage insurance (PMI) premiums each month. The lender agreed, provided they submitted a formal appraisal which supported their claim of house valuation. The Andersons had an appraisal done for $275 and the lender dropped the PMI charge. End result: reduction of monthly payout by $31 a month. The appraisal would pay for itself in about nine months and the savings would continue forever.

Here's what the Andersons projected as their income for wealth-building year number 10. Gradually they were using more and more money for personal expenses. They now had to pay almost 15% self-employment tax on their commissions. Also, over $400 a month for a family health plan through a health maintenance organization. In addition, they now had day-care expenses and were trying to meet the seemingly endless needs of two children.

Income Projection Statement
December 31, Wealth-Building Year #10

Forecast of Joe's commissions	$ 8,000
Forecast of Jane's commisions	27,000
Cash flow from Hall St.	6,100
Cash flow from Shalimar	6,600
Cash flow from Bigelow St.	5,900
Cash flow from Lauren Ct.	5,900
Cash flow from Mayfair Apartments	37,200
Total Anderson family gross income	$ 96,700
Budgeted for normal living expense	60,000
Fresh funds available for investments	$ 36,700/yr

The fact that neither Joe nor Jane were working for salaries anymore gave them immense satisfaction. They were closing in on one of their goals, too, achieving $100,000 household income. In addition, they were keeping more of the money they did take in because of the tax sheltering provided by depreciation. Here's the depreciation they were entitled to take for each full year:

Tax Sheltering Depreciation
For Upcoming Wealth-Building Year #10

Shalimar Quad	$ 4,772
Bigelow Quad	4,931
Lauren Quad	4,931
Hall Quad	4,400
Mayfair Apartments	16,640
Total Shelter	$35,674

In addition, they were paying down loan principal on their rental properties with rental income. By checking their amortization schedules, they could see rental mortgage payments in year 10 would pay down $17,632 in loan principals. They really could add $17,632 to their projected income figure but decided not to. It wasn't money they had free use of since it was dedicated to loan reduction through mortgage payments.

The Andersons used calculations of cash flow to estimate their income. Cash flow, by definition, meant after debt service. Debt service meant mortgage payments that embodied both principal and interest. By leaving principal paydown out of income they were focused on freely useable income. All of it was spendable as they wished, with the exception of taxes. They did, however, see the beneficial effect of principal paydowns as increased property equities on their net worth statement.

While the Andersons were content with their lives and their progress toward becoming millionaires, they realized they still had a long way to go. Nevertheless, they felt the need to take a breather from acquisitions to adjust to their new lives.

They still didn't know it but millionaire status for them was within six years.

Looking back over the year, the Andersons were not only astounded by their progress, but how much they had learned. Shortly after the start of the year, they were attracted to a 24-unit apartment building but the asking price seemed to put it far beyond their reach. Then mentor Fred explained a method that included an assumption and seller financing to result in a purchase with virtually no money down. Through hard work and perseverance they turned the tired, mediocre performing building into one which was attractive and highly profitable. Fred also explained a shortcut method of updating the values of rental property already owned. The Andersons now owned 40 apartments and were blessed with a second child. Their net worth and income were increasing nicely.

19

A Grand
Slam Buy

Wealth-building year number ten was a consolidation period for the Andersons. They solidified their positions by making sure all rental properties were in good shape, all accounting and maintenance procedures were working smoothly and all arrangements were made for side issues.

One side issue was a reciprocal agreement for out-of-town coverage made with another couple who were also striving to build rental property wealth. Peter and Angela Miles were about five years older than the Andersons, also had two kids and owned 22 rental apartments. Like Joe and Jane, they went away occasionally for a long weekend and for an annual vacation of one to two weeks. In the past, their travels had been limited by the need to provide maintenance coverage for their rentals.

Both couples used telephone recorders to collect messages from tenants and others. Once or twice a day, regardless of how far they were from town, they would call their recorders and make notes on the messages. Naturally, they carried lists of tenants, vendors and phone numbers. Depending upon the situation they would call the tenant or a vendor, such as a plumber, or both. Action on calls for non-essential maintenance was deferred until their return, but the tenant was called and so advised. Repairs for anything critical such as lack of heat or air conditioning or an inoperative toilet, were arranged for by long distance.

The reciprocal arrangement meant that when either the Miles or the Andersons were away, apartment maintenance needs of the other would be handled by the couple that stayed at home. Each couple gave the other telephone recorder access codes, tenant and vendor lists and access to apartment keys. The out-of-towners could more completely enjoy their time away. The at-home couple had authority to act for the absent landlords if there was critical need.

Both couples avoided going out of town in the first nine days or the last four days of a month. At these times it was "all hands on deck" to handle incoming rents, pay bills, renovate apartments after move outs, plus show and rent apartments. From the 10th to the 26th of every month relatively little happened so this is when the Andersons or the Miles took off if they wished.

Joe had met the Miles at a meeting of the Tri-City Apartment Association to which he had belonged for three years. Monthly dinner meetings were primarily social but usually had a speaker imparting words of wisdom on some aspect of effective apartment operations. Association committees kept up with such things as local and state legislation that could impact apartments, utility issues and other relevant member education.

The social part was particularly valuable, Joe thought. You got to know other landlords or managers and vendors on a face-to-face basis. In the casual times before and after dinners and speakers it was easy to discuss commonplace problems and incidents and find out how others had handled them. Joe learned a lot at association meetings; the dues were well worth it. Fred had encouraged the Andersons to join years ago but they hadn't immediately done so. Fred urged them to get involved on an association committee to really get to know some interesting people. Fred had been president of the local association just after it was formed.

Jane had become a real estate broker and had set up her own company called Personal Attention Realty, or PAR. She felt the name suggested the close attention she was prepared to give buyers or sellers who worked with her. Since she didn't have or want a large agency with lots of salespeople she felt she ought to emphasize individual attention. She rented a two-office suite and put up the legally necessary signage. Of course

Joe placed his salesman's license with Jane's agency. Now, they both had an office away from home, which was to their liking.

A primary reason Jane became a broker was that she wanted to be fair to her previous broker, Kathleen Chennault. For the past year, Jane had been spending an increasing amount of time on their own apartments. She handled most showings and most accounting. This took away from the time she could devote to selling for Chennault's agency. Since Jane knew she was no longer giving Chennault 100%, she felt she ought to become an independent broker and establish PAR.

Joe either did or arranged for all apartment maintenance and cleaning. He had rented quite a few apartments himself but conceded that Jane did it better. She had amazing people skills. Joe was friendly to a degree, but Jane could put people at ease and they warmed to her instantly.

For the first four months of their eleventh wealth-building year the Andersons were not looking for anything new to buy. Their plates were full. However, as they got comfortably on top of things, they again started to think of acquisitions. Their investment war chest had grown to about $55,000. Jane again began to stay alert for any rental property coming on the market but nothing of interest was evident. Fred had taught them to be patient, to wait for good properties that could be bought right, so they bided their time.

In late June at a Tri-City Apartment Association meeting, Joe had an interesting conversation with Jaime Okola, the local head of an apartment management company. Locally the company managed 15 properties having a total of about 2,000 apartments with the company itself owning about 50% of them. The company had a strong presence in twelve states and was headquartered in Atlanta.

When Joe happened to mention he was looking for apartments to buy, Jaime offered to contact his head office to see if any owner of local apartments had an interest in selling. He invited Joe to drop by his office in a few days to see if anything might be available.

Joe dropped by. Jaime said two properties they managed were available for purchase, although they weren't currently on the open market. Joe eagerly asked for details but was dismayed to hear they were a 118-unit and a 106-unit property located in the college student rental area. Both were too large for the Andersons to consider and he and Jane had no interest in student rentals. He relayed this to Jaime and asked him to see if anything might be available in the 40- to 60-unit size in a non-student area.

Two days later Jaime called to say a 48-unit and a 58-unit were available and gave Joe the addresses. Subsequently, Joe and Jane drove by both properties. They were apparently both built in the era of the Beacon Arms apartments. Both seemed enormous to the Andersons and somewhat tired. Curb appeal was definitely low. Nevertheless, they decided to ask Jaime to obtain details on the 48-unit property.

Jaime did, and the Andersons again drove by the property, known as the Flamingo Apartments, on Caladium Parkway. The apartments were in three two-story buildings arranged in a U-shape. Parking lots were situated around the outside of the U as well as inside its open mouth that faced the rear of the property. In back was a swimming pool. Asking price for the 48 units was $1,170,000. Actually there were only 47 apartments; the 48th unit was a laundry room containing four coin-op washers and four dryers.

Listed expense items were typical but, at first glance, the amounts seemed high. Of course, there were special expenses related to the swimming pool. Not surprising were management fees, head office overheads, computer system fees and maintenance overheads. Clearly, the management company was allocating its expenses to all properties it managed. It didn't matter to Joe and Jane, however, since they would manage the property themselves and wouldn't apply overheads.

Joe and Jane estimated true vacancy loss was running at about 8% for most months but at about 13% for May, June and July. This suggested the complex housed a number of college students though it wasn't in the traditional student housing district

The Andersons did their usual preliminary analysis as they had for so many prospective properties over the years. The results looked promising so they arranged for a preliminary physical inspection. They looked through one-third, or 16, of the apartments—every third one. Plus, they looked closely at the laundry room, a storage room, the pool and the pool equipment room. Then they did some more figuring since they could now see where more money ought to be spent and where money could be saved. They decided to discuss the property with Fred.

Fred and Wendy liked the idea of the Andersons moving up to a larger multi-family property. "It's twice as many units as you've got in your Mayfair Apartments," intoned Fred, "but you won't find it twice as hard to handle. Maybe half again as hard, which is a pretty good thing when you think about it. Presumably you'll get twice the Mayfair cash flow with only one and a half times the Mayfair work."

Wendy agreed. "Once you get used to it and have it the way you want it, you'll find it is relatively simple to take care of. It's roughly equivalent to twelve quadraplexes but it will be like managing seven quadraplexes."

"But how do you suggest going about buying it, assuming we figure we want to try to get it?" Joe asked. "We think it could be good, but we can't do a complete analysis until we've blocked out how we can finance it. You know debt service has a lot to do with it. We should have close to $67,000 cash in our investment war chest by the time this ever closes, even if we put it under contract today. And then there's commission. They'll probably pay 5% to a selling broker so that's another $58,500. Good thing Jane's a broker so we get to keep it all! In addition, maybe we could somehow trade in one of our quadraplexes. We've got anywhere from $35,000 to $52,000 equity in each quad. Or, maybe we should ask them to hold a second mortgage. What do you think, Fred?"

Fred asked questions about their existing four quadraplexes—what they were worth, what was owed and so forth—plus the state of their relationship with their primary lender. Jane thought their main lender probably had a good opinion of them because they had never been late on any mortgage payments and they had several accounts with growing balances.

"Good," declared Fred as he stroked his chin. "I've got some ideas but I want to mull them over tonight. Tell me again about the Flamingo numbers. If you want it, my advice will be ready for you tomorrow. Can you guys come over about 1:30 P.M.?"

"We can."

And they did. "So, Fred," Joe started, "how are we going to do it?"

"You're going to get rid of *all* your quads."

The Andersons gasped. Fred continued. "And you're not going to take any commission." Jane's mouth opened in a look of alarm. Joe just stared, mouth slightly agape. Fred looked at one Anderson and then the other then shrugged and declared, "Well... you asked me."

Wendy urged Joe and Jane to be seated and poured iced tea for all. Once everyone had had a sip or two, Fred started again. He had a pad of paper in front of him and jotted numbers on it for others to see as he spoke.

"First of all, forget $1,170,000. You know they don't expect to get full price. The question is . . . what do they *plan* to get? Knock 10% off the asking price. That's $117,000 and I'm going to assume that was their dickering pad. The reduced price is $1,053,000.

"Also," added Fred, "you don't want to take commission on this deal, because you'd end up paying too much income tax on it. In this case, just state no commission in your offer and drive down the price accordingly."

"Being in the real estate business, I'm sure they planned or expected to pay a brokerage commission. I'm sure, Joe, that your friend Okola passed on the fact that your wife is a broker. When realtors hear about a broker being involved, they naturally know a commission has to be in the deal. Probably the owners in Atlanta figure they'll have to pay 5% to any selling broker and built that much into their asking price."

"What's 5% of $1,053,000?" Fred already knew the answer so he wrote $52,650 in large numerals on his pad for the others to see. "Take that away from $1,053,000 and," he paused for effect as he made the subtraction, "you get about $1,000,000 on the nose. Bingo! I'll bet our Atlanta friends decided they wanted a million after commission so they added commission and dickering room on top of a million to get their $1,170,000 asking price. The numbers work out so plausibly I would be surprised if that wasn't their thinking. We may be wrong but it's interesting to try to double think your competition.

"If you got Flamingo for a million, you ought to be thinking of $200,000 or 20% cash as down payment. Plus, maybe another 15 to 20 thousand for closing costs. And no, I don't think they'll take a second mortgage. My guess is that from the seller's standpoint, Flamingo is a marginal property at best. It's not large enough to take all the overheads they want to apply and still make a decent profit for them. Of course, simply absorbing some of their overheads helps their overall operation, but my guess is they're also not satisfied with Flamingo's cash flow. So, they would like to cash out. If so, they won't want to take back a mortgage."

Fred continued. "You said you were closing in on $67,000 in your investment war chest. You're short of the $220,000 needed. My recommendation, then, is that you plan to dispose of your four quadraplexes to get the equity out of them. Of course, it's got to be by trading so you won't have to pay any capital gains tax at this time. You probably have at least 160 in equity in your quads, don't you think?"

"Probably, but we'd have to check," Jane responded.

He continued: "Okay, check on quad equities as part of your homework assignment. Your homework also includes putting on your thinking caps to figure out who would like to buy your quads. Could be one person or it could be four. Also, touch base with your banker and just say you're thinking seriously about a deal worth $1,000,000. Ask the banker what terms they would offer if you put up 20% in cash. Talk in a presumptive manner. Let them think the deal's going ahead one way or another, and you're giving them first chance to be a helpful part of it. Without saying it, let them know if they don't come up with some pretty good terms you'll be going to one of their competitors. Can you do this homework?"

"We can," said Joe and Jane. "Give us a few days. We'll call you and plan another get-together once we've got a handle on things."

A week later, the foursome got together again. Jane reported: "We set some realistic market values on our quads and subtracted what we owe according to our amortization schedules. As of right now, here are our equities." She laid out the following list:

Quadraplex Equities

Bigelow Quad	$ 41,000
Lauren Quad	40,000
Shalimar Quad	57,500
Hall Quad	48,500
Total Equity	$ 187,000

"Our equity is greater than we thought it was. Of course, we'll have transaction expenses even if we don't charge commission. What with taxes on deeds, facilitator fees, legal fees, recording and so forth we're talking about $2,200 to close each one. That drops our net to about $178,000. That's assuming we could sell them at the value we set on them. But if we could, 178 plus the 67 already in our chest gives us 245. So, we're okay as far as cash is concerned."

"Got anyone in mind to buy the quads?"

"Yes. Yes, we do. I called three people and Joe called six. Between us we think we've got four different buyers chomping at the bit. We both knew people who were looking for some rental property providing something good came along. When we told them we were considering selling one or more of our own quads, four of the nine names were more than interested. They like what we've done and kind of see themselves doing something similar. They also know we keep our properties well maintained and full. That helps a lot."

"You didn't tell them any prices did you?"

"No, not at all and not even which quads let alone all four of them. We said we were just thinking about doing some dealing. We've got four excited, enthusiastic prospects who just want us to count them in—if the price is right—when the time comes."

"Good. When the time comes, give them the prices you think are right without padding them. Show them analyses to prove they're fair prices. Now, what about your banker?"

"Good news and bad news. He said right off that they'd want to take a good look at the details and do it with us if the numbers looked good. Said the rate would be competitive. It would be an adjustable rate and right now about 8 5/8%. The bad news is that he said 20 years is the maximum term they would go. I told him we liked 30 years, but he said an $800,000 loan could be 20 years at the most. Oh, well."

"Sounds like you guys have all your ducks in a row and sounds like it's getting to be time to shoot!" declared Fred. "Now, since you have a basic plan and the wherewithal if everything falls into place, have you completed your purchase analysis? If so, what's the maximum you should pay for this place? Don't forget, cash-on-cash return is the key."

"We have," said Joe. "$975,000," added Jane.

"That high?" questioned Fred. "Well, whatever. I recommend you start with an offer of $910,000. They won't accept but you'll find out how much resolve they've got. But with this size deal you won't make a formal offer anyway. Instead, you'll start with what's called a letter of intent or, in this case, what you might call your letter of hope." They all laughed.

"Seriously, you use a letter of intent as a softer, less formal version of an offer. Sort of like giving your girl a friendship ring before you actually get engaged. Easier to revise. Speaks in plain language. Doesn't have the detailed legalistics an offer or contract has to have. Once you've agreed on a letter of intent, then you go to an offer. But by then the terms have all been pretty well agreed to, so the offer easily becomes a contract. Get it?"

"We do."

The Andersons prepared a letter of intent and sent it with a short cover letter to the Atlanta-based owners of the Flamingo Apartments.

The intent letter to create a contract for sale/purchase described the property and listed all the special stipulations and contingencies that the Andersons were used to putting in their offers. The Andersons clearly stated that no real estate commission was to be paid on the transaction before stating the price, $910,000 and cash down payment, $182,000. Also, the letter listed in straightforward terms who would pay for what closing costs. Naturally they put in a version of the special "IRC Section 1031 Exchange" clause they had first used when they traded their duplex for their Hall Street quadraplex. Deferment of capital gains taxes on their quads was critical to the success of their plan; they needed to use all their equities to put together the needed down payment.

One contingency clause gave the Andersons 30 days after a contract was signed in which to obtain purchase/sale contracts on properties they planned to include as the buyers' portion of the intended exchange. Joe and Jane could work on lining up third party buyers for their quads right away, but they couldn't sign any agreements until Flamingo was safely under contract. At this stage it was by no means certain that their grand slam deal—as the bridge-playing Wendy dubbed it—would ever come to pass. There were a lot of "ifs" involved. It would be disastrous if they put their four quads under binding contract and then couldn't reach agreement with the Atlanta people. If they couldn't acquire Flamingo, they had no wish to give up their quads.

The letter of intent was faxed to Atlanta and a hard copy mailed. In less than a week a response was received. Several of the Andersons' terms were adjusted but none were rejected except the price. Atlanta countered at $980,000.

Fred advised them not to accept the counter. "After all," he said, "your analysis showed you $975,000 was the maximum you could pay in order to get a cash-on-cash return equaling three times the current annual CD rate. It was $975,000, wasn't it?"

"It was. So what should we do?"

"Sit on it. For maybe a week and a half or two weeks. Just look how much their price has dropped already—$190,000 from $1,170,000. Now, I realize they would think of some $58,000 of that as commission they had been planning to pay anyway, but we may have touched a nerve. I'll bet Flamingo just isn't that good for them anymore. It doesn't fit in with their preference for larger properties. It could very well be that the sellers are already thinking it's pretty much sold to you guys. They're already counting their chickens, so to speak. Let's let the deal dangle a bit. It'll maybe make them more receptive to a counter-counteroffer."

A little over two weeks later the Andersons sent a letter to the Atlanta sellers. It stated that the Andersons accepted all the changes the sellers had made to the earlier letter of intent with the exception of the $980,000 price. After careful re-evaluation of the income and expense figures supplied by the sellers, the Andersons were prepared to pay $955,000. If the sellers could accept this counter-counteroffer, a suitable formal contract would be drawn up immediately for signatures.

Atlanta accepted. Jane accordingly prepared a formal offer and sent it to the sellers. An administrative assistant at the sellers' office called Jane to say the offer was verbally accepted but that it had to be reviewed by their legal department and this may take a bit of time. It did. Three weeks later a thick document arrived at Personal Attention Realty. It was Jane's offer, signed, but with a massive addendum added by the sellers' legal department. With careful reading they could see all of their points, terms, conditions and contingencies were in there and not really changed, but each main point seemed subject to pages of legalese in the addendum. Jane turned it over to the attorney they planned to use if there was a closing.

The Andersons' attorney finally advised them to go ahead and sign to accept the contract, including addendum, without changes. His opinion was all would be fine so long as the deal proceeded as the Andersons envisioned. However, if the Andersons tried anything funny, or if unforeseen problems arose, the sellers had written in "wiggle room" that would allow them to get out of the transaction.

Given a signed contract on Flamingo, the Andersons presented analyses and partially completed sale/purchase contracts to each of the four persons who had expressed strong interest in one of their quads. The first couple approached was given their choice of the four possibilities. Once they had looked at each building and made their choice, the contract was completed with the buyers' names then signed by all parties. The second potential buyer was given their choice of the three remaining quads. The third prospect had a choice of two properties and the last prospect had no choice. Because the prospects had, in effect, been pre-sold and were generally familiar with the Andersons and their operations, all four quads were under contract three weeks after the Flamingo contract was finalized.

None of the buyers asked the Andersons to help with the financing by holding a second mortgage loan. Good thing they didn't because Fred had told Joe and Jane they shouldn't take any notes since they needed all the equity released to be applied against down payment and closing costs for the larger building.

Joe and Jane were busy conducting inspections of each Flamingo apartment, along with the manager. Joe had made a check-off sheet for each unit so it was easy to note the condition of each key item such as stove, disposal, refrigerator, window treatments, paint, carpet, etc. Anything non-functioning that was part of a mechanical, electrical, heating, A/C or plumbing system was listed for the sellers to repair, at seller's expense, before closing. The Andersons were well aware that they were buying a used car rather than a new car, so a good amount of wear and tear was to be expected. However, by agreement, everything mechanical was to be in operating condition prior to closing.

The heating and air expert they had used for years, and who had become their friend, was asked to look at the heating/cooling equipment for each apartment. He declared it okay except for a few units needing immediate repair. He pointed out that while it appeared from the outside that most of the equipment seemed to be original, and therefore about 25 years old, it really wasn't. Inside each original housing he found newer compressors, fan motors, relays and sometimes wiring. Evidence of normal maintenance over the years. Joe likened it to the old story about the hammer that a carpenter and his son and grandson had used almost daily for 60 years. Yes, it had lasted 60 years but the handle had been replaced six times and the head five times. Some things could last indefinitely providing they were properly maintained.

An appraisal was obtained for $2,450 (payable at closing) and a survey for $575. The appraisal, which was required by the bank, gave a valuation of $970,000. This meant the Andersons had done well negotiating a price of $955,000. The bank required one point—1% of the $764,000 loan—as a fee, payable at closing.

Two and a half months passed from the date of the letter of intent until the days for transaction closing. It involved some tricky scheduling and coordination but overall everything went off without a significant hitch. During the morning of closing day number one, two quad buyers came in to close, one at 9:00 and one at 10:30. In the afternoon, the remaining two quad buyers came in. Everything was signed and all buyers presented their cashier's checks. The closing attorney cut checks for the surveyors, insurance companies and the appraisers, but the Andersons' proceeds were given to an exchange facilitator. It was important, from an IRS exchange rule standpoint, that the Andersons not take constructive possession of the proceeds; they would be turned over to the Flamingo seller as the exchange was completed.

On the second closing day, representatives of the seller arrived for closing of the Flamingo. One rep had power of attorney for the specific purpose of signing closing documents. Within 40 minutes the exchange was complete. Joe and Jane were now owners of the Flamingo Apartments and were not owners of four quadraplexes.

The closings were in mid-November. This meant all property taxes had to be paid no later than the closings since tax bills had been issued. Sellers were responsible for taxes from the first of the year until closing date, buyers were responsible for the remainder of the year. It was presumed that all rents had been collected for occupied apartments, and, at closing, November's rents were prorated. Joe and Jane had collected $9,066 in quadraplex rents and turned over $5,440 to the new owners. On the other hand, the Andersons received $9,406 in November rents from the former owners of Flamingo.

Aside from prorations, the Andersons' cash aspects of the deal were:

20% down payment on Flamingo	$ 191,000
Flamingo closing costs	19,865
Total	$ 210,865
Less proceeds from quads	-176,842
Fresh cash needed from Andersons	$ 34,023

Since Joe and Jane had accumulated $69,000 in their investment war chest by the time of closing, they had roughly $35,000 left over. They knew a good chunk of it would be needed over the ensuing months to renovate apartments when they became vacant. Of course, they were still adding about $3,000 a month to their war chest.

Immediately after the closing Joe and Jane mailed letters for each tenant that they had prepared in advance. The letter was to arrive just after the former manager hand delivered a notice to each tenant telling them of the ownership transfer to the Andersons. The letter from Joe and Jane introduced themselves as new owners, gave a number to call to report apartment problems, told who their December rent checks should be made payable to, and where they should be sent. The letters also specified what the rent was and how much deposit had been transferred from the previous owner. It was important that these numbers jibe with the former owner's records. Putting it in the letter would ward off any claim by a resident of lower rent due or higher deposit paid.

Naturally, the Andersons were in for a few surprises. For one thing they had to immediately pay the utility company $2,800 in deposits as they had utilities transferred to their names. The apartments were separately metered for water and electricity, and tenants paid for what they used. However, there were house security lights around the building, laundry room lights and hot water, pool water and electricity for its pumps, and lawn water all to be paid for by the Andersons. While Joe and Jane were expecting the monthly utility bills, they had simply overlooked the requirement for deposits.

A worse surprise, discovered in December as rents were coming in, was that in addition to the two known vacancies, four apartments were occupied by tenants who had not paid November's rent! They should have anticipated it since it was almost identical to their experience at Beacon Arms. Evidently, with the pending sale the departing management had let down its guard. In addition, these tenants, becoming aware of a management change, may have decided to "test" the new system. Since, at closing, the Andersons had gotten a proration based on rents for all occupied apartments at closing, they had no loss—yet. But they'd have to act fast concerning December's rents. Three-day notices were immediately delivered. One paid up; the other three quietly vacated their apartments after business hours. By now, the Andersons were experienced enough to expect that whenever a new property was taken over some bad apples might have to be tossed out.

At the time of purchase, scheduled monthly Flamingo rents averaged $362 whereas, due to vacancy loss, the average collection was $331. Other monthly income—from the coin-op laundry and a vending machine—brought in an average of $225 per month more. If these figures held they would take in $189,384 in twelve months. However, the Andersons considered it was of primary importance to work toward improving all three income averages. At the same time, they would work toward reducing expenses.

Many operating costs were cut as general renovations began. Exterior trim was painted and units brought back to very good to excellent condition whenever vacated. The costly swimming pool was filled in and a large deck for sunning was installed in its place. A major landscaping project, featuring flower and shrubbery beds plus flowering trees, was started. Curb appeal was considerably enhanced. All in all, the Andersons spent about $33,000 on condition and fix-up work in their first ten months of ownership. New tenants were more carefully screened than before and higher rents were introduced. Average monthly rent and laundry room receipts were rising.

An attractive new sign was erected in the middle of one of the new flower beds. Joe and Jane, as was their prerogative, renamed the Flamingo the Parkview Apartments.

A small city park located nearby was visible from some apartments, so the new name had a practical rationale. Mainly, though, the Andersons wanted to convey the idea of fresh, changed and improved to their newest acquisition.

Net annual income (after vacancy loss) by the end of their first full year of operation was at the rate of $207,024, up $17,640 or more than nine percent.

In addition, operating costs had been reduced by more than $300 a month. The Parkview Apartments were becoming quite profitable for Joe and Jane.

They drew up the following Parkview forecast of cash flow for their 13th wealth-building year.

NET ANNUAL INCOME	$	207,024
OPERATING EXPENSES		
Advertising		1,375
Insurance		3,000
Routine Repairs & Supplies		18,800
Expected Renovations		11,250
Taxes		16,116
Utilities		5,480
Yardwork		3,200
TOTAL OPERATNG EXPENSE		59,221
NET OPERATING INCOME		147,803
DEBT SERVICE (P+I)		80,289
CASH FLOW	$	67,514

Taking the realized gain from the four quadraplexes exchanged for Parkview away from acquisition cost of the bigger property resulted in a substitute tax basis of $686,880 for Parkview. Taking away the appraisal's $104,395 valuation for land resulted in $582,485 value for depreciable improvements. This meant $21,181 in income tax sheltering depreciation could be claimed each full calendar year. Thus, of the $67,514 cash flow from Parkview only $46,333 would be subject to income tax.

The figure of $80,289 used as Parkview's debt service included $14,977 in loan principal paydown. This *was not* a tax-deductible expense and would be considered by the IRS as income. The Andersons continued to prefer simply using cash flows from their properties to estimate their income for a coming year. While principal paydown was income it wasn't immediately spendable since it went directly to the loan company. However, since it reduced loan liability it had an elevating effect on net worth.

At the time of closing the Flamingo had a scheduled or gross annual income of $208,320 although, due to vacancy loss, the net was $189,684 a year. Joe divided the gross into the appraisal value of $970,000 to obtain the gross income multiplier of 4.7. This seemed too low to the Andersons. They considered Parkview was very similar to Mayfair, although twice as big, and Mayfair's multiple was 5.4. After some debate, they decided to use a multiple of 5.1 for the purpose of determining a reasonably accurate value to use on their net worth statement. The test, as always, would be to consider whether the property could be readily sold at the valuation obtained. In the case of Parkview, the Andersons knew it looked a whole lot better than when they bought it, and the bottom line number was much better as well.

The Andersons' scorecards for the end of their twelfth wealth-building year were:

Rental Property	Gross Annual Income Rate	Gross Rent Multiplier	Developed Valuation
Parkview 47 units	217,740	5.1	1,110,474
Mayfair 24 units	115,800	5.4	625,320
TOTALS	333,540		1,735,794

Joe & Jane Anderson Net Worth Statement
December 31, Wealth-Building Year #12

ITEM	ASSET VALUE	LIABILITY	EQUITY
BANK ACCOUNTS (CASH)			
Regular checking account	3,300		3,300
Rainy day fund	3,900		3,900
Big routine items fund	2,400		2,400
Major apt. items reserve	6,000		6,000
Investment war chest	31,000		31,000
Cash Subtotal	46,600		46,600
REAL ESTATE			
Lakeview home	183,000	115,286	67,714
Parkview Apartments	1,110,474	749,023	361,451
Mayfair Apartments	625,320	Mrt 1 357,200	178,487
		Mrt 2 89,633	
Real Estate Subtotal	1,918,794	1,311,142	607,652
MISCELLANEOUS			
Household furnishings	8,500		8,500
Joe's minivan	8,700		8,700
Jane's SUV	11,000		11,000
Misc. Subtotal	28,200		28,200
TOTAL ASSETS	$1,993,594		
TOTAL LIABILITIES		$1,311,142	
NET WORTH (Assets-Liabilities)			$682,452

Jane was spending less time at her real estate business due to the time demands of Jennifer and Rachel. However, she was becoming more effective—improving her batting average as they say—so her real estate brokerage income was rising. It also helped that she was a broker rather than a salesperson. She kept 100% of the commissions she brought into her company, PAR. She had business expenses, but these were not high. In projecting family income she used net commissions, meaning after business expenses, as the contribution from her real estate business.

At the start of each month, Jane got heavily involved in the bookkeeping relating to the operation of their 71 rental units. She recorded rents, deposited them, chased after slow payers, paid bills and reconciled bank accounts. She also produced a few of the reports they found useful. Her rental property involvement was usually wrapped up by the 10th of the month except for loose ends that kept cropping up throughout the month. Both she and Joe showed vacant apartments to prospects.

Joe no longer did any real estate selling work but he kept his license active. He was pretty busy maintaining apartments or overseeing others who were doing the actual work. Most of his work was at the beginning and ends of the month; mid-month was slack time. He really liked what he was doing. It was wonderful to be your own boss, he thought, and to set your own schedule. Naturally, he got aggravated from time to time at either a tenant or a maintenance problem, but, he reminded himself, he got annoyed regularly at his salaried job. And operating rentals paid so much better than being a salaried employee. Most important was the feeling that all his efforts were for the benefit of Jane, Jennifer, Rachel and himself.

Income Projection Statement
December 31, Wealth-Building Year #13

Forecast of Jane's commissions	$ 36,000
Cash flow from Parkview Apartments	67,515
Cash flow from Mayfair Apartments	40,700
Total Anderson family gross income	$ 144,215
Budgeted for normal living expense	68,000
Fresh funds available for investments	$ 76,215/yr

They had greatly exceeded their goal of having in excess of $100,000 annual household income. However, due to their ingrained frugal ways, they were budgeting the use of only $68,000 for family expenses. Even that amount was almost more than they felt comfortable spending. Their ability to set aside over $76,000 for investments simply astounded them. Their surplus, for investments, was about as much as their friends the Repaskys and Archers each took in as total household incomes. Of course, the Repaskys and Archers continued, most months, to spend more than they earned so their debts continued to mount. Luckily, both owned their own homes; it was about the only reason the net worth of each couple was slowly increasing.

In addition, the Andersons figured they paid proportionally less income taxes than anyone they personally knew. Joe and Jane felt they paid enough—through quarterly estimated tax payments—but considering all the money they had use of, their effective tax rate was relatively low. The explanation was all the tax-sheltering depreciation they were entitled to take:

Tax Sheltering Depreciation
For Upcoming Wealth-Building Year #13

Parkview Apartments	$21,179
Mayfair Apartments	16,640
Total Shelter	$37,819

The future looked very bright to the Andersons. They had no money worries. Their income and net worth was rock-solid secure; no one could fire them or lay them off. And all four of them were enjoying good health. They were immensely pleased with their wealth-building plan. They planned to stay the course.

Joe was now age 42. Jane was 40.

The last two years had proven the value of active involvement in a local apartment association. It led the Andersons to a 47-unit apartment building. It seemed impossible for them to buy it, but their mentor guided them through successful negotiations. A letter of intent led to a contract involving three-way trades to provide tax-deferred money.

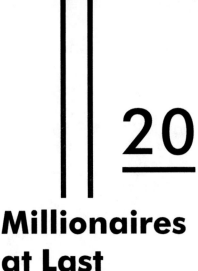

Millionaires at Last

It was now inevitable that Joe and Jane would become millionaires in just a few more years. It was as if their wealth-building process was on auto-pilot. As if they were in an airliner and had entered the coordinates of their destination into some kind of economic positioning device and life was taking them there. Oh, there would be twists, turns, dips and dives on the way but they would get there. That is, unless they did something really stupid or an unexpected tragedy happened. By now, experience had molded the Andersons into the types of people whose mistakes turned out to be minor rather than monumental blunders. Only divine intervention of a tragic nature could keep them from their goals.

They simply needed to stay the course. Everything was in place for wealth-building and it was just a matter of living it out—carefully. Over time, the inexorable appreciation of well-located and well-maintained rental property combined with the programmed paydown of mortgage loans would get them there. It had to. At the end of their twelfth wealth-building year, they owned $1,993,594 in assets, mostly real estate, offset by $1,311,142 in liabilities. As market values were appreciating, they were paying off mortgages virtually automatically, month after month. Considering just those two factors alone—property appreciation and loan balance paydown—becoming millionaires was assured.

As they were starting wealth-building year 13, Joe and Jane developed a chart showing after-inflation appreciation of their assets at a very conservative 2.5% increase year by year, and their loan balances dropping in accordance with their amortization schedules.

As can be seen from their chart, Joe and Jane will become millionaires in four more years. The sought-after brass ring will be grasped in wealth-building year number 16 when they are ages 46 and 44, respectively. Besides having a net worth of over $1,000,000 they will have an annual household income of over $160,000. Their primary goals will have been achieved.

Projecting the Andersons' Net Worth

Wealth Building Year	Value of all Assets	Liabilities	Net Worth	Ages of Joe/Jane
12	1,993,594	1,311,142	682,452	42 /40
13	2,043,434	1,278,421	765,013	43 /41
14	2,094,520	1,242,875	851,645	44 /42
15	2,146,883	1,204,276	942,607	45 /43
16	2,200,555	1,162,360	**1,038,195**	**46 /44**
17	2,255,569	1,116,844	1,138,725	47 /45
18	2,311,958	1,067,417	1,244,541	48 /46
19	2,369,757	1,013,742	1,356,015	49 /47
20	2,429,001	955,452	1,473,549	50 /48
21	2,489,726	892,152	1,597,574	51 /49
22	2,551,969	823,405	1,728,564	52 /50
23	2,615,768	748,746	1,867,022	53 /51
24	2,681,162	667,665	**2,013,497**	**54 /52**
25	2,748,191	579,606	2,168,585	55 /53

But wait! Look down the chart and see that the Andersons will have a net worth of *over* $2,000,000 by the end of wealth-building year 24. That means they will be multi-millionaires! At that time Joe will be 54 years old while Jane will be 52.

But can an avalanche be stopped before it dies naturally?

The figures show what will happen if the Andersons do nothing except operate their rental business in a routine manner. But, for twelve sometimes difficult and always hard working years, Joe and Jane were activists in building wealth. Can they suddenly turn away from what has become almost second nature? Can an avalanche be stopped . . . before it dies naturally?

Whether Joe and Jane were born frugal or the trait became ingrained during their early years of wealth-building is unknown. The fact was they were very frugal now. They always looked for the best value in anything they bought. To them value was the right mix of quality and price. For an inexpensive, throw-away type item the main ingredient was price, provided, of course, that the item was appropriate to the task and likely to last the short life until disposal time. For an item to be used repeatedly, even constantly over a long period, the main ingredients were quality of design, materials and construction. Price, within reason, was no longer a factor. So, to the Andersons, being frugal was by no means a matter of buying only the least expensive item. Sometimes they bought the most expensive item if it offered the best value over expected life usage.

Neither did being frugal mean they deprived themselves of anything they needed. Quite the opposite. They readily bought anything they needed, after checking for the best value amongst variations of the item.

Now that they were close to becoming millionaires, did they buy everything they wanted? Yes and no. No, in the sense that they didn't snap up every appealing newfangled item that appeared on the market, and they didn't adhere to fashion fads. On the other hand, yes, they indulged themselves with the latest and best—in terms of value—of anything they thought they needed. It was their frugality, or being frugal, that seemed to cause them to automatically distinguish between a need and a want. Most wants were considered briefly, then dismissed.

Concentrating on needs did not preclude purchasing luxuries. For example, when they felt they needed to properly record, for their present and future enjoyment, the events and development of their daughters, Jennifer and Rachel, they didn't hesitate to get the latest and best mini-camcorder and digital camera. Since they were needed for their objective of recording and distributing family event photos, they didn't hesitate to get a scanner and six-color printer for their home computer.

An avalanche cannot be stopped mid-run. So, despite having their day-to-day living needs satisfied and attainment of their goal to be millionaires assured, the Andersons looked for more wealth-building opportunities. It was not a matter of greed; it just had become their normal way of life.

In April of their 13th year, their war chest had fleshed out to about $56,000. They were adding to it at the rate of over $6,300 a month. They were considering looking for an additional rental property to buy. However, in reviewing where they stood on their various mortgages, they were reminded of the balloon on the second mortgage held by Kathleen Chennault on the Mayfair Apartments. The balloon was set to burst in two years, in April of year 15. At that time they were scheduled to pay Chennault $87,075.

Maybe they should put funds aside to pay the balloon on schedule. Or they could wait until year 15 and do a full refinance of the Mayfair. They could get a new first mortgage large enough to allow payoff of the second mortgage. Getting a new first wouldn't be much of a problem. They would need about $412,000 to cover their existing two notes, but the property would be worth over $650,000 by then. However, getting a new mortgage would cost them 3 to 4% in closing costs—$12,360 to $16,480. They may be able to finance the closing costs, meaning boosting the new loan to 425 or so to cover them, but it was still a cost to be paid sooner or later. Joe and Jane decided to talk to mentor Fred.

It was no longer easy to meet with the Madisons. Fred and Wendy were in their late sixties now. Years earlier they had turned their apartments over to a management company and were traveling regularly all over the place. They took an overseas trip once a year and rented condos two months at a time twice a year in different parts of the U.S. and Canada. Depending upon the season they might be found for extended periods in Idaho, Arizona, Southwest Florida, the Muskoka region of Ontario or North Carolina. In between major trips, the Madisons made week-long trips to the cities in which their children and grandchildren were located. Life as retired multi-millionaires suited them just fine. Joe and Jane were slightly envious, but they knew their time was eventually coming.

As luck would have it, Fred and Wendy were home when Jane called. They would be leaving town in three days but were pleased to set up an immediate meeting with the Andersons.

The gathering made all of them think of the many times over the last twelve years they had gotten together to discuss apartment operations and acquisition strategies. There were many purely social gatherings as well. Joe asked Fred how the management company idea was working out.

"Very well, indeed," replied Fred. "Although it took maybe six to nine months for us to work out the kinks. We wanted our apartments managed in the same manner as we had managed them, but that didn't always mesh with the approaches the management company used. But truthfully, sometimes they had better ideas than we did. Gradually, with compromises on both sides, we got things worked out so we're quite satisfied. Now the management company handles everything for us. They charge a significant fee, but it's a fair one so we have no complaints. Cash flow even after payment of the management fee is still terrific. Owning rental real estate is the best possible retirement plan of all as far as we're concerned. Plus, our properties are still appreciating. Why, our net worth goes up more than $200,000 each year and would do so even if we stayed in bed all the time!"

"Any thoughts of selling?" asked Jane.

"Not for the foreseeable future, although we've set up a living trust and all our rental properties have been put into that trust. But that's a long story; maybe I'll write a book about it sometime."

"Oh, Fred!" interrupted Wendy. "You're always going on about how you're going to write a book! First, it was going to be on how to buy rentals. Then you were going to write about how to operate rentals. Now you're going to write about how to get rid of rentals before you die. Give it a rest! You haven't written a damn thing. Why in the world would you think you're going to start writing now?"

"You never know, my dear, you never know. Maybe I'll get myself one of those laptop computers and start plunking away while you drive us on trips. But let's hear what's on the minds of Joe and Jane."

Joe outlined the balloon mortgage situation and what they saw as the alternatives. Fred asked questions about their available money and about what Kathleen Chennault was up to these days. That question surprised Jane.

"Well, Kathleen and I keep in touch but not regularly. However, I believe she's involved in some deal concerning putting together enough adjacent property to do something big downtown. She's buying a bunch of decrepit old buildings and plans to bulldoze them and put up something new. She's 'Ms. Urban Renewal' at the moment. It'll probably work out; she's very good. Always has something on the go."

"Good, if she's got something on the go it means she needs cash money. Developers always do. You may be in luck. You might be able to work out an early payoff of the second mortgage she holds. At a discounted amount, of course. If you have an individual as a loan holder it's often possible to work a discounted payoff deal. People are always coming up with reasons why they need cash money. Banks, on the other hand, won't discount their loans for early payoff. Their business is to have money loaned out earning interest. They don't want you to pay off early except in connection with refinancing or you taking out an even bigger loan. But I have a hunch Ms. Urban Renewal would like an unexpected chunk of change to present itself on her doorstep. Did you bring your amortization schedule on the loan she holds?"

"We did. It's right here."

Fred studied the amortization schedule, started clicking away at his calculator and occasionally jotted down some figures.

Finally he spoke. "Right now you owe Kathleen Chennault $89,296, and you're obligated to pay her $87,075 in two years. I suggest, Jane, you go see her and offer the following. Say you and Joe are considering buying another rental but thought you might like to pay off Kathleen's second mortgage instead. Ask her if she would accept $55,000 cash immediately and another $20,000 in four months as payoff in full. In other words, you pay her 75 now instead of 87 two years from now. Whether she'll do it or not depends on how much she could use the cash at the moment. In rough terms, you're discounting the current value of her loan by almost 16%. Plus, if you pay off the loan you'll be saving the 8% interest you're paying her. Sounds good to me."

"Oh, Fred, do you really think she'll go for it?"

"Don't know, Jane. But we do know there's only three things she can say, don't we!"

"Yes! No! Or hell no!" shouted the Andersons.

"Bingo!"

Two days later Jane reported that Kathleen Chennault wouldn't accept the $75,000 offer but would accept $80,000, payable $55,000 immediately and $25,000 in no more than 120 days. Jane asked Fred if they should accept the counteroffer.

"Yes, by all means. You currently owe $89,296 and you can get away with paying 80. Your $80,000 gives you an immediate gain of $9,296 which is 11.6% cash-on-cash return. Plus, you mustn't forget that by getting rid of the loan you'll be saving the 8% interest you've been paying on the whole amount. Not only that, you'll save the $12,000 or so that you would have to pay to refinance to get a new larger first mortgage.

"Draw up a simple modification-of-loan agreement setting out the terms you've agreed to and how they replace terms of your existing mortgage loan. Also, put in that she will give you a satisfaction-of-lien document once you've paid the final $25,000 in four months. You guys and Kathleen Chennault will need to sign and date it. Once you get the satisfaction-of-lien, take it to the county courthouse and get it recorded officially."

"Okay. We'll do just that." And they did.

Paying off the mortgage immediately increased their net worth by the $9,296 by which the loan had been discounted. The $80,000 had been eliminated as a liability, too, but their assets decreased by $80,000 in cash at the same time so it was a wash resulting in no net worth gain. All but $1,000 of their war chest was wiped out. However, by getting rid of the second mortgage, their cash flow increased by the $681 a month it had been costing them as mortgage payments of principal and interest. This meant they could, thereafter, put a little more than $7,000 a month into their investment war chest. The good old treasure chest would be replenished quickly.

The Andersons' chart of wealth growth had assumed all assets would grow by 2.5% after inflation. This grossly underestimated the rate at which their cash assets were increasing. Seven thousand dollars a month into the war chest was a rate of $84,000 a year; close to double their balance sheet cash sub-total at the end of year 12. The question was what to do with the cash. Should they buy another rental property? Buy some luxuries? Or pay down the principal on other mortgages? What to do with your excess cash was a nice problem to have, but it really was somewhat of a problem. Joe and Jane wanted to do the right thing. They also wondered whether they should diversify into stocks, bonds or mutual funds.

They decided to do several things. First, they decided in the spring of year 14 to have a swimming pool installed in their backyard for $19,000. The whole family could enjoy it, Jennifer and Rachel especially. It was a luxury from the wish list devised long ago. In terms of wealth-building, they figured the pool with nice landscaping would increase the value of their house by about $13,000. Secondly, they started college education funds for their daughters who were ages six and four. Thirdly, in the spirit of counting their blessings and being grateful, they increased their charitable giving dramatically. Since monthly funding of the education and charitable giving plans was a commitment, household expense went up and funding for investments went down accordingly.

Finally, they decided that in November of year 14 to try to acquire more rental property. By then their war chest would be back up to about $75,000. At a minimum that would enable them to buy a property worth $300,000, putting $60,000 as 20% down and having $15,000 for closing costs and immediate fix-up. Of course they would be looking for a special situation that would result in a larger property for the same cash. They had learned from Fred to try to find special situations and to be imaginative in their financing. If, for example, they found a seller who would take back a second mortgage they might be able to get a $500,000 property for the same amount of cash. One never knew.

Fred, as he had several times over the previous years, strongly advised them against diversifying. He pointed out that they were having considerable success acquiring and operating rental real estate. They were becoming experts. If they were on to a good, profitable thing, why would they want to start in on an investment type unknown to them, uncontrollable by them and risky? While they were being successful during the property acquisition mode of their lives, there wasn't adequate justification for diluting their investment efforts. Since they were doing well with rentals they should stick with them. Diversification could wait until they were about to retire, at which time completely passive investments might be a good place for excess cash.

As it turned out, early in year 15, with the help of another realtor, they located and became owners of an additional rental property consisting of twelve one-bedroom apartments and six two-bedroom units. The sellers did, in fact, take back a second mortgage at a fixed interest rate of 7.5%. Joe and Jane immediately went into their new property routine that started with the purging of undesirable tenants and fixing up apartments as they became vacant. In addition, they worked on the curb appeal of the property by having the building repainted by Lincoln, the parking lot seal-coated and fresh parking lot striping applied. Just as at Mayfair and then as at Parkview, new, properly-screened tenants readily paid higher rents. Turnover dropped, too, causing cash flow to increase significantly.

No, an avalanche cannot be stopped before it runs its natural course. In point of fact, Joe and Jane Anderson became millionaires in their 15th wealth-building year when they were ages 45 and 43. They made it a year sooner than their chart had indicated. And although Jane had cut way back on her brokerage activities their gross family income still topped $155,000. Of that, close to $50,000 was sheltered from income taxes by depreciation. At the end of year 15 they estimated they would become multi-millionaires in year 21 when they were 51 and 49. However, since they were still wealth-building activists, chances were they would achieve the "multi" goal in fewer than six years.

The Andersons had proved that ordinary folk, like themselves, starting with ordinary incomes and ordinary abilities, could become millionaires within a reasonable number of years through residential rental real estate. It took budgeting, the setting of specific, desirable goals, discipline, a means of keeping score and always living below their means. Living below their means enabled them to save at least 10% of their gross income year by year. The savings became their investment war chest. Gradually, as net worth went up, they enjoyed more of all of life's pleasures and luxuries. Fifteen years after they started their wealth-building program the Andersons lived as well as they wished and acquired anything they needed without hesitation. But by no means were they living ostentatiously and never would.

While none of the methods used by the Andersons to build wealth are complicated or remarkable, they still had to learn them. Trial and error and common sense could have led them to winning techniques, but major errors early on could have led to crippling discouragement. Real estate books and realtors are a good source for initially learning techniques but the Andersons were fortunate in having Fred and Wendy Madison as mentors. The Andersons continue to make mistakes as does everyone else, but they don't make big ones.

One of the most important things they learned from the Madisons was how to properly analyze and determine maximum price to be paid for whatever properties they thought might be nice to own. For the small investor, the absolute key was cash-on-cash return on investment. All monies needed for down payment, closing and for essential immediate fix-up had to be considered as the total cash investment. As accurately as possible, operating costs plus mortgage payments had to be subtracted from net property income to obtain cash flow. Annual cash flow, as a percentage of total cash investment, had to be at least three times the current annual certificate of deposit interest rate for any property they were going to manage themselves. Once they knew the maximum price to be paid, the job was to try and buy at a lower price.

Fred taught them that while in the acquisition mode (which would last until they were approaching retirement) they should maximize their use of financial leverage. The best strategy was to not try to own any property free and clear but to obtain ownership of as much profitable rental property as possible by buying with minimum down payments. He also advised them not to diversify into multiple types of investments. Providing they were having success in acquiring and operating rentals they should not dilute their real estate buying power.

"You should concentrate your resources," Fred had said. "Become expert at the endeavor which is working best for you."

The Madisons taught them to buy in well-maintained, stable locations convenient to areas of activity appealing to renters. They taught them to aim for the broad middle band of tenants rather than the high end or lower tier of renters. They taught them to start with whatever size of rental they could afford but to move into multi-family apartments as soon as practical. They taught them to avoid outright sales that trigger capital gains tax in favor of tax-deferred exchanges as they upgraded to larger properties. They taught them to be imaginative, but scrupulously honest, in their dealings. Also, they should try to double think the motivations and true desires of buyers, sellers and lenders; then, try to satisfy those desires in the deal.

As to operating rental properties, Fred and Wendy taught the Andersons to remember that every business has aggravations and to accept that fact with good spirit. Accordingly, they should not get upset when tenants reported problems. Instead they should impress their tenants with rapid, thorough responses.

Fred had explained that things wouldn't fix themselves, so if they had to fix something anyway, they might as well do it as fast as possible to create a pleased resident out of an annoyed one.

The Madisons taught them to treat tenants fairly as customers. Most, in turn, would then treat the landlord right, pay rent properly, take care of their apartments and stay longer before moving out.

Fred suggested that Joe and Jane become licensed realtors in their quest for wealth. There are advantages to being a realtor, but Fred emphasized it was by no means essential. He and Wendy also delighted in pointing out to both Joe and Jane that either of them could have become millionaires without their partners. Of course, it's easier and more enjoyable to become wealthy with a companion who shares your point of view.

Perhaps the most important thing the Madisons taught them was to set a goal, such as becoming millionaires, set out a rough plan as to how to achieve the goal and then *get started.* Plan to adjust your techniques along the way as necessary but keep after your goal. And, *get started!*